SOCIAL MEDIA AS SURVEILLANCE

Social Media as Surveillance
Rethinking Visibility in a Converging World

DANIEL TROTTIER
Uppsala University, Sweden

ASHGATE

Published by
Ashgate Publishing Limited
Wey Court East
Union Road
Farnham
Surrey, GU9 7PT
England

Ashgate Publishing Company
Suite 420
101 Cherry Street
Burlington
VT 05401-4405
USA

www.ashgate.com

British Library Cataloguing in Publication Data
Trottier, Daniel.
 Social media as surveillance : rethinking visibility in a
 converging world.
 1. Social media. 2. Facebook (Electronic resource)
 3. Electronic surveillance.
 I. Title
 303.4'833-dc23

Library of Congress Cataloging-in-Publication Data
Trottier, Daniel.
 Social media as surveillance : rethinking visibility in a converging world / Daniel
Trottier.
  p. cm.
 Includes bibliographical references and index.
 ISBN 978-1-4094-3889-2 (hbk) ISBN 978-1-4094-3890-8 (ebook) 1. Online social
networks. 2. Social media. 3. Internet--Social aspects. 4. Electronic surveillance. 5.
Eletronic intelligence. 6. Privacy, Right of. I. Title.
 HM742.T76

Reprinted 2013

ISBN 9781409438892 (hbk)
ISBN 9781409438908 (ebk – PDF)
ISBN 9781409484264 (ebk – ePUB)

Printed in the United Kingdom by Henry Ling Limited,
at the Dorset Press, Dorchester, DT1 1HD

Contents

Acknowledgments

This work would never have come to fruition without support from the following individuals. I am deeply indebted to David Lyon. Your mentorship and unwavering encouragement are the reasons why I chose to pursue and was able to complete this research. But your guidance went beyond academic concerns, and this is no more evident than in the success and happiness of your former and current students. This project would be severely lacking without Martin Hand's continued encouragement. Your office door was always open, you trusted me to teach your courses, and you were willing to lend books that you had just obtained. I am also grateful for Vincent Mosco's contributions through supervision and teaching. You have fostered a wealth of perspectives for me to approach my research, but have kept a sharp eye on the underlying concerns and relevance. This produces a sociology that is as nuanced as it is assertive.

I am extremely thankful for Laura Murray's interest and patience throughout this project. Likewise, Rob Beamish has helped tremendously by holding my work to a high standard during my time as a doctoral student. Mark Andrejevic's contributions through published research as well as direct feedback have also been invaluable. I would not be in this field were it not for all the stellar individuals in Surveillance Studies at Queen's University and abroad. I am especially grateful for Kevin Haggerty's guidance during the transition from graduate student to post-doctoral fellow, and Christian Fuchs' support in my continued journey as a postdoc. This book was also made possible thanks to the Department of Sociology at Queen's University, the Blakely Fund, the Ontario Graduate Scholarship, and the Social Sciences and Humanities Research Council.

This project was greatly enriched by all the friends and colleagues I met as a graduate student and postdoctoral fellow. I am honoured to include you in my social network, and have every confidence in your future accomplishments. Finally, this book would not be possible without my family's confidence and patience. Thank you.

Chapter 1
Introducing Social Media Surveillance

Introduction: Dwelling in Social Media

Social media complicates relations between individuals, institutions, businesses and police, by acting as a platform where all these groups converge. This book looks at the rise of surveillance practices on social media, using Facebook as a case study. Drawing on in-depth interviews with different types of users, it underscores new practices, strategies, concerns and risks that are a direct consequence of living on social media. Recent scholarship has considered social change stemming from social media (Miller 2011, Turkle 2011). These works point out the way that social relations are transformed by virtue of being mediated on platforms like Facebook. Issues of privacy, exposure and visibility clearly matter in these studies. This book follows from these concerns by concentrating on the process by which users manage their personal information on social media, while taking advantage of the information that others put up.

People increasingly live their lives on social media, suggesting that these services are a kind of dwelling. Framing social media as dwellings leads to several questions: Who lives on Facebook? How do they interact with each other? How does this co-habitation impact how they share their lives? This chapter addresses issues of exposure and visibility on social media, including the seemingly conflicting desires for privacy and publicity. It argues that different groups dwelling on Facebook lead to a mutual augmentation of their surveillance practices, a claim that is substantiated in later chapters. This chapter locates social media surveillance alongside scholarship on social media in general, as well as other types of new media.

I had the pleasure of spending my twenty-ninth birthday in an airport. If nothing else, this experience was a great thought exercise. Airports are transitory non-spaces. We use them as a means to connect with others. An increased reliance on airports produces the feeling that we dwell too much in them, rather than the locations that they connect. This becomes an opportunity to reflect on transient communities, and the importance of maintaining social ties. Most of the important people in my life are scattered around the world. While thinking about this distance, I began to receive notices on my phone, all of which directed me to birthday wishes on my Facebook wall.

These messages persisted for the rest of the day. I began to wonder: what if these were guests at a birthday party? I would need to rent a large hall, for one thing. Also, there would be potential for social discomfort. Work colleagues would be mixing with high-school friends, exes, and family members. Worlds would collide. What kinds of problems would arise? More specifically, what kinds of exposure would come from this? These concerns are not rooted in speculative fiction. Social convergence is a reality: it is a condition with which social media users cope.

Scholars commonly talk about social media as a kind of digital space. But based on its uptake, we can take this description further in saying that it is a kind of dwelling. We live through social media, and we live on social media. Moreover, this dwelling is characterized by social convergence, and this social convergence has distinct effects on our visibility. Social convergence refers to the increased social proximity of different life spheres. This provokes discomfort because we maintain different representations of ourselves, and these may clash or directly contradict one another. This discomfort suggests that we live compartmentalized lives, and that we perform differently in each context. Whereas most online spaces maintain these borders, social media, and Facebook in particular, are eager to demolish them. Social media like Facebook have the effect of making different fragments of our lives visible to all other fragments. If I solicit career advice on my Facebook wall, this may provoke a debate between an unusual assembly of social ties. Moreover, details from these various spheres are likely to leak elsewhere. Users are not prepared for this kind of exposure.

Early discussions of digital media claimed that it would revolutionize domestic life (Turkle 1984, Poster 1990). Indeed, proclamations about the profound impact of technologies are not uncommon. Today, social media appear to be a kind of dwelling in their own right. In abstract terms, this means they occupy more time in our lives, that we use them extensively without really noticing them. This is a consequence of the ubiquity of digital media: they are perpetually operational, and they assume an ever-greater presence in our lives. For users who live on these services, their continued creep is an inevitable development. We revel in the benefits of these technologies and cope with the drawbacks. Sites like Facebook become an extension of our interpersonal lives. But what they allow us to do in terms of social relations set them apart from the rest of the Internet. Earlier sites and services allowed us to bridge temporal and spatial gaps as well as overcome barriers. However this happens on a staggering scale with social media, for both local and global ties. This is partly due to their popularity: hundreds of millions of users – including hundreds of known peers – ensure that we never leave.

Dwellings matter for sociologists. They are a terrain for social life. They are the households and institutions where individuals are socialized. They are also the terrains where cultural meanings are constructed and negotiated. Their progressive migration online raises concerns over surveillance and exposure. Even casual Facebook users develop a presence that matters. Their profile is increasingly the default means by which they are known by others. Furthermore, issues of ownership and control are a source of concern for users. They invest time and energy in social media spaces, even if unsure as to whether they own or merely rent them. Sites like Facebook are used for social coordination. They are also spaces where users author their biography and their identity. Though these sites are usually free to join, prolonged investment in them produces a kind of social dependence. In facing this dependence we ought to consider the terms of our lease. These terms include unwanted visibility that is amplified by social convergence. Users are exposed in ways that cause immediate shock and embarrassment, but this visibility is multi-faceted, with long-term consequences that users do not anticipate.

Looking at how people use Facebook provides insight into the extent that we rely on these services. There is a user culture here, but it is pervasive in everyday life. Users connect with other users and share personal information with them. They rely on these sites as an everyday communication platform. But these services are changing quickly, and users are growing more comfortable with them, without knowing much about their long-term consequences. Users are moving more and more of their lives onto social media, without knowing who else is dwelling there. We can consider components that are central to Facebook. A Facebook presence is made of numerous parts that users employ.

First, the social media profile acts as a repository of personal information, a body of information that stands in for the actual body (boyd and Heer 2006). The profile marks the individual user's presence. But this presence depends on social connections. Upon creating a personal presence, users are invited to 'friend' people they know. This typically involves submitting a request to another user – be it friend, family member, acquaintance or stranger – who then accepts or denies the request. Users often accumulate hundreds to thousands of friends, and personal networks are thus created. Interestingly, these friendships become a kind of personal information that is displayed on the user's profile. To 'friend' another user means more than acknowledging that you know – or want to know – them. Friending also involves sharing personal information with that person. This includes biographical details, photographs, interests and virtually anything else the user is willing to share. Sites like Facebook have developed extensive privacy settings so that users can customize how much information they share with others.

Upon creating a profile, making friends and sharing with a personal network, users can coordinate social movements through social media. Facebook in particular has a few components to facilitate social activity. The 'events' feature allows users to publicize upcoming parties, protests and other events. Likewise, the 'groups' feature enables users to rally around a particular cause or belief. By joining a group and making that membership visible on one's profile, the user can explicitly support anything from a Haitian earthquake relief fund to a local coffee shop. This feature has been supplemented by the 'fan' application. Being a fan instead of a member suggests a commercial rather than organizational structure. If a Facebook user's contact list is composed of people who are socially relevant, it stands to reason that this site becomes a central resource for planning and coordination. University students who use the site report that it is an easy way to contact people about formal events, but also for pedestrian social coordination like planning study sessions. Organizations benefit from Facebook through its ability to harness pre-existing 'friend' networks to augment membership. Local businesses are expected to maintain an online presence. Consultants will gladly do this for them.

As a result of these features, Facebook plays a central role in users' lives. Their activities and personal details are housed on a medium that brings together so many different audiences, who in turn may contribute to that presence. The possibilities for exposure are staggering. These moments of exposure, whether performed by individuals or institutions, are often treated as transgressions. But these activities are built into the very fabric of social media. These sites are designed for asynchronous relations of visibility. The user – with the help of friends – builds a presence that others can visit at their convenience. Users regard this as one of the creepier aspects of Facebook. But its aggregate effects are no less disturbing: they bring about a convergence of social contexts. Unexpected consequences are common.

In practice, Facebook is contextual. Users make themselves visible by sharing information with others at a specific moment. But these moments add up, and a vast presence is accumulated. What's more, this presence is networked, as users help sustain each other's visibility. As this becomes our default representation, groups and organizations are increasingly referring to this once-casual profile. And in focusing on these concerns, we run the risk of mistaking Facebook for an empty shell that contains our presence. True, its valuation rests mostly on our contributions. However, those who design, own and control social media have their own agenda and intentions. They deliberately engineer the site to foster the kinds of social convergence and exposure that in return foster so much surveillance.

We depend on dwellings for privacy. Walls are supposed to shield from public scrutiny, to ensure dignity and to protect from worst tendencies. In the age of Facebook, walls become a public display of our personal lives. What happens when 'connecting' and 'sharing' take precedence over other values and needs?

Social Media: A Brief and Incomplete History

Social media are the focus of the following research. In their short tenure these services have become central to a lot of social, political and cultural upheaval. Their effects on mobilization and collective and individual identities are especially profound. But they are only the latest kind of technology that people have used to this end. It is therefore useful to consider a brief history of social media. This will help identify the novelties of recent sites like Facebook, as well as where they draw their influence. It will also give us a richer idea of online dwellings, and how they evolve over time. For this purpose, online communities from the 1970s and 1980s are an appropriate starting point. While the precursor to the Internet was restricted to the technological elite like military and scientists, they provide an early insight into the features that make sites like Facebook such popular dwellings.

Early examples of online dwellings include bulletin board systems (BBS), where users connected by dialup and exchanged data. They would return to the same BBS and maintain ties with other users. One notable community is the WELL, which was organized into thematic sub-communities. Users recognized the communicative value of these services, and invested a heavy presence in them (Rheingold 2000). Though restricted to a more tech-savvy population, BBSs anticipated social media's value for exchanging information. Around the same period, Usenet was also attracting a lot of attention. Like Facebook, it had origins in the post-secondary sector. It was used primarily for news and discussion, covering a broad range of topics. These were locations where people could discuss things that were otherwise dismissed as eccentric, and even stigmatizing. At the time the Internet was treated as something distinct from the offline world, meaning it was easy to separate these two spheres. Yet Google's acquisition of Usenet in 2001 saw this relatively obscure content leak into the public (Google 2001). Previous understandings of privacy and anonymity were compromised, setting the tone for new kinds of exposure.

Other online spaces have emerged since Usenet. The continued growth of the Internet, coupled with increasingly affordable home computers, contributed to the rise of the web. Web-hosts like Geocities made it easy for a broader population to build an online presence. These were often personal in nature, and while the audience had the potential of being global, these sites also attracted people who were known to the author. Meanwhile, chat rooms and message boards carried the use and function of BBS communities into the mainstream. While these were celebrated for allowing connections between virtually anyone, this connectivity was also framed as a risk. The fact that youth could interact with child predators was presented as a very real danger, and a reason to police these spaces with greater intensity.

The emergence of sites like LiveJournal in 1999 was another step towards social media. While LiveJournal was a weblog service, it shared two features with contemporary social media: personal profiles and the ability to add other users as friends. In its early days, users could only join through invitations from their peers. Users were generally known to one another in other contexts, meaning the audience was less anonymous and more situated. In terms of design and reception, LiveJournal was treated as a kind of online diary. Other features anticipated the rise of Facebook: privacy settings, and the ability to aggregate friends' content into a stream. These had the effect of simultaneously hiding and exposing user content. Friendster was launched in 2002 as a more prototypical example of a social media dwelling. The emphasis shifted from diary entries to the profile as a site of activity and interest. Despite a sudden rise to popularity, Friendster was restricted to key subcultures and communities, such as Burning Man enthusiasts. While Friendster eventually garnered one hundred and fifteen million users, its success was eclipsed by MySpace, which took on a more mainstream following. MySpace also saw a pronounced investment by the media industry and was purchased by News Corporation in July 2005 for over a half-billion dollars US. This compromised its success as a standard dwelling, as it developed a reputation for having more aspiring entertainers than conventional users.

When Facebook was launched in 2004, it was only accessible to students at a few Ivy League universities. Facebook is currently the largest social networking site in terms of users and activity, although older services are still used extensively. In addition, other sites have emerged that target specific populations. Sites like CyWorld, Orkut and StudiVz were designed for users in specific countries. Sites like LinkedIn and ASmallWorld have a pronounced emphasis on the kinds of professional networking that have previously occurred on golf courses and in cigar lounges. While Facebook continues to grow, other services have emerged that have capitalized on its success as well as its mistakes. Twitter has long been touted as a 'Facebook killer' though these two services work remarkably well in tandem. Twitter resembles Facebook's 'status update' feature, with followers instead of friends. This makes it ideal for quickly dispensing social commentary. Foursquare marks the rise of geo-locational social media, as users can 'check in' to stores, restaurants and other locations. Facebook has since adopted the 'check in', marking a further dissolution of the barrier between the Internet and real life. These services mark a progression towards users being increasingly located and profiled. Moreover, as it becomes customary to use multiple services, this presence takes on further breadth. The advent of mobile web technology has further linked these services with everyday life through increased portability. Facebook has gone on to gather nearly one billion users, who upload nearly eight billion photos per month, to say nothing of text-based updates and other kinds of content (FB Statistics 2011).

This is only a partial history of online sociality, but it provides some guidance in terms of key features that have shaped the use and social effects of these services. First, they become more open over time. This is a product of information and communication technologies being more affordable, but it also speaks to the permeability of the content shared by users. These services are increasingly explicit about sharing, and are designed to solicit more information. But users also shape social media: online activity becomes more accepted and even expected in order to be social, with fewer barriers to access and publishing.

The services outlined above share a common theme. They have always been a kind of interiority. They are all spaces that users turn to for psychological and cultural comfort. People invest time and energy because of these rewards. Yet these services change over time. Online spaces used to be a refuge from offline scrutiny. But now people go offline for respite from online visibility. These spaces have become a lot more social, in the sense that they have more numerous and profound connections to the user's social environment. All the while, users have grown accustomed to this technology. They are more comfortable with its presence in their lives. They are more accepting of the fact that so many people use it. More users mean a broader audience for an online presence, more social applications. It also means these services are less insular, providing less respite and more connections to real life consequences.

Marketing and journalistic hype about these technologies relied on heavy-handed claims. They promised connections between social realms, the reunion of dispersed families, in addition to a competitive advantage for businesses. These early promises might have overstated social effects, but they are indicative of the end state: a digitally mediated dwelling, one with considerable sociological relevance and social clout. Social media overcomes distance not only by bridging gaps, but by creating a spaceless space. It may have contextual cues, it may even be geo-located, but that does nothing to hinder its portability. Sites like Facebook are growing to an extent that they are locations in their own right. To be sure, they are not replacing offline spaces. But domestic life, identities and reputations undergo a radical transformation when the most minute personal details are searchable and archived indefinitely.

The Trouble of Social Media Surveillance

Social media are services where users dwell. They do this to connect with peers, and to share their lives with these peers. But they also have to consider the unanticipated consequences of sharing on new dwellings: namely, that otherwise transient activity is made permanent. The risk of exposure is tempered by privacy settings and other tactics at users' disposal. But users cannot control their peers, nor can they control the intentions of those who control services like Facebook. The longer that users dwell on Facebook, the more their lives are exposed.

Surveillance refers to the sustained and targeted collection of personal information. It is a loaded term, and is often associated with closed circuit televisions and international espionage. But these visions overlook the fact that surveillance is so pervasive in everyday life. Not only do people routinely give up their information in everyday life, but they also take advantage of the visibility of others. Surveillance is also an enduring process. It is not just individual moments of exposure, but the basis of relations between individuals, organizations and the state. This is also apparent when considering the longue durée of social media. Surveillance evokes concern because of privacy violations. But other consequences are equally pressing. Surveillance is the driving force behind social sorting, the allocation of life chances and business models in the information economy.

Social media is best understood as a series of practices surrounding the authoring of personal information, creation of interpersonal networks and the development of coordinated activities. These practices are largely based on information sharing and perpetual visibility. In order for the site to function, users are expected to routinely submit information. The rapid adoption of social media by individuals and collectives suggests that social life is increasingly mediated by these services. A sociological perspective highlights four dilemmas brought on by the rapid adoption of social networking technology. These dilemmas correspond to four distinct phenomena: individual usage, institutions that attempt to manage these individuals, marketers that are seeking new ways to harness (or 'monetize') personal information and police as well as other investigators who are turning to social media.

The first dilemma is that individuals struggle with changing language, norms and practices. Users feel a tremendous social pressure to join social media. Mary, a student we will meet in Chapter 3 states: 'I just thought Facebook was complicated and stupid, but my friends completely pressured me into it because they all had Facebook, so I got Facebook, and it wasn't too bad.' Even those who wilfully join report that their presence is, at least partly, beyond their control. Users have to manage connections with hundreds of peers. This involves a calculated public image, withholding certain types of information from certain friends and a heavy degree of self-censorship to cope with a heterogeneous audience. To complicate matters, a user's friends are more than an audience. These peers are actively involved in constructing the user's identity both in obvious and, as we shall see, non-obvious ways. They can offer commentary on any kind of content provided by the user, either endorsing or questioning the user's self-presentation. They can take an even more active stance by posting on a user's wall or tagging the user in a photo or video. It stands to reason that an individual's identity is increasingly a collaborative endeavour. Self-presentation is ultimately beyond individual control, and undesirable details may leak out because of an individual's peers. This has led to arguments between users over social norms on social media. But while comparisons to stalking gained prominence during Facebook's initial ascendancy, this has arguably given way to descriptions that take a more casual and accepting approach to sharing personal information.

Similarly, terms like friendship, privacy and visibility need to be reconsidered in light of relations now mediated through Facebook. While users are developing practices and protocols for social networking, they can barely keep up with features and privacy settings that are routinely introduced. The fact remains that more users are sharing more personal information with a rapidly growing audience of colleagues and strangers. Terms like 'public' and 'private' no longer suffice to describe the information, the users or the venues. In light of these developments, sociologists must shift their attention to the seemingly contradictory reproach and enthusiasm that is characteristic of social media users.

Second, institutions struggle with risks associated with social media, but also take advantage of the visibility of its user base. Individuals and institutions are made more visible to one another. Individuals increasingly maintain a detailed presence on sites like Facebook. All sorts of socially relevant conversations occur on these spaces. This extends beyond any particular social sphere as it becomes technologically possible and increasingly normative to be 'always on'. Moreover, users can publically affiliate themselves to institutions like workplaces, universities and government branches. Individuals on Facebook who are affiliated with these places are a potential liability. A disgruntled employee may publicly denounce her workplace. Likewise, an employer may deem photographs from a user's weekend inappropriate and misaligned with their corporate image.

Individuals also treat social media as a source of knowledge about schools and workplaces. New students may consult their university's homepage to find out about courses and residences, but they will certainly join Facebook groups like 'class of 2015' and 'must knows about courses' to learn from their peers. Potentially undesirable aspects of these institutions such as a reputation for being a 'party school' are publicized. Institutions face a complicated challenge in that their reputations on social media are in the hands of the user base, and misinformation can potentially go unchecked. Yet there is a student backlash against institutions having a visible presence and involvement on these sites.

The exposure described above is not appealing for media and communications officers, or any other institutional employee now burdened with social media. But there are tremendous opportunities for institutions that successfully utilize this technology. Institutions are often charged with the task of closely observing populations. Social media offer unprecedented access to their personal details, with users having little to no awareness when this information is being gathered. Institutions are thus chastised if they make a visible presence, but it is increasingly a possibility that they loom in the background and watch over user activity and personal information. Students, it seems, are living their lives online. But employees also have a professional and personal presence on these sites. Infractions and other events of concern are made visible and searchable. Institutions see their jurisdiction extending to sites like Facebook, and thus into their members' personal lives.

Third, social media are a risky opportunity for businesses. Like institutions and individuals, they are changing their practices in response to the exponential increase in visibility of their clients and markets. But they are also made visible to their clients when users upload opinions, reviews and experiences with their products and services. The ability to know populations and social aggregates is rapidly changing businesses that value knowing their market as well as their own reputation. The claim that any publicity is good publicity needs to be revisited as personal details about everyday life are cast into the public eye. Facebook users can effortlessly share their views about brands and products. They can also create communities based on the shared dislike of a business. The ease with which these groups gather members, coupled with the fact that they are searchable on the site as well as on Google, suggests that this is a growing concern for corporations. More than just a collection of individuals, Facebook makes its user population searchable through attributes. Groups and fan pages contain detailed conversations about brands and products. For better or worse, businesses are actively involved, along with a new category of experts, consultants, 'gurus', and 'rock stars'. Old work is refitted with new media.

Social media services have an incentive to cash in on this growing body of information. Facebook offers a series of 'business solutions' to companies wanting to utilize the social network. This corresponds to a wealth of social engagements, ranging from creating fan pages to in-depth advertising schemes where information is collated about users. By harvesting personal information, businesses acquire knowledge about users that users themselves may not possess. Amid this discussion, we should not forget that Facebook itself is a business. While it presents itself as a free service to its user base, it exploits the resource it collects: personal information. Users are left wondering who owns and collects their information, although they are certain that it is of significant value to whoever does use it. Clancy, another student claims: 'You can have some stupid little game or something, but it can be run by Nike and you just don't know, so you're using some satellite company.' Finally, social media presents new challenges as well as opportunities for police and other investigators. Policing has always been centred around information collection. Cases are built on the basis of good evidence, and contemporary police tactics are centred on this. One way to gather evidence is to maintain strong ties with the public. Community policing has a long history, and has undergone a particular revival in recent years. But investigators also sought to bypass face-work by turning to digital technologies.

As social life continues its migration onto social media, it stands to reason that criminal evidence would find its way on sites like Facebook. When Facebook was restricted to university students, evidence of student parties would inevitably leak onto the site. Underage drinking and other transgressions took on a new public venue. While it came as no surprise that students occasionally abused alcohol, its presence on Facebook warranted a more public response. These services became another terrain for investigators to monitor, with an accompanying learning curve. But by virtue of the ease with which they gathered and distributed information, they are also a powerful tool for retrieving evidence. A typical profile contains personal information authored by an individual and their peers over a prolonged period of time. Moreover, the social qualities of social media are a tremendous asset. The 2011 Vancouver riot is distinguished from the one that took place in 1994 because of the ubiquity of digital cameras. Thousands of photos were submitted to sites like Facebook, and facial recognition technology as well as human volunteers put names to faces. While new developments are constantly emerging, it is clear that police work on social media takes advantage of as-yet unnamed qualities that are unanticipated by most users.

Research Questions

Compared to celebratory and damning accounts of new media, user interactions with Facebook are astonishingly mundane. The exchange of text and images between users is by no means a new development. Yet it is the fact that much of the technology involved has been around so long that makes Facebook so interesting. Newer services like Facebook are modelled on earlier ones, often with minor changes. They also undergo perpetual revisions that ensure an immersive user engagement. Likewise, users' own practices change with time. Some users will disable key features on the site like the wall and photo albums. Others will rely on pseudonyms and multiple accounts.

Through their familiarity with social media, users have become accustomed to sharing personal information online. Facebook is an increasingly refined interface for authoring and exchanging social and personal information. New conditions of information exchange, fuelled both by finely tuned technology and a rapidly growing user base, create extensive new visibilities and as such demand examination from a Surveillance Studies perspective. More and more personal information is circulating online; what are the new conditions and dynamics of this exchange? Two key questions govern this research.

First, how are sites like Facebook used to exchange personal information? A broad range of social actors is using this technology, which begs scrutiny of the most appropriate diagrams for conceptualizing information exchange. To assist the analysis that follows, four models are proposed.

First, lateral – or peer-to-peer – information exchange refers to a decentralized exchange between individuals through Facebook's servers. This includes providing personal information to users who make up a 'friend' list as well as to strangers who may have access to this information. Thus, lateral surveillance includes the harmless exchange of information between trusted peers as well as stalking and other harmful transgressions.

Second, institutional information exchange occurs when institutions monitor key populations. Corporate and government bodies are a prominent feature of the new information landscape. Their reputation is recast in light of the domestication of information technology. But they now have the increased ability to collect information about the individuals whom they serve or govern.

Third, aggregated data mining is used primarily by businesses to study key markets. Not only are individuals made more visible to corporate entities, but social media also allow marketers to pinpoint specific fragments of a population. It has never been easier to track college-educated men between the ages of 25 and 34, or politically conservative Yale alumni who reside on the eastern seaboard of the United States. On Facebook personal identities give way to sortable data and aggregated knowledge.

Finally, police and other investigators use Facebook and other social media to enhance their investigative scope. These organizations are no strangers to surveillance, but social media conditions provide new opportunities to watch over populations. Police may have a presence on these sites, usually for public relations reasons. But a lot of their investigative efforts are covert. Investigators may pretend to be someone else, they may remain hidden from public view, or even bypass the interface through legal channels. These strategies take advantage of unknown or understudied features of social media. These practices are interesting for the study of crime and policing, but they also tell us a lot of the social features of social media.

The second question considers what kind of dynamic exists between these four diagrams. I propose that a kind of 'mutual augmentation' exists between individual, institutional, aggregate and investigative forms of surveillance on social media. This dynamic stems from the fact that these four diagrams co-exist within the same informational platform. By sharing not only the same body of information, but also the same interface used to access that information, formerly discreet surveillance practices feed off one another. As an example, consider how marketers now benefit from 'user-generated value' when individuals exchange relevant information amongst themselves. Likewise, university-age users have adopted new criteria of 'employability' and 'liability' to assess their peers as well as themselves. This is a logical extension of the assumption that employers, the police and other typical 'watchers' may access their personal details.

What Do We Already Know About Social Media Surveillance?

We know that social media are a dwelling, and that this introduces problems for its users. The research in this book queries the kinds of surveillance that take place on Facebook, and their relation to one another. Other scholarship helps situate these queries. The research presented in subsequent chapters addresses new media and Surveillance Studies. It is therefore necessary to consider how these two fields situate this topic. Following this, we turn to recent scholarship that addresses surveillance practices that use social media. In talking about technologies and devices, I take an anti-essentialist approach to their social effects (Grint and Woolgar 1997) that recognizes a mutual co-construction of technology and social reality. While designers, marketers and users inscribe values, uses and possibilities into technologies, these technologies become crystallized, constraining and shaping how we use them. In the case of social media, they shape how we interact with each other.

Social Media as 'New' Media

Before reviewing literature on social media, it would help to briefly consider the insights offered by recent literature on new media cultures. This will not only illuminate key features of social life in the digital age, but also illustrate the principal frameworks through which social media surveillance has been made meaningful.

Social media are still new. We are still coming to terms with their presence in our lives. But this is not the first time that we are coping with new technology. Social media are only the latest kind of new media. In fact the term 'new media' is quite old, and arguably has fallen out of favour. But the broader category of 'new' offers a context to understand technological growth, the visions that surround them and their social consequences. For one thing, new technologies are always accompanied by claims and promises of social upheaval (Mosco 2004). And while these promises often fall short, some curious developments can be discerned when these technologies take root. Below we consider some frameworks that help make 'new' meaningful. Three specific frames provide insight: convergence, ubiquity and the rise of Web 2.0. These terms are rooted in computer science, but comment on the broader social effects of new media. With a working understanding of these terms, this section then considers the sociological impact of social media.

Convergence as a concept illustrates the social impact of new media saturation. Its sociological relevance is demonstrated by connections between formerly distinct practices and contexts (Jenkins 2006). Convergence refers to a series of phenomenon that must be considered separately in order to develop a full appreciation of the sociological novelty of new media. Technological convergence is manifest at the level of hardware as well as software. Regarding the former, the recent proliferation of mobile devices demonstrates how formerly distinct functions are now handled by a single device. At the turn of the twenty-first century, a technologically savvy individual would carry a multitude of mobile devices. In addition to a cellular phone, the user might also carry a digital camera, digital music player and personal digital assistant. None of these devices would offer the user access to the Internet. A few years later, a single device – be it an iPhone, Blackberry or another kind of smartphone – can stand in for all these gadgets, all while connected to the Internet. This transition suggests a shift where several functions have converged to a single device. This does not imply that smart phones have achieved a kind of technological hegemony. Digital music players now record video and connect to the Internet. Digital cameras offer seamless access to photo and video sharing websites. Tablets and netbooks have been introduced as more portable counterparts to desktops and laptops.

These devices are the platforms upon which users engage with software. But software like Facebook also demonstrates a socially significant kind of convergence. Prior to social media, users would visit specific sites to read news items (cbc.ca; bbc.co.uk), to upload photos (flickr.com), watch videos (youtube.com), reconnect with erstwhile colleagues (classmates.com) and pursue romantic interests (match.com). Facebook markets itself as performing all these functions. This is not to suggest that this social networking site has eclipsed the above sites, although it has long surpassed Flickr as the largest collection of user-submitted photographs. Rather, it operates on an 'either/or' logic that is illustrative of software convergence. Convergence is a misleading term because it suggests that all are collapsed into one (Manovich 2008). It is more appropriate to think about multiple accumulations of functions, or information. Facebook is internally equipped to perform any of the above features. In addition, it offers connections where content from any of the above sites can be accessed. This can be done automatically though third-party applications, or manually if another user brought this content onto Facebook. This is sociologically relevant because separate practices now coexist on the same artefact. The fact that Facebook offers a breadth of services suggests that it creeps into numerous social spheres for the average user. With academic, professional and personal relations being directed through Facebook, we can also speak of a generic social convergence of social spheres (Gates 2006).

Convergence is accompanied by a saturation of technologies that produces a specific kind of environment. The spread and saturation described above resembles ubiquitous computing. Mark Weiser first envisioned ubiquitous computing while working at the Palo Alto Research Centre in 1988. As a principal scientist at a private research and development company, Weiser was enlisted to envision a new manner to market computers. Ubicomp rests on the claim that the minutiae of everyday life are increasingly managed by computing devices. These devices operate by pervasively collecting information from users, performing tasks and providing services in response to this information.

Weiser considered the hardware requirements for an ambient engagement with computers. Computing hardware is recast as smooth surfaces that are integrated into already mundane things. Computers are thus materially downplayed as either something that easily disappears into pockets and book bags, or are entirely assimilated by kitchen appliances and coffee tables. A disappearing interface is not simply another accomplishment of computing devices, but rather part of the ongoing deployment of technology manifested by users and devices alike. In many respects, this process resembles blackboxing, whereby 'the scientific and technical work is made invisible by its own success' (Latour 1999: 304). So long as the proper functioning of ubiquitous devices is assured, the various acting components which constitute a ubiquitous system may come to be recognized as a single agent. Attention can be shifted from the sets of devices that are employed within everyday life to the higher-order abstractions. Adam Greenfield (2006), a self-described critical futurist, suggests that ubicomp will act on abstract concepts such as 'the body', 'the room', and 'the city' through its ability to put computers into the things that make up these things. Thus, ubicomp not only suggests the embedding of computers in all spheres of social life, but a particular deployment that shifts attention away from these devices back onto the user. Ubicomp is about the disappearance and subsequent invisibility of computing, enabling the totality of everyday life to be made visible and knowable. Distinctions between online and offline recede as users experience a perpetual engagement with information and communication technologies (ICTs). These are the ideal conditions for social media to have a ubiquitous reach in social life.

Facebook exemplifies a software corollary of ubicomp through its spread onto mobile phones and other portable devices with wireless capabilities. In fact, many of these devices bear a striking resemblance to the pads, tabs and boards that Weiser (1993) envisioned. These mobile interfaces enable users to send and search personal information through a growing range of wearable and 'always-on' devices. This ensures a more pervasive engagement with social networks, with ubiquitous visibility and broadcasting stemming from a ubiquitous proliferation of technology. As well, this development echoes Microsoft developer Dave Stutz's endorsement of software that operates 'above the level of the single device' (O'Reilly 2005).

The mobile development marks one path towards social saturation, but ubiquity goes beyond the ubicomp framework. Its ongoing development reflects a calculated attempt to saturate its presence in a variety of social settings, but also to draw attention away from this presence by making the interface as intuitive and responsive as possible. Increasingly robust privacy settings and a customizable interface have the explicit purpose of enhancing the user's experience of – and integration within – Facebook. One developer describes ongoing developments as 'making it easier to get to the information you want to see' (Abram 2007).

Elsewhere on Facebook's weblog, new features are said to reflect the 'intention of making the profile cleaner and simpler and more relevant, while still giving you control over your profile' (Slee 2008). Furthermore, the devices that connect to Facebook require less user intervention as they assume a greater presence in domestic settings.

By deploying a pervasive, yet unobtrusive platform for the exchange of personal information, social media are located within the ubicomp framework. By facilitating its pervasiveness (increasing the number of users who engage with Facebook through computing devices) as well as its apparent passivity (an invisibly transparent presence that enables users to focus on uses, not devices), Facebook stands to become further embedded in everyday practice. The growing pervasiveness of wearable computing devices foreshadows an ambient social networking functionality. As such, a watershed moment for the ubiquity of social media is when the focus shifts from its interface to its content (that is, when it will be possible to use Facebook without talking or thinking about Facebook itself). The trajectory envisioned by Weiser also suggests that technology that is popularized and saturated becomes quite banal (Mosco 2004). Facebook relies on banal technology at the level of hardware and software. Ubiquitous computing speaks to a long-term projection of the future of computing. In contrast, Web 2.0 is a more short-term projection of the shape of things to come, and speaks directly to the advent of sites like Facebook.

Web 2.0 describes a variety of online platforms and services that rely on users submitting information. This has led to the prominence of user-generated content as a feature for online presences. In addition to providing original content, web users are also invited to provide content in response to content already online. This includes rating and commenting on items on Amazon and eBay, but also offering the same input on news items. Most conventional news sites have made this a standard feature, and TV news programs direct their viewers to these sites. Although some authors have questioned the value of user-generated content (Keen 2007), others have maintained that the 'wisdom of crowds' is a tangible resource through Web 2.0 (Thompson 2008). Likewise, Twitter streams and Facebook profiles, by virtue of being a series of innocuous bits of information authored over a long period of time, eventually add up to represent something more significant. They provide greater insight in terms of identifying and profiling users.

O'Reilly (2005) considers other features of Web 2.0. First, these services are always subject to revision. New functions are introduced, and old ones are revised. These changes are often in response to user complaints and requests. While this does not render software testing redundant, much of this labour is offloaded – explicitly and implicitly – onto the user. Explicitly because software developers release a beta version of a program, making revisions based on user feedback. But this is also a less obvious process when sites like Facebook and Amazon harness user feedback to revise the services they offer. Second, information is increasingly 'pushed'. Notifications on mobile devices and news feeds on Facebook seek and display relevant information for the user. Upon identifying a relevant individual, weblog or topic, these features will present the user with the latest content from these sources. This has proven to be an effective way to manage the sharp increase of user-generated content, especially when taken in aggregate. Third, software operates above any single device. As software is designed to function seamlessly on multiple devices, it is rendered mobile. This enables an ease-of-use associated with convergence, in anticipation of prolonged and seamless user experience.

Beer and Burrows (2007) recognize new conditions of Web 2.0 for the social sciences, both as a topic of and tool for research. They argue that consumption is now bound to production, which necessitates a reconsideration of these concepts. A key dilemma is whether consumption becomes labour if it is a value-adding process. This development is also tied to online dwellings having a greater involvement in users' personal lives. Thus, active involvement on these sites is tied to authoring private and personal information in the public domain. Web 2.0 services generate a wealth of content for analysis, although ethical concerns are raised. Lately, the term 'social media' has come to replace Web 2.0 as a catchall for the above features.

The features illustrated in a Web 2.0/social media framework help situate information exchange through new media more broadly. Following public criticisms that social media mark a 'dumbing down' of information exchange (Keen 2007), recent scholarship shifts from the content to the exchange itself by underscoring the phatic value of these services (Miller 2008). Instead of dialogic communication, new media are used to convey social linkages. These exchanges are not communication for information's sake, but rather communication for communication's sake. Consider a series of brief text-messages between long-distance lovers meant to acknowledge affection rather than convey any specific message. A chief scientist at Yahoo claims: 'No message is the single-most-important message. It's sort of like when you're sitting with someone and you look over and they smile at you' (Davis, in Thompson 2008: 5). We may speculate that social ties are maintained or kept idle in case they need to be used. While relevant information can be exchanged on Facebook, the Facebook culture of status updates, pokes and gifts is more akin to phatic exchange. From this perspective, the information in contemporary information exchange is heavily downplayed. Yet information that is light on content still holds social weight by conveying that the sender is thinking about the receiver. More importantly, it is disassociated from immediate context, suggesting an ever-present but unobtrusive flow of information between people. Likewise, Grinter and Eldridge (in Miller 2008) attribute the popularity of text messaging among adolescents to the fact that weighty narratives give way to bits of immediately relevant information.

This suggests that contemporary information exchange is based on a rapid production and consumption of content. While a social presence via authored information is tied to use-value, it also creates new conditions of visibility that require further inquiry. The new baseline requires users to maintain co-presence (Zhao and Elesh 2008) by continually submitting social information. It may initially seem devoid of content or meaning, but might carry meaning at a later point. The rise of 'trending topics' in Twitter demonstrates how a short-term cultural climate is now more visible and searchable. These trends are built from tags that describe any single message, but point towards a zeitgeist when taken in aggregate. For example, Peter Falk, Nicki Minaj and Marriage Equality all featured prominently among over three hundred million Twitter users during the week of June 24, 2011 (Silverman 2011).

While earlier literature suggested that computer mediated communication was decontextualized from the material world, the advent of new media services has strengthened the connections between online and offline environments. Thus, a dramaturgical approach based on self-presentation has more purchase than postmodern approaches to online sociality (Robinson 2007). New media technologies are not divorced from user context, but actually refer back to it. Indeed, they are embedded in contemporary social relations. This is a key feature of a networked social morphology that scholars have described in great length. Networked sociality shapes contemporary labour through individualization, the blurring of work and play, and social ties that oscillate between dormant and intense (Wittel 2001). New media technology makes these developments possible, and these conditions leak from the workplace to everyday life.

The changing nature of information as a kind of social currency suggests that narratives have been displaced as a key imagery. Lev Manovich (2001) offers the database as a more accurate representation of contemporary information. Whereas narratives frame information as linear and situated, databases are not confined to any single context or framework. The narrative's inherent stability gives way to the perpetual input that feeds the database, which itself is extracted from any local context. Scholars like Knorr Cetina (1997) describe the post-social features of new media technology. This is not meant to suggest that humans are absent from social engagement, but rather that various layers of software and hardware dehumanize human-to-human relations. While this perspective offers insight, research on emergent media should not shift attention away from the user, especially as they are negotiating with these layers. Even if they do not initiate engagement, the chain of interactions that follows still reflects on them.

Introducing Surveillance Studies

Surveillance Studies refers to a growing scholarly field, one that is borne out of several disciplines, including sociology, law, policy studies, information science and computer science. Surveillance implies watching over others, and is performed by individuals as well as organizations. David Lyon refers to surveillance as 'processes in which special note is taken of certain human behaviours that go well beyond idle curiosity' (2007: 13). Surveillance processes can be broken up into various steps: the collection of personal data, processing that data and the social consequences stemming from that assessment. This distinction is important because of temporal as well as contextual gaps between these steps.

Popular understandings of surveillance stem from dystopian literature and movies, including George Orwell's *1984* and Steven Spielberg's *Minority Report*. It also stems from the panopticon: a prison model by Jeremy Bentham, a nineteenth century English utilitarian philosopher, made famous by Michel Foucault, a twentieth century French postmodern philosopher. In the panopticon, all prisoners are made visible to a central tower while the guards cannot be seen. Surveillance becomes all encompassing, but also uncertain as inmates never know when they are being watched by the prison guards. This uncertainty pushes inmates to watch over themselves (Foucault 1977). This self-scrutiny is evident in contemporary society, as individuals become their own watchers and police their own behaviour. They know the extent to which their lives are visible to others. Of course, we can think of instances where a lack of self-awareness led someone to do something embarrassing, such as post a jeopardizing photo on Facebook. But these horror stories push everyone else to be vigilant in their self-scrutiny.

In addition to Orwell and Foucault, Surveillance Studies stems from the study of police practices (Marx 1988), emerging technologies (Norris and Armstrong 1999, Lyon 2009) and micro-level interactions to manage one's identity (Goffman 1959). Surveillance occurs in different contexts, and for different reasons. Yet these practices are similar in their collection of personal information. Gathering personal information is a dominant logic for modern governments and organizations (Dandeker 1990). Surveillance is ubiquitous, not just because of ubiquitous technologies, but because watching and assessing pervade nearly every social relationship. Surveillance is concerned with personal information, which is increasingly seen as a resource for corporations, evidence for investigative agencies and a liability for individuals. Personal information refers to biographical data like a date of birth, but also transactional data like online purchases. Virtually anything that can be linked to an individual – and to which they may be accountable – can be treated as personal information.

Some concepts are particularly relevant in Surveillance Studies: Oscar Gandy (1993) and others consider the importance of the profile. The profile is the principal interface between an individual and other individuals, but also with corporations, governments and other organizations. Individual profiles range from online identities on social media, to customer profiles in loyalty card systems. Profiles refer to any accumulation of information of an individual by an organization. Profiles are crucial to online sociality, as they enable users to build and maintain a consistent identity. But they also have a more nefarious element for users, who may lack control of their data, or even the ability to see their profile. Individuals routinely encounter troubles with their individual profiles, including credit reports, customer profiles with utility and telecom companies. These profiles operate on behalf of the user, who in turn struggles to fix disparities and cope with the consequences.

Profiles are a quasi-involuntary construction and representation of the self. But they also refer to broader categories, including racial profiles for policing and geodemographic profiles based on postal codes (Burrows and Gane 2006). By moving to a specific postal code, an individual may be categorized by a market research group as a 'newly wed or nearly dead' or as embracing a 'shotguns and pickup trucks' lifestyle. Again, these profiles serve as stand-ins for – or simulations of (Bogard 1996) – the actual person, and these simulations have rigid consequences for individuals. Cumulative disadvantage occurs when an individual is negatively profiled, and the consequences of this profiling impact life chances, further reinforcing the negative profile (Gandy 2009). The expansion of surveillance schemes is fuelled by a 'phenetic fix' (Lyon 2002): a desire by organizations to collect, classify and sort social life. Surveillance is a concern not only because people's social lives are visible in ways that are unanticipated, but also because models, profiles and simulations stand in for individuals, who in turn endure the consequences.

Many scholars contend that the rise of surveillance is a product of the rise of modernity. Large-scale migration to urban centres led to anonymity and a loss of interpersonal trust. This contributed to a climate that favoured new forms of verification and security. When reputations become less tangible, we turn to other measures for verification. This is most apparent in digital media, including eBay reputation systems, testimonials from colleagues and security measures on online dating sites. Some social media users suggest that Facebook marks a return to a small town dynamic, in the sense that everyone knows everyone else's business. But social media are a more enhanced form of surveillance when compared to the small town, as this information is retained indefinitely, rendered searchable and linked to a growing and volatile dwelling.

Another theme that cuts across Surveillance Studies is the balance between care and control. Surveillance practices are assumed to be a branch of social control, but many of these are implemented for the sake of ensuring a safe environment. This serves as a reminder that not all surveillance is negative. For instance, ask a cyclist what they think of aerial cameras that monitor speeding motorists, or ask a motorist what they think of the CCTV camera in their parking garage. Yet the semblance of care is also used to justify increasingly invasive procedures, and a greater concern with personal lives. The boundary between care and control is also blurry, such as when a parent who once used a baby monitor now installs a tracking device in their teenage child's car. Some of it may simply be benign, and this is made apparent when discussing exposure and visibility on social media.

Surveillance Studies identifies the convergence of formerly distinct surveillance regimes as a key concern. This includes merging databases and individual profiles, through technological innovation (Jenkins 2006) or through post 9-11 legislation like the 2001 USA PATRIOT Act that facilitated information sharing among security agencies. This suggests a kind of surveillant assemblage (Haggerty and Ericson 2000) that leads to all-encompassing and seemingly irrefutable profiles and by pushing information from one context to another. The notion of the assemblage is tied to a postmodern contribution to theories of social control. Although censorship still happens, as when Egypt recently invoked their Internet 'kill switch', pushing individuals to speak and implicate themselves is a more effective strategy. This can be traced back to confessional processes (Foucault 1980) but extends into contemporary culture through reality television tropes, empowering notions of interactivity and other attempts to solicit information. Quoting Gilles Deleuze: 'Repressive forces don't stop people expressing themselves but rather force them to express themselves. What a relief to have nothing to say, the right to say nothing, because only then is there a chance of framing the rare, and even rarer, thing that might be worth saying' (Deleuze 1995: 129).

Finally, 'surveillance creep' refers to spread of surveillance practices from one context to another. Invasive technologies typically emerge in airports, casinos and other locations that can justify a heightened scrutiny of individuals. This scrutiny is then normalized, and spreads to other contexts. Likewise, exceptional events can justify the unveiling of surveillance technologies. For instance, the 2004 mugging of Canadian figure skater Alexandre Hamel led to the establishment of a municipal surveillance camera project (Hier et al. 2007). These cameras were initially purchased in 2001, but were not rolled out until a public outrage could justify an initially unpopular move. Facebook's ability to crosscut social spheres makes it an especially fruitful platform for surveillance creep.

While the following section addresses privacy, already we see that surveillance and data collection are a concern for reasons that go beyond privacy. Surveillance regimes are indeed ubiquitous, multi-contextual and increasingly converging. Exposure is a concern, but surveillance also brings about profiling, a foreclosure of life chances and reinforces discrimination.

Privacy: A Very Brief Primer

Scholars struggle with privacy as a concept. For this reason we return to it on a few occasions in this book. Privacy is a legal concern that is linked to individual and collective rights, but it is also performed through everyday social interactions. In practice, individuals operate with various models of privacy, and these understandings are balanced against other concerns. Privacy is central to the study of surveillance, as well as the personal experience of surveillance. Its relevance in modern law was identified by Warren and Brandeis, who defined it as 'the right to be let alone' (1890), that is, freedom from surveillance and scrutiny. Alan Westin also shaped the contemporary understanding of privacy in his 1967 *Privacy and Freedom*. Westin describes privacy as 'the claim of individuals, groups or institutions to determine for themselves when, how and to what extent information about them is communicated to others' (1967: 337). This definition implies a degree of control over personal information flows, a process that has been greatly complicated since the 1960s.

The contemporary social value of privacy is nebulous. It conjures a sense of dignity as well as autonomy. Autonomy refers to a psychological sense of wellbeing, but also an instrumental ability to control the flow of personal information. Scholars like Nippert-Eng (2010) have elaborated on the social value of privacy by describing how individuals manage secrecy and avoid exposure in everyday situations. Bennett argues that while privacy is a vaguely defined value, it is also a cause that is championed by activists and policy makers (2008). Macro-level advocacy shapes laws, policies and best practices through an international network of governmental and non-governmental actors.

A micro-level understanding of privacy is informed by Erving Goffman's (1959) work on self-presentation. His dramaturgical approach expands on Shakespeare's notion that 'all the world's a stage' by framing social life as a series of performances. Individuals are deliberate and strategic in their social interactions. This is partly for the sake of cooperating with others to maintain a cohesive understanding of the world, but also to remain in good standing with others. Goffman makes a distinction between front and back stages. Front stages are locations and contexts where social performances occur and back stages are where these performances are managed. These regions map very well with a cursory understanding of 'the public' and 'the private', and are built into architectural design, as well as software interfaces.

The construction and performance of identity gains salience when considering another one of Goffman's sociological contributions: stigma (1963). Stigma refers to personal attributes that an individual wishes to hide from others, ranging from biographical details (a criminal record), a physical trait (a skin condition) or a social quality (an inability to follow a football game). Goffman contends that individuals go to great measures to hide stigmatizing information from public scrutiny, and that the privacy of the back stage is paramount for concealing these stigmas. Moreover, stigmas are as ubiquitous as the technologies and processes that risk uncovering them: '[T]here is only one complete unblushing male in America: a young, married, white, urban, northern, heterosexual Protestant father of college education, fully employed, of good complexion, weight and height, and a recent record in sports' (Goffman, 1963: 128). An oft-repeated critique of privacy is that 'if you have nothing to hide, you have nothing to fear'. Goffman makes a valuable contribution by stressing the fact that we all have something to hide.

Surveillance in Social Media

This book extends from the above findings by treating surveillance as a guiding dynamic on social media. While some surveillance is totalizing and hierarchical, it can also be lateral and diffuse. The advent of social media has caused a sharp increase in the amount of personal information online. The audience for this growing body of information is itself growing rapidly. This leads to new kinds of exposure and visibility that researchers are ill prepared to understand. What is perplexing about this visibility is that users are actively engaged in generating and distributing personal information about themselves (Beer and Burrows 2007). The routine, taken-for-granted nature of social networking is juxtaposed against a growing, searching and sortable body of information. This suggests a further expansion of the age of an information-based, or 'knowing' capitalism (Thrift 2005).

Scholars like boyd (2008) have assessed exposure on ubiquitous social networking. By drawing a link between technological convergence and a convergence of social spheres, she suggests that users' values associated with privacy are rapidly changing. While users could previously assume that personal information flowed through stable pathways, social media require a reconsideration of assumptions. In terms of assessing who was most willing to develop new privacy values, Fogel and Nehmad (2008) reported that those with profiles on social media were more likely to have greater risk-taking attitudes. While the public exposure of personal information is linked to risky cultural values, the mainstreaming of social networking – coupled with ever-changing privacy settings – is reversing this perception. Not being visible on social media is increasingly tied to an atrophy of social capital and a denial of life chances such as employment or meeting a romantic partner.

The extent to which social networking has augmented the amount and range of personal information made available online clearly has broad legal implications. Grimmelmann (2009) offers an in depth review of Facebook's privacy policies in accordance with the practices of its users. He suggests that users routinely harm each other's privacy interests as a result of the peer-to-peer nature of information exchange. He proposes a greater resonance between user practices and safeguards offered by social media to maintain their interests. Even with these recommendations, Facebook poses a challenge to existing legal frameworks. Steeves (2008) recommends that legal approaches recognize the social context in which personal information is handled on sites like Facebook. Given the kinds of social convergence reported in the above literature, this recommendation is as challenging as it is urgent.

By virtue of their networked morphology, services like Facebook pose unique challenges to users wanting to conceal their identity. Even if users hide information like their political affiliations (Wills and Reeves 2009) or sexual orientation (Jernigan 2009) reasonable estimates can be made based on their friends. Even if users never provide this information to their social network, their more public friends reflect on how they are identified. Research in this field needs to further explore the surveillance implications of increasingly public knowledge about social ties.

Users' ties to their peers are also a means for interpersonal forms of surveillance. Andrejevic (2005) notes that lateral types of surveillance have emerged through a wealth of domestic technologies including search engines, low-cost background reports and nanny cams. Beyond simply being visible, Albrechtslund (2008) contends that the act of sharing information on sites like Facebook can be a deliberate and empowering process for users. While users often confirm these positive outcomes, the acts of watching and being watched are coupled in a way that also augments conventional surveillance practices. Far from levelling the playing field, it is possible that increased scrutiny and visibility among Facebook friends renders everyone more visible to institutions like employers and governments. Users are deliberate in their decision to go on sites like Facebook.

They do receive benefits from their presence. Yet their visibility on these sites has many consequences, and some of these may not be apparent until much later. The complexity of social media, triggered by an increased involvement of social actors from different contexts, is fuelling the mutual augmentation of different kinds of social media surveillance.

Using Facebook as a Data Source

A growing body of scholarship suggests that Facebook is an increasingly relevant topic of academic inquiry. Its rapid growth has implications for the social sciences and humanities, legal studies and policy studies, among other disciplines. Yet in addition to being a topic for inquiry, Facebook already has a significant legacy as a device for scholarly research. That is, Facebook and other social media services are increasingly used as a source of research data. This was inevitable, given the vast amounts of personal information that these sites collect and host. Yet this development raises significant ethical and methodological issues to be addressed in order to assess this trend appropriately, and to temper the push toward turning personal information on social media into research data. Moreover, this is only the latest manifestation of the surveillance practices in the social sciences. This is often – perhaps conveniently – overlooked: the social sciences rely on the visibility of their target population. Empirical sociology has long rested on data collection from its subjects.

Facebook initially drew academic attention as a rich description of university populations. A lot of early scholarship involving Facebook used it as a window into undergraduate sociality (Ellison et al. 2006, Hewitt and Forte 2006). This focus follows a legacy of using students as a sample base in the social and behavioural sciences. As Facebook is wildly popular and spreading throughout an increasingly diffuse population, it is an increasingly de facto choice as a window into contemporary sociality.

Some other features need to be considered to contextualize this shift. Savage and Burrows (2007) report that the social sciences are in trouble. In an age of knowing capitalism, market research is surpassing academia in its use of the tools and techniques once championed by the social sciences. This development calls into question the role and value that sociologists can claim, as they are increasingly unable to match the scale of research performed by non-academic agents. In light of these concerns Savage and Burrows call for a 'politics of method' where these techniques are reappraised 'not simply as particular techniques, but as themselves an intrinsic feature of contemporary capitalist organization' (2007: 895). To be sure, social media contain potential for social scientists. Social networks can be used to assess taste patterns, and provide insight for the study of the dissemination of culture as well as a better optic for knowing social structure. Social media are part of a growing assemblage of domestic technology that gathers information on consumer behaviour and everyday life. This is 'knowing capitalism' in its clearest manifestation, and marketers and advertisers are the early adopters. Beyond corporations, computer engineers are demonstrating the sociological potential of the data found on Facebook (Thelwall 2010). It would be negligent for academics not to shift their attention to this emergent sociality.

Scholars have turned to the potential use of social networks in general and social media in particular as a source of research data. As 'the most explicit representation of social networks on the Internet' (Hogan 2008: 155), accessing sites like Facebook means accessing social networks as they are manifest in everyday life. Ostensibly, capturing a snapshot of a participant's social ties on Facebook is the most direct way to reproduce this data. Some scholars use this data to consider how health and taste patterns are manifest through social networks. The intersection of culture and social structure is especially relevant and germane in this context. When describing the potential for sociological insight of sites like Facebook, Lewis et al. state that they:

> are historically unique in the amount and detail of personal information that users regularly provide; the explicit articulation of relational data as a central part of these sites' functioning; and the staggering rate of their adoption. As such, they constitute a particularly rich and attractive source of network data – one that social scientists have only just begun to explore. (Lewis et al. 2008: 330)

Sites like Facebook are thus identified as an unprecedented source of relevant sociological information. Yet this does not resolve how this information should be collected. This research team elects to bypass the participant, and instead obtains their personal information directly from the source. A host of methodological reasons are cited as justification:

> By downloading data directly from Facebook.com, we avoid interviewer effects (Marsden 2003), imperfections in recall (Brewer and Webster 1999; Brewer 2000), and other sources of measurement error that may accompany survey research (see Bernard et al. 1984; Marsden 1990; Feld and Carter 2002; Butts 2003). At the same time, Facebook provides users with a standardized profile template that facilitates data cleaning, coding, and comparison across respondents. (ibid.: 331)

Facebook is treated as a canvas for the study of social networks insofar as users can continue to build their networks as a pervasive activity. Yet the authors acknowledge that users will not build their network with the intention of mirroring their real life network. They also identify the shift from 'public' to 'private' profiles as a complication for longitudinal studies. This stands out as a consequence of relying on the covert collection of personal information as a methodological approach. Despite these concerns, many scholars endorse using social media as a source of sociological data, stating that they provide 'a wealth of new opportunities for social scientific inquiry' (ibid.: 341).

For all the supposed benefits of research using social media, this approach has a number of limitations. First, Facebook was not designed for data collection. Taste patterns are not inputted as they would be in a survey, leaving vast discrepancies in the extent that users submit information on social media. The above authors are quick to point out that users 'differ tremendously in the extent to which they "act out their social lives" on Facebook: both the level of social media participation and the meaning of this activity undoubtedly vary across individuals and settings' (ibid.: 341). In addition to issues of generalizability, this kind of research makes assumptions about how concepts like friendships and social ties are operationalized. Researchers need to consider the kinds of actions on Facebook that constitute an act of friendship, or the manifestation of a social tie. Requesting or accepting a friendship connection seem like obvious choices, yet researchers scarcely understand the motivations that underlie these actions. Can a user with eight hundred Facebook friends maintain eight hundred friendships?

Contemporary research using social media rests on assumptions about their interfaces and practices. Based on the descriptions offered in this research, one would be led to believe that Facebook profiles are a kind of enhanced survey. Yet for all the scholarship surrounding Facebook, little is known about the epistemological status of the information-as-data. Little is known about the degree of consensus among users regarding the meanings that underlie activity on the site. This is not to exclude the possibility of research using Facebook, but rather a call to develop a better understanding of how users interface with Facebook.

The research described above raises ethical concerns. By collecting information from social networks, researchers are effectively sidestepping their participants and not obtaining consent. While behavioural research has long collected data using some degree of deceit, social network users submit information for purposes entirely unrelated to scientific research. Some users will object to their personal information being used to study taste patterns or social structure. Informed consent is an important cornerstone for contemporary social scientific research (Moreno et al. 2008). These concerns lead to fundamental questions in terms of the status of personal information uploaded or transferred through ICTs insofar as researchers are only one of several parties that are making use of this information. In the case of this research, the appropriateness of use rests on the perceived intention of participants. Researchers need to ascertain whether or not participants are publishing their content for a global audience. Moreno et al. contemplate the extent to which this information can be considered public or private. Users may publish it online, and not consider this content to be private, yet may object to this content being used in scientific research. This objection is central to concerns over privacy and visibility, and need to be explored further before giving carte blanche to this methodological approach. The fact that this research takes place without user consent furthers concerns about surveillance in the social sciences. Regardless of its empirical value, scholars need a better understanding of the interface from which they are drawing this data. At the very least, the sociological lens should shift its focus on social media users, and not just their digital traces.

Researchers also need to consider the harm that can be committed through research. Most scholarship on social networking and social media cites privacy concerns as a product of information being difficult to contain. Surveillance creep and information leaks mean that the misuse of information and compromised privacy are constant concerns. Thus, research that directly addresses privacy and visibility should be especially mindful of misusing information that users/ participants place online. Even anonymizing identities cannot be guaranteed, as researchers only scarcely understand the potential to re-identify people based on other criteria. For example, a researcher may remove participants' names, but publishing their social ties or location still identifies them to some degree. This is largely an emergent field, and so researchers should act with caution when it comes to using personal data.

Situating the Research, Situating the Researcher

Contemporary scholarship on social media has focused on the kinds of input that Facebook can provide as an interface. There is a pressing need to foreground social media users by having them describe the interface and their position in relation to it, instead of only using the interface to describe users. This will illuminate surrounding issues that are not visible when focusing exclusively on the interface itself. By placing users and not the interface as the point of departure, this research is able to point to the social effects of social networking technology. In focusing on users and their relation to Facebook, this research foregoes a direct exploration of how users are represented online. Research that focuses on users themselves will complement the research described above by placing a focus on the social context in which traces are authored. By developing a better understanding of the meanings and values that inform social media use, this research will help operationalize databased work. It also helps researchers situate themselves among other 'watchers' of social media by producing a better understanding of the agents involved in this kind of visibility.

The research in this book focuses on the factors that compel users to be on Facebook, how they justify this presence, how they conceptualize their privacy, how they conceptualize social relations like friendship, how they conceive of visibility, and how they manage their identity accordingly. This focus is founded on ethical concerns. One of the central purposes of sociological research is to give a voice to individuals and groups who are otherwise unable to do so in a scholarly forum. For all the talk of self-expression in celebratory discussions of social media, very little is known about how users themselves are balancing identity management and the interpersonal scrutiny of others. The call to prioritize the person in interpersonal management becomes all the more pressing when approaching this topic from a Surveillance Studies perspective. Considering how people are subject to unanticipated exposure while privileging their online traces reinforces the problematic effects of social media and contemporary surveillance. Studying Facebook by facing its users in an interview setting is also grounded in practical reasons. The purpose of this research is to study the interaction effects of social media interfaces and their user base. This necessitates not only knowledge of the ongoing development of the social media service, but also – perhaps especially – knowledge of how users are reconfiguring interpersonal exchange. This is best accomplished by approaching users directly.

This research describes the process by which conventional and atypical surveillant agents use social media to scrutinize personal information. In doing so it augments the visibility of those who take advantage of the augmented visibility of others. By no means is this the first time that Surveillance Studies has endeavoured to watch over the watchers (Norris and Armstrong 1999, Smith 2007). In exposing social media surveillance, the findings presented in the following chapters are an important contribution to the social sciences. But knowing about asymmetrical relations of visibility is the first step towards coping with them, and consequently this work contributes to advocacy and public awareness efforts.

Watching those who watch Facebook does not contribute to a levelling of visibility. As virtually all social actors are invited to engage with Facebook, addressing information flows does not remedy a simple 'watcher/watched' binary. However, raising awareness of relations of visibility is an important component of research on domestic surveillance technologies. With Facebook in particular, the technology and surrounding practices are still in formation, and it is important to cast light on conditions to which users are growing accustomed.

The above section outlines the importance of having knowledge of social media users in addition to the knowledge of the interface. Grounded knowledge of the interface will emerge by speaking with users. A preliminary and situated understanding will also come from the researcher's own use of and presence on Facebook. Social scientific research does not operate distinctly from social processes, and so the call to operate 'outside' of the social (Black 1995) is suspect as a prescription. Being a Facebook user does not compromise critical scrutiny. This engagement offers experiential knowledge, but subsequent research is still largely disinvested from the interface. Existing research on social media is pivoted along experiential knowledge, which is used to fuel critical inquiry (Boon and Sinclair 2009). In accepting one's position within the social, a Surveillance Studies researcher should endeavour to render visible processes by which others – particularly subaltern others – are rendered visible.

I joined Facebook in August 2006, roughly a month before choosing it as a topic of inquiry. I was not a heavy social media user prior to enrolling, but was curious as to the kinds of communities that were built on these sites. After using the site for a month, I was also struck by the kind of visibility of others that was offered to me as well as the visibility of myself to others. When taking it up as a topic, the controversies surrounding its expansion offered two perspectives: that Facebook and social media in general are a blatant violation of privacy, and that they offer unprecedented social affordances. These perspectives are not contradictory, but maintaining some distance from both is a sound point of departure.

Having a reasonable familiarity with Facebook as a user provides an initial grounding to understand how the interface operates, but also how its producers have revised its functionality over time. This experiential knowledge does not compromise empirical research, though it is important not to privilege this situated knowledge over how the topic of study is understood and practiced elsewhere. The researcher's experiential knowledge of terms like 'wall' and 'friend' serve as a point of entry to understanding what others are saying, but the researcher also endeavours to privilege the participant's use of these terms in order to underscore the fuzzy and often contradictory nature of using and understanding Facebook. Inside knowledge is a helpful starting point (Lash 2002, Beer and Burrows 2007), but so is using the inside knowledge of others. Indeed, researchers should be sceptical of their own status as an insider. Using services like Facebook does not mean having some privileged access to the surrounding culture, particularly when studying a feature of contemporary youth culture (Beer 2009b). Facebook has grown so much that being 'inside' Facebook has largely lost any significance. But deferring to digital youth is necessary to understanding digital youth culture.

Methodological Description

Two key questions govern this research. First, how are social networking sites like Facebook being used to exchange personal information? A broad range of social actors uses this technology, and so this research needs to consider the most appropriate diagrams for conceptualizing information exchange. Four models stand out: interpersonal, institutional, aggregate and investigative. Second, what kind of dynamic exists between these diagrams? The research in this book proposes that a mutual augmentation exists between different forms of surveillance on social networking sites. This dynamic stems from the fact that these diagrams co-exist within the same informational platform, and work with the same body of information. In order to answer the above questions, my research uses qualitative data collected from selected populations that use Facebook.

Key themes for interviews are shaped by what is already known about these activities. These interviews are semi-structured in order to account for emerging practices. Preparing for this research involved a scrutiny of key academic literature on social media as well as surrounding topics. This provided some indication as to broad themes underlying this research, as well as situated understanding of what is currently known about surveillance and social media. Three sets of semi-structured interviews were completed.

First, thirty undergraduate students who use Facebook were selected for study. These interviews were conducted between November and December 2008. These students were all enrolled at the same mid-sized Canadian university at the time of study. The decision to focus on undergraduate students was an obvious one in that universities were the first institution to use Facebook and many of the students interviewed report being users since it first became available in 2004. Although it has since grown to a more mainstream status, these students make up the population that is the most familiar with the service. As such, they are the most likely to notice changes in the interface, changes in the context surrounding its use, and would have been the first to experience consequences associated with prolonged use. These students are also relevant because of their immediate context. Many students use Facebook to maintain social relations with friends and family elsewhere, as well as foster new relations with other students. Yet they are also entering adulthood as well as the job market or postgraduate studies. For these reasons they become increasingly concerned with their public exposure.

Institutional surveillance on social media is also a growing concern. A second set of 14 semi-structured interviews was conducted with university employees who use Facebook as a workplace service. These interviews were conducted between February and June 2009. These employees worked at the same Canadian university as the first set of interviewees. While some participants had personal experience with Facebook and other social media services, they were all beginning to use these services in a professional setting. Key agents were contacted following meetings with two vice-presidents at the university. Snowball sampling was also used to contact further participants in specific offices. These interviews lasted 45 to 90 minutes, and were conducted at the participant's office. In order to produce a detailed account of Facebook's growing use as a business service, a third set of thirteen semi-structured interviews took place with employees and self-employed consultants who use Facebook as a business tool. These interviews took place between July and October 2009, and once again ranged from 45 minutes to an hour and a half in duration. These three sets of interviews provide a framework from which the recent rise of investigative surveillance is best understood. These interviews are supplemented by a review of recent journalism, policy reports and criminological literature on police work, technology and social change. Given the sheer novelty of these developments, this research focuses on social media policing primarily to develop a theoretical framework as well as research questions that anticipate its development.

Chapter Overview

Facebook is especially complex, and provides users with a lot to consider. We live with technology, and increasingly live through technology. Chapter 2 unpacks the notion of Facebook as a kind of dwelling with perspectives that are rooted in scholarly material from related fields. First, this chapter reviews the sociology of software, which highlights the importance of these interfaces for social life. Facebook is treated as software that enables the ubiquitous flow of information. Next, it considers the network as a diagram for social life. Social ties and social capital have become more tangible in the age of social media. This chapter then considers the dwelling as a means for publicity, exploring the presentation of self as well as contemporary branding practices. It then considers labour. In the twenty-first century users become the driving force of the information economy. Leisure becomes labour, as Facebook's owners rely on user engagement in order to achieve financial maturity. Social media are treated as sites of labour and exploitation, signalling an emerging surveillance economy. These four perspectives each contribute to the idea of the enclosure (Andrejevic 2007) as a model for life on social media.

Young users dwell in a Facebook that they no longer recognize. After building an extensive presence on Facebook, new guests, intruders and co-habitants complicate that presence. Facebook began as an extension of the campus dorm in that it was mostly harmless and inconsequential. 'Creeping' and 'stalking' were a mild concern, but also an enjoyable pastime. Suddenly, parents, professors and professionals joined Facebook, forcing young users to rethink their exposure. This impacts how they are watched, but also what they upload, and how they watch over each other. Chapter 3 examines interpersonal surveillance, that is, people actively watching and being watched by family, friends and former lovers. It unpacks everyday practices that have become complex in light of Facebook's expansion. It describes the soft coercion involved in using Facebook, including peer pressure to join the site. Users dwell on Facebook because their friends dwell on Facebook. Social media users balance cross-contextual transparency with a deliberate performance of public exposure. Users make themselves visible to each other, but also to their employers, government and law enforcement agencies. This chapter draws from a series of interviews with Facebook users. A thematic analysis focuses on the perceived risks associated with social media as well as measures taken to protect personal information. These interviews also consider how participants shape their engagement with social media using publicity and privacy as conceptual guides. As well, this chapter explores how these practices are made meaningful and even augmented through concurrent forms of surveillance that occur on the site.

The early days of social media proved challenging for universities. Faculty and staff were the subject of public criticisms, and school reputations were in the hands of outspoken students. Other institutions faced similar risks. Yet these institutions are responding to this exposure with a mix of official mandates and grass-roots expertise. Chapter 4 focuses on institutional surveillance practices that have been facilitated through Facebook, using the university sector as a case study. Institutions respond to new conditions of visibility offered by social media. While the abundance of user activity on Facebook complicates how these institutions are represented, they are better suited to watch over target populations. This chapter draws from a series of interviews with university administrators and employees that use Facebook in order to watch over student populations. As Facebook first emerged in an academic context, these findings provide a rich description of how institutions can scrutinize populations using social media. A thematic analysis chronicles the conditions that lead to the institutional scrutiny of Facebook.

With so many people on social media, it was only a matter of time before businesses got involved. Sites like Facebook present them with a dual challenge: fear of missing out, but also a fear of messing up. Amidst the social media gold rush, businesses were enthusiastic, but uncertain about how to exploit – or monetize – Facebook. Simply watching users? Simply broadcasting to users? Some mix of the two? Businesses' presence on social media implies a different kind of watching. Whereas interpersonal surveillance concerns the known acquaintance, and institutional surveillance sets its gaze on the members of a fixed organization, market surveillance targets relevant demographics. It is an aggregate surveillance based on the collection and processing of information on all Facebook users. Chapter 5 focuses on a new kind of visibility that is made available to organizations through social media dwellings. A broad set of organizational tasks – including market research, public relations and customer service – are augmented through a growing body of searchable personal information. This chapter describes emerging practices by organizations to cope with new relations of information exchange on social media. It offers findings from a series of semi-structured interviews with professionals who use Facebook as a business tool, including market researchers, brand managers and communications officers. Findings are organized along strategies used by businesses to capitalize on Facebook's data.

Chapter 6 considers policing and other kinds of investigations on social media. If Facebook makes it easier for friends to stay in touch with each other, what benefits does it offer police? At this point, virtually everyone dwells on social media. Police and other investigative agencies are thus handed a tremendous resource. Personal information and incriminating details are time stamped and made searchable on an ever-growing dwelling. Based on interviews with various kinds of Facebook users, coupled with emerging reports by advocacy groups and journalists, this chapter describes how police, intelligence and national security agencies use social media for investigative purposes. In addition to emerging practices, this chapter considers the features that make social media such a valuable resource for investigative agencies. These developments force a reconsideration of investigative practices like undercover policing (Marx 1988) and the use of criminal informants (Natapoff 2009). The fact that these agencies rely on the same service as so many other social spheres augments their ability to police social life. In particular, these agencies are able to exploit suspects' interpersonal networks in order to access otherwise inaccessible information.

The previous chapters consider a range of social media surveillance. But Facebook continues to grow as a dwelling, bringing in new inhabitants as well as new kinds of scrutiny and visibility. Researchers need to keep up with this complexity, as it has important scholarly, but also practical and policy implications. Chapter 7 considers the broader implications of the distribution of personal information through social media. Having covered extensive empirical and theoretical material on social media surveillance, this chapter returns to the term 'social' as it applies to social media. This understanding is rooted in the sheer complexity and volatility that scholars, users and policymakers face. After outlining the key features of social media surveillance, this chapter presents agenda-setting concerns for researchers, recommendations for users and directions for policymakers.

Chapter 2
What Kind of Dwelling is Facebook? Scholarly Perspectives

Introduction

There should be little doubt in the reader's mind about Facebook's importance for its user base. But saying that users dwell on it leaves many questions unanswered. Even if this imagery has an intrinsic appeal, we must ask what it means to 'live' on social media software? Just how much of their lives can users offload onto programming code and search algorithms? We share these spaces with our peers as well as strangers, with whom we are connected via social networks. How do these networks shape our relations to other users? If users are housing their identities on sites like Facebook, what kind of publicity does this produce? Privacy matters to users, but it becomes difficult to maintain when Facebook's developers seek so much publicity. Dwellings also require a lot of effort in their upkeep. Users may not consider it, but their everyday activity on social media is a kind of labour. Moreover, users merely dwell in a space that somebody else owns. What kinds of labour go in to building a presence on a site like Facebook? Looking at the above concerns builds a case for treating social media as a digital enclosure, that is, a model for containment, social control and visibility.

Social media are a new object of analysis. Literature on the social effects of new technologies offers insight, but we need to consider what Facebook's growth tells us about the category 'social media'. For this reason we need to examine the broader categories that describe Facebook. This chapter offers a multifaceted and conceptually thorough description of Facebook. Much of the existing research on Facebook is based on a single perspective, such as self-presentation, online communities or privacy violations. Rather than attempting a definitive account of its emergence, this chapter offers five answers to the question 'What is Facebook?' Facebook is first approached as a kind of software, and some key features of software in contemporary life are considered to clarify this. Next, Facebook is approached as a social network manifest through networked technologies. Thirdly, the site is also considered as a brand that in turn promotes the branding and publicity of its user base. Fourth, Facebook is described in terms of labour and exploitation. This chapter concludes by turning to the notion of the digital enclosure as embodying these four features. The digital enclosure is synonymous with the dwelling, but offers a more detailed account of social media's social effects.

Each section is rooted in a particular line of scholarly work. The material considered below dovetails with a selective description of Facebook's key features.

While this does not produce a single chronological account of Facebook's growth, these complementary accounts leave fewer conceptual and substantive blind spots. They underscore pressing concerns about surveillance and visibility, and justify the approach outlined in Chapter 1.

Facebook is Software

Facebook, and social media in general, are a far cry from ubiquitous computing. Whereas Weiser imagined that we would come to overlook the computers that saturate our lives, we are still very much fixated on our devices. Users have strong opinions of interfaces, and the slightest revision may upset them. But despite policing the interface, users rarely pay attention to the software that governs it. Facebook's software is what organizes and makes sense of information. It is the driving force behind social consequences like unwanted exposure and social convergence. So much social life is processed by software, and these processes are not value-neutral. And despite seeming intangible, software manages so much of the material world. It both transcends and regulates social life on social media.

Social media software is sociologically relevant. It transcends any single hardware device, maintaining a prolonged engagement with its users. It is embedded in the social world, and it regulates our lives. It is subject to ongoing revisions by its authors and in response to user feedback. This enables a rich engagement with services like Facebook, but also facilitates surveillance creep and unanticipated consequences when these services assume increasing command over our world. Software is extending its reach into social life, such that we need to consider the values that structure software, which in turn structure social life. Scholars looking at software treat it as a kind of information architecture. It shapes social encounters and possibilities, yet it easily escapes scrutiny by virtue of being backgrounded. A sociological understanding of software rests on two paradoxes.

First, software is seemingly immaterial, yet it has material consequences. Software situates users. For instance, the rise of geo-locational features on social media means that users can be plotted and mapped out in real time. Its enables more visibility and greater social sorting, and contributes to the information sector, or knowing capitalism (Thrift 2005), as well as a 'new new media ontology' (Lash 2007a). This reflects a postmodern commitment to localized contexts (Van Dijk 1999), particularly when storage and transmission are augmented by a globalizing time-space compression (Harvey 1990). Second, software is decidedly non-human, yet it is increasingly woven into human relations. Software is often tied to the rise of non- or post-human sociality, and information exchange within interpersonal relations is increasingly interfaced through software like Facebook. Users are deemed responsible for the effects and consequences that software produces, even when these users are largely uninvolved in the process.

Facebook's programming code facilitates information exchange between its users. Its software augments the visibility of its user base. As a portable – almost liquid – platform for information exchange, Facebook extends the scope of any surveillance practice. Personal information becomes more volatile. Whereas information leaks (Lyon 2001) were previously thought of as unfortunate incidents, they are a standard feature in social media. The circuits that manage social life are less visible, yet they amplify the visibility of social life. This complicates attempts to be a responsible user. When damaging information is uploaded, it is not always clear who put it online.

Software Ubiquitously Governs Social Life

Facebook is associated with material objects like laptops and mobile devices, but its software is what is most uniquely 'Facebook'. It is software code that enrols devices, users and their personal information. A conventional view of software frames it as a programming language that commands a specific hardware. For this reason Lawrence Lessig contends that software code has legislative properties in the way that it governs over social life (2006). This governing effect has been complicated with an ongoing decoupling of software from hardware. Services like Facebook, Twitter and YouTube are designed to function on a range of fixed and mobile devices. Through perpetual revisions and an increased reliance on outside programmers on open source platforms, software is more akin to an ecosystem (Thrift 2005) rather than to a script or a machine. Not only is software dynamic, but programmers and users maintain precarious control over its functioning, especially when coping with unanticipated 'bugs' and 'crashes'.

With Facebook, the fact that its users focus on its output rather than on the software itself contributes to its pervasiveness. Software's overlooked presence in contemporary sociality provokes a technological unconscious (Thrift 2005). Users maintain pervasive relations with software, but they are unaware of its importance in regulating social life. Software is a 'layer that permeates all areas of contemporary society' (Manovich 2008: 7). It organizes and presents information in specific ways, but this enables users to respond and develop their own practices. It does not simply present fixed content, but rather 'dynamic outputs of a real-time computation' (ibid.: 15). Software does not simply retrieve a file, but often compiles and creates it in real time, just in time. The rise of contextually relevant user-generated input suggests that users are increasingly involved with that construction. This performance requires that software be in a state of ongoing construction and revision. Social media are never a finished product. This also speaks to the indeterminacy of software and producers' reliance on its user base to shape software. Recent literature on software has underscored the governing logic of the remix. Manovich states that users are able to modify not only content exchanged through software, 'but also their fundamental techniques, working methods, and ways of representation and expression' (ibid.: 25). For example, the Open Office suite of programs allows non-professionals to propose and implement changes to the functioning of the software. Producers will make software accessible to the public, and see what features become popular with users, and by extension what kind of service the software performs.

Software's pervasive engagement and surveillance creep means that techniques used for one medium can be used for others. Anyone who is familiar with Facebook can easily adopt Google+. Diverse kinds of personal information can easily become content, as the learning curve for users to submit information is quite small. While it has spread to a heterogeneous population, the act of using Facebook is restricted to a narrow set of actions centred on browsing and entering content. This logic is extended when activity outside Facebook is integrated as content on the site. Media are increasingly modular and mobile. These conditions enable the kinds of networking described in the following section, but also explain how software can have such a ubiquitous reach.

Software sorts and orders content based on algorithms whose criteria are opaque to most users. For example, new connections and content are recommended as a purported convenience. These possibilities resonate with Kittler's (1996) distrust of GUI (Graphical User Interface) as well as his prescription to seek the 'essence' of computers. For Kittler, the increased focus on software obscures our understanding and awareness of hardware. Focus on the interface enables the invisibility of more fundamental layers, which are then taken for granted. When looking at Facebook, content provided by other users obscures software, which in turn obscures hardware. Of course awareness quickly returns if any of these layers break down.

Software's Material Consequences

Software's importance in social life is typically understated. It structures urban life (Graham and Marvin 2001), but instead of direct governance, this is a more subtle regulation of the ground-level functionality of streets, neighbourhoods and buildings based on their access and positioning on networked transportation and information systems.

A growing body of academic literature considers software's impact through social media. This amounts to a greater sorting of social life (Beer 2009a) through participatory web cultures. These services increasingly constitute our lives rather than just mediating them (Burrows 2009). Facebook merely organizes our personal details, yet users experience and describe themselves as dwelling 'on the site'. This mode of being goes beyond an online/offline binary where the user removes themselves at will. Abstention is an increasingly remote possibility. Rather, users always maintain a presence through software. Software is a way to connect social spheres. Yet contemporary software goes beyond mere mediation: it is more than a point of transfer. Software is more intimately involved in the 'making up' (Hacking 2002) of lives. Software now directs ubiquitous flows of information that are difficult to avoid. Their deep presence in social life connects them to the classificatory power (Bowker and Star 1999) that commands our lives. This is a post-hegemonic power that, rather than manifest strictly as a top-down imposition, is immanent and embedded in everyday life.

An increasing reliance on software is tied to the emergence of new laws, or rules (Lash 2007b). But whereas rules for social life have typically been constitutive (determining who is entitled to play) and regulative (determining how the game will unfold), these rules are algorithmic. The shift to algorithmic rules implies a shift from normative power to a power based on fact. These rules, Lash argues, become the pathways through which capitalist power operates. Lash also describes top-down searching taxonomies as displaced by user-generated folksonomies. Yet it is too early to assess what will happen to conventional kinds of classification with the rise of user-led tagging and sorting. A more likely outcome is that the latter will augment the former by infusing categories with contextual relevance. Conventional categories will be more dynamic and responsive to popular input. However, we have no reason to believe that these categories will be any less rigid when it comes to sorting individuals. For this reason we can anticipate that software obscures new kinds of control, sorting and organizing and ought to further the study of protocols embedded in software (Galloway and Thacker 2007).

Software's Human Consequences

Software partially obviates the need for human agency. Relational databases in particular (Gane et al. 2007) contribute to the visibility of the social life. Social media underscore these features. Facebook is fundamentally about human affairs: users communicate with people who matter to them. Yet most of the interpersonal legwork is subsumed by software. Software is becoming more social, in the sense that it now regulates relationships based on the pervasive submission of personal information.

Algorithms sort and stratify people (Graham 2004) in order to, for example, offer them different kinds of services. Facebook's increased presence in users' biographies means it will feature more prominently in the allocation of life chances. Following Manovich: 'The new paradigms that emerge in the 2000s are not about new types of media software per se. Instead, they have to do with the expansion of the amount of people who now use it – and the web as a new universal platform for non-professional media circulation' (2008: 191). What is remarkable about social media like Facebook is not their functionality, but their user base. The rapid growth of the number of social media users leads to a more granular and situated kind of governance. These users routinely provide information about themselves and their surroundings. This presents a contradiction: this authorship is manifest as a kind of empowerment, but also as exploitation, ordering and social control. Users are free to disclose information and describe the social world as they wish. Yet it is actually a foreclosure of possibilities. On social media, everything is named, and this production of knowledge does not need to be permanent to have permanent consequences.

Humans matter less when they offload the management of social life onto software, but they are still subject to the consequences of this management. Further, conventional power based on capital and control is not displaced by ubiquitous software. While classificatory power often operates independently of human intervention, this makes identifying the watchers and watched who are backgrounded by this automation all the more important. In terms of watchers, venture capitalists, software developers, marketers, security agents and many others benefit from social media by exerting control over information flows when deemed necessary or beneficial.

Key Features

As a flagship of social software, Facebook is a key example of interpersonal sorting in that it allows users to search, author and otherwise manage their social networks. It is indicative of a greater social sorting in social media. These components are a kind of information infrastructure: they make raw data functional. Consider some of its key features for navigating through personal information.

Facebook's search function makes its public content accessible. It first emerged to locate users by name. It has since expanded to locate virtually any text-based content on the site. Searching is used primarily to locate other users who have not been added to a friend network. In practice this facilitates online connectivity by making users searchable by name. It is also possible to locate users based on identifiable features such as schools they attended, movies they enjoy, favourite activities and interests. Searching also locates people who are only known based on these criteria, as well as to look for strangers who fit these criteria. It is not used simply for navigating outside one's friendship network. The search bar has an auto-complete feature that suggests a user's friends. This facilitates locating friends, a tedious act when a user has hundreds of contacts. Other text-based content – including pages, groups, events, applications and postings by friends and strangers – is searchable. Searching thus enables multiple points of entry to content on Facebook. Users can be located by who they are, as well as through what they say. Hundreds of millions of users are thus accessible through search algorithms. Users can restrict this access either by changing their name or by electing to be unsearchable in Facebook's privacy controls.

Feeds organize information for public display. User activity is translated into brief news items that are broadcast on prominent locations for the purpose of distributing that information. Much like searching, this is an example of software-enabled visibility. Yet it surpasses searching in that it automates the flow of personal information between users and their friends. This feature was introduced as news feeds and mini feeds in September 2006. Users' activities would be displayed on their own profile's mini feed and on their friends' news feeds. The news feed became the welcome page for users, meaning that users would know what their friends were doing when they would first log on, and vice versa. This caused some discomfort and protest, and Facebook implemented privacy settings allowing users to withdraw from this feature. Since then it has been adopted as a standard feature for gathering information.

News feeds have been bifurcated into two features: top news and most recent. Top news sorts information according to popularity whereas most recent sorts news items chronologically. These features are prime examples of Lash's (2002) observation that information is increasingly pushed to the user, that it finds the user rather than vice versa. Facebook's software augments the ability for users to find out about each other through searches, but offers the feeds as a counter-point that initiates scrutiny and visibility. Feeds make order out of complexity, with the effect of sorting interpersonal sociality. A complex set of information dispersed on different profiles becomes a linear set of events that welcomes users. This also automates 'stalking' on Facebook, as users are by default made visible to their peers when Facebook pushes their information to each other's news feeds. In 2008 Facebook merged the mini feed with the wall. Walls will be discussed later, but suffice to say that this merger directs attention and subsequent conversation to one key location on the profile.

Third party applications greatly complicate the question 'what does Facebook do?' In its early days Facebook was used to facilitate a contextually specific kind of sociality. Much of this new software – especially social games – lacks any apparent social function, other than collecting user information. In May 2007 Facebook released its Application Programming Interface (API), allowing software developers to build their own applications within the Facebook platform. There are now over seven million additional applications and websites integrated into Facebook (FB Statistics 2011). While online games are very popular, other applications allow users to submit or solicit additional information about themselves. By enlisting external developers, Facebook opens up its software to unanticipated growth. A software studies perspective frames Facebook as a broad set of services that further automates the visibility of personal information.

Facebook is a Network

We may be forgiven for thinking that Facebook created social networks. It reconnects us to so many lost friends, and displays all those friends before us. But these networks predate social media. Moreover, the study of social networks sheds light on the kinds of living arrangements users are coping with on sites like Facebook. To claim that we live in a networked world can refer to a number of different social conditions, brought on by ever-expanding technologies, work conditions and so on. Social life involves flows, exchanges and travel. In all aspects of our lives we rely on networks. These networks transport people, information and capital. Facebook is the latest exchange of information, but its use only makes sense in a broader culture of ubiquitous networking.

Facebook is perpetually revised communication software. Yet its information exchange relies on a vast range of networked hardware. In doing so it also connects individuals to each other, although describing these connections is no simple task. Attempts to qualify friendship ties on Facebook have perplexed scholars and users alike. Other questions emerge in terms of the social morphology made possible through Facebook: What kinds of capital circulate through Facebook? Does Facebook replace or augment face-to-face connections for users? As a web-based service, Facebook users submit information about their social networks through networked technology.

Networks, especially decentralized and distributed ones, are often described as complex structures (Urry 2003). Yet networks are also sites of monolithic force, both as bottom-up manifestations of protest and top-down censure or denial of service. Networks – whether they are large groups of individuals or Internet architecture – are both pliable and heavily structuring. Facebook is a digital manifestation of social ties, and these ties structure social morphology. Not only are users' impressions of social networks like Facebook entirely based on the composition of their personal social network, but these networks also contribute to the overall composition of the site in its entirety.

The network is also an increasingly salient diagram for Surveillance Studies. Distributed connections matter more, and are manifest through domestic technology, the popularization of surveillance culture and individual motivations. But centralized and privileged optics are still featured prominently in networks, and thus retain their sociological relevance. In using social media like Facebook, the interface's focus on peer-to-peer communication means that decentralized nodes are foregrounded, while any awareness of a central hub is typically obscured.

Networking literature extends from earlier sociological material on social ties and social structure, including group affiliations (Simmel 1955) and broader social transformations (Tonnies 2002). Even while coping with the novelty of networking on social media, we can ascertain three perspectives to ground our analysis. The first perspective addresses the co-existence of technological networks and egocentric social networks. This provides foundational insight about the uptake of networked information and transportation technologies in everyday life, and how social networks have been shaped in late modernity. The second perspective further scrutinizes macro-level consequences of information technology in late modernity, using the network as a key social morphology. Here, the contours of a network society are explored in terms of economic activity, state autonomy, and emergent forms of sovereignty. The third perspective extends from the second by considering some of the micro-level dynamics of these social shifts. Here, network sociality is seen as emanating from the workplace, transforming the workplace, and blurring the boundary between labour and leisure.

Technological and Egocentric Networks

Networks are a useful way to visualize the social world. Social network analysis is 'neither a method nor a metaphor, but a fundamental intellectual tool for the study of social structures' (Wellman 1988: 4). Social structure is quite simply described in terms of nodes (social system members) and ties depicting their interconnections. Because of limitations in 'knowing' social networks, this perspective rests heavily on egocentric – or personal – networks. Concerns of spatiality and culture are managed by having tangible units as the composition of social life. As Wellman states: 'We look for the social essence of community in neither locality nor solidarity, but in the ways in which networks of informal relations fit personas and households into social structures' (ibid.: 131). All of this resonates with a user-centred engagement with Facebook. The idea of a personal network of friends presumes that the individual user is located as a central node. The individual – not any kind of cohesive networked community – is the point of departure when logging on Facebook. Social network analysis posits that sociality – including social problems – tends to manifest through networks, according them a key ontological quality. Networks are framed as a kind of sociological canvas in that clusters of social ties are treated as a locus of social activity.

This tradition also states that social ties are augmented by emergent technologies. This is a remedy to earlier perspectives that position technology as a radical altering or displacement of social relations. Rather, we can imagine more of a symbiotic relation between network technology and personal networks, with some types of capital – be they social, fiscal or technical – augmenting others. Network analysis helps position technological networks *vis-à-vis* social networks. They are not pitted against each other; rather, technology augments and occasionally dampens interpersonal relations.

Information technologies complement – rather than replace – face-to-face exchanges. Along with automobiles they privatize network relationships. Here, privatize refers to the creation of interiorities or enclosures for information exchange, as opposed to public spaces like village squares. This shift offers insight regarding the role of information and transportation technology. It is not just a matter of closing distance gaps, but also offering refuge from public scrutiny. Technology has long been used to create enclosures. The current task for scholarly research is to assess who else beyond immediate users are involved in the construction of these enclosures, as well as the terms under which they are maintained.

Social Network analysis treats the popularization of the Internet as furthering the transition from house-to-house sociality to person-to-person sociality (Boase et al. 2006). This brings a rise of networked individualism, where users' social reach is vastly extended. Instead of relying on any single community, individuals draw from multiple groups for capital. This speaks to the kind of diversification valued in career literature on 'networking': having many ties in heterogeneous networks means greater social capital.

Macro-Level Consequences

Social networks are a useful analytic concept for fusing technology and sociality, specifically using an egocentric perspective. This offers guidance about how communities are complicated and sociality is augmented through social networking sites. But what about broader sociological changes? For more macro-level concerns, we may consider how networks are a key social morphology. Sociologists increasingly treat state and economic relations in terms of networks. This is tied to a paradigmatic shift from industrial to informational economies. Again, the term 'network' does refer to information technology, but the scope and reach of institutions as well as inter-institutional relations are understood as a product of nodes and ties. With nodes and ties as the building blocks for network relations, they enable social exchanges, which are described in this literature as flows. The flow is a fairly amorphous concept, referring to the circulation of information, capital and people.

A macro-level networked sociality had a profound impact on spatial and temporal relations. Castells (1996) refers to the space of flows to describe the linking of vast locations through transportation networks as well as information networks. This is often experienced as an eradication of distance, such that otherwise distant urban nodes are closely linked through features including frequent and inexpensive air travel, satellite offices for large corporations and dense fibre optic infrastructures. As a result, cosmopolitan areas resemble each other more than their immediate surroundings. Likewise, other spaces – whether suburban neighbourhoods or shantytowns – are increasingly similar. An increased reliance on transportation networks means that being 'in-between' spaces is a common experience. While this has initially been described in terms of disconnectedness and a negligible sense of spatiality – the continued domestication of mobile communication and GPS technology suggest a reversal of this experience. Timeless time emerges as a mutation of biological and mechanical time. This involves both the compression and de-sequencing of time, with events like production and consumption cycles being a lot faster and often disjointed. The advent of new technological affordances is coupled with new expectations, most importantly of labourers by corporations producing goods, services and content.

When abstracted, the conditions described above contain a vaguely generic 'revolutionary' character, such that any actor or interest group could benefit from an increasingly networked world. Authors have extolled Facebook's potential for citizen (Zhuo et al. 2011) and consumer (Shirky 2008) empowerment. Yet in practice the information society is heavily linked to late capitalist development (Castells 1996). Though consumers and activists groups use ubiquitous and networked ICTs, telecommunication companies as well as other sectors of the information economy are increasingly free of regulatory constraint. In addition to its heavy rooting in military history, contemporary ICTs are also linked to the 'circulatory system of economic processes' (Barney 2004: 73). Castells notes that corporate entities are less constrained by nation states in the network society. Connections between regional offices may flow regardless of government interventions, while the sovereignty of state actors is challenged.

Micro-Level Consequences

The shifts described above have consequences. Network sociality is spreading from key workplaces in the information sector to workplaces more generally (Stadler 2006). The flow of social capital tied to corporate, 'old-boy' spaces like the golf course and cigar lounge have gone mainstream, with management and creative classes now expected to attend networking events after work hours. These often mark a hybridization of social and corporate intentions, and mark a furthered attempt to harness social ties for employment and workplace opportunities (Grannovetter 1974)

But before accepting this account of the network society, we may turn to a close examination of contemporary workplace conditions, which are said to extend to everyday sociality. In response to the scholars who lament the loss of long-term enduring ties, media scholar Andreas Wittel suggests that the microdynamics of networking need to be more carefully studied before drawing this conclusion. Indeed, concepts like hierarchy and power also require further inquiry in response to Richard Sennett's claim that the network society is largely the domain of a minute elite. In response to claims that modernization is tied to a kind of de-socialization, he states that this does not necessarily result in 'a retraction of social principles and structures' (2001: 64), but is rather a shift from closed to open social systems, where boundaries and identity may not be as apparent.

Focusing on micro-level patterns lends support to the idea of a networking 'attitude'. This attitude emerges in response/conjunction with broader socio-technical and socio-economic conditions. As such it sheds light on the reason why users are so willing and able to adapt to online social networking. In describing network sociality, Wittel offers five features that underscore micro-level experiences that stem from the workplace to everyday social life. The first feature is the continued push towards individualization. This refers to an absence of any shared narrative. Much like ubiquitous computing's shift towards many computers per person, this suggests a transition from one narrative for many towards many narratives per individual. While this has prominently been described in terms of a loss of social bonds (Putnam 2001), Wittel remarks that individualization demands a heightened concern with relations with others. For instance, nomadic work patterns oblige a more deliberate maintenance of network ties among labourers. Second, Wittel claims that social ties are increasingly ephemeral as well as intense. This is evidenced in work projects where strangers are partnered for eighteen hour shifts, as well as speed-dating and other in person social networking events where protocol leads to intense, three minute conversations. This comes off as a kind of strategy to extract the most value/capital from as many network ties as possible. Third, Wittel describes a shift from narrative to information. This refers to a loss of trust based on mutual fatedness, leading instead to what Giddens (1994) calls 'active trust'. Information also denotes a kind of social literacy, which is also crucial to balancing risk and trust. Fourth, the assimilation of play and work suggests elements of play are creeping into the workplace. This is tied to the rise of creative/information economies. This is often celebrated in terms of foosball tables and beanbag chairs in corporate offices, but is also tied to the further expansion of work: long work hours during peak seasons and the expectation of being 'always-on' through wireless technology. The blurring between work and play is also tied to the complication of other binaries, such that private ties and spaces are now subject to public (corporate) scrutiny, and peers are increasingly thought of as business colleagues. Finally, Wittel cites the rapid proliferation of technology as an expansion of face-to-face sociality. Here, social media like Facebook is centrally located in terms of managing social relations.

These changes suggest an ongoing expansion of networks that marks a furthered coupling of social ties and information technologies. The degree of networked information exchange made possible by this deployment in turn facilitates information flows and structures based on complexity and decentralization, while concurrently augmenting the capacity of surveillance regimes (Lyon 1994: 41). The above developments suggest social structures where nodes/actors operate free from hierarchical constraint. This is most obviously evidenced by the rise of open-source software and web-based services that promote the autonomy and creative capacity of its user base. Yet these systems are able to house decentralized activity because of protocols that guide and regulate network sociality (Galloway and Thacker 2007). These protocols are often obscured and taken-for-granted, thus allowing the co-existence of social control on networks that are shaped by discourses of freedom and open access.

Finally, the expansion of ubiquitous ICTs and networking forces a revision of our understanding of digital divides. Access to information networks is less of an issue, as individuals are frequently encouraged to join telecommunication networks. The issue today is bandwidth. Whereas exclusion from information networks was an earlier concern, Saskia Sassen (2002) points to a potentially worse situation where less privileged users are tied to socio-informational networks, but lack sufficient resources to manoeuvre and exploit these networks. Here, technological capital has a direct impact on social capital, as a disadvantaged position in networks has a direct impact on a user's quality of life.

Key Features

When people joined Facebook in the past, they were invited to affiliate themselves with specific networks. These networks have been phased out, but for years they structured interactions on the site. Although these were first mapped along the academic institutions, their expansion lead to regional and workplace networks. These networks determine flows of information. According to default privacy settings, users were able to access other network members' information, and have their own personal information accessible to others in their network. Communication within networks was limited in the sense that a user could not simply send a message to all members of the Toronto regional network. Regional, workplace and academic networks were a preliminary way of organizing users into clusters, and according each other with varying degrees of access and visibility.

Facebook's current organization is decidedly egocentric. Egocentric networks are a more salient way of understanding how users experience social media. Facebook instructs users to make connections with other users, and to think of the accumulation of these connections as a personal network. Friends do not need to belong to the same institutional or regional networks. Again, following default settings, Facebook friends will be mutually transparent to each other. In its early days Facebook invited friends to qualify how they knew each other through a series of drop-down menus. This feature has also been removed, and the information it contained is no longer accessible by users. This suggests a simplification of ties, with diverse social relations being collapsed into a single category: the friend. Other than privacy settings regulating flow and access, a friendship is a friendship for Facebook. Facebook does enable users to sort their friends into groups, though this is more for the sake of access and privacy as opposed to qualifying how they knew each other.

Friend networks are diagrams where information about connected users can flow to one another. Facebook's privileging of sheer connectivity over the clarification of specific ties suggests that its founders have an interest in having as much information accessible to as many people as possible. These networks also hold a fundamental epistemological and ontological quality in the sense that knowledge of Facebook as well as a user's experience within and without it are directly shaped by the composition of her ego-network as well as other network affiliations. The friends that a user adds on Facebook determine the kind of content she receives and produces. This perspective also sheds some light on our understanding of the term 'friend' in Facebook. Here, the friend is not an actual friend but instead resembles a generic node. The Facebook friend is not an empty signifier, but rather is a base unit, or currency.

Facebook enables other kinds of networked connectivity beyond affiliate and personal networks. Users can also join groups and communicate with strangers. Groups can be formed on any conceivable basis: pet peeves, political causes, fan clubs and so on. While many users do not engage with groups beyond joining them – and making that membership visible on their profile – groups do represent a clustering of strangers based on a particular interest or cause. Conversations and other exchanges do take place on group pages, and users will make themselves visible to each other either intentionally by adding them as a friend, or unintentionally by sending them a direct message. Facebook has also introduced fan pages, which follow a similar structure. The main difference between fan pages and groups is that fan pages have users take a more audience-like engagement with the page, and also offer the creator of the page with statistics about its user base. Facebook has recently changed its profile structure such that activities, interests, workplaces, schools and cities that users list will be linked to related fan pages. Facebook events have a similar membership structure as groups and fan pages, although being affiliated with an event ostensibly means being linked to a social event situated at a particular time and location.

The above are examples of structures and spaces within Facebook that contain a networked quality. Yet content on the site is also networked in the sense that tags and other hyperlinked content connect related content to each other. The act of describing content also has a networked and collaborative quality: one user may tag a second in a photo that a third person uploaded to a fourth user's wall, to which a fifth and sixth user may add commentary. Offering content about yourself or others is often a group endeavour that visibly links users to that content. On a broader scale, Facebook's API has a networked quality. Programmers otherwise unaffiliated with the site are encouraged to produce content for the service that will then be linked to it. Much like a user's friend network will shape their experience and understanding of the site, the cluster of applications they add to their account will also shape the activities they engage in on the site, and consequently the kind of user they are. Third party applications also contribute to Facebook's networked structure. The site benefits from new services stemming from decentralized control, yet still retains ownership over the network, and can deny access to applications that do not meet its criteria.

Facebook is a Device for Publicity

We are concerned with the fact that Facebook pushes our personal information onto other people's screens. This is not meant to overlook the importance of Facebook holding on to this information for its own purposes, but the fact that this information is made public is precisely what makes social media socially meaningful. Indeed, what would Facebook be without its nearly one billion public faces?

Facebook is software that enables coexistence among different kinds of networks. But Facebook is also a device for branding and visibility, as well as a brand itself. The relation between its status as a brand and the branding services it offers speaks to the kind of visibility it advances. Facebook wants to be known as the predominant location for networked sociality. In doing so it needs to render user social life visible. Its own visibility rests on the visibility of its user base. The way Facebook promotes social visibility influences how social life and personal identities are manifest online. The logic of the brand extends to the individual, as Facebook is inseparable from interpersonal content. Facebook seeks recognition through the primacy of profiles, which shapes social presentation.

Facebook serves to publicize personal information, while seeming to offer users control over access. As a site for multiple agendas, desires and values, Facebook pits privacy against public representation. By soliciting personal information, it promotes visibility by pushing as much information as possible to as many audiences as possible. It appears to offer privacy, but only insofar as this will promote its brand as a safe social space. Indeed, these developments occur along claims by its founder that privacy concerns are 'overblown' (Allen 2010).

This section considers how Facebook brands and publicizes social life. First, contemporary branding strategies are used so that corporate identities circulate and gain visibility through information networks. This has the effect of producing personal branding, where these strategies are spilling from corporate to individual identities through the popularity of online profiles. The ensuing personal visibility pits publicity against privacy, pushing digital media users to reconsider goals and risks associated with online services like Facebook.

Facebook as a Brand

Before accumulating nearly a billion users, Facebook was a struggling startup alongside many competing services. Its success rested on the visibility and prominence it garnered. It sought to be a default location for social contacts, social images, social news and social events. When looking at Facebook and similar services, growing over time and spreading to new devices, its recognisability as a branded service seems crucial. The changes and revisions it has undergone risk alienating its user base. In order to maintain its prominence, brands are an increasingly important component to social media as well as to capitalism, commoditisation and symbolic exchange. The brand as an identity is decoupled from any tangible commodity and follows trans-media trajectories, not unlike how social media operate on numerous hardware devices.

The brand is an object, specifically an interface that regulates the interactivity between product and users (Lury 2004). Brands may be immaterial, but they also direct feeling and action. Their dependence on consumer input suggests an open-source interface, not unlike open-source software. Further, the brand's near-immateriality resonates with Facebook's near-immaterial information exchange, reliant on near-immaterial labour. This is true when thinking about conventional brands like Nike, Coca-Cola. It becomes all the more explicit when considering a product that collects and distributes information. The Facebook brand is about little else but this interactivity. It is helpful to think of Facebook as a meta-brand: a platform for promotion, which itself is heavily promoted. It is a platform that focuses on other people's publicity, with the implication that their publicity cannot proceed without buying into Facebook. Brand activity is centred on generating information about consumers to reconfigure production (Lury 2004: 17). This is especially relevant when describing a company like Facebook that serves to generate information about its users. Marketing is insinuated in social media. This resonates with bringing new services under Facebook's enclosure (ibid.: 8) including consumer profiling (Elmer 2004). Brand awareness and branding strategies are a recent development of the contemporary culture industry, placing an emphasis on the flow of cultural products. For Lash and Lury (2005) culture is heavily entrenched in manufacturing, and vice versa. In taking this approach to the study of Facebook, it resembles a venue for the circulation of cultural objects, and it is itself a cultural object that circulates.

Branded cultural products are tied to everyday sociality and information exchange between peers. These are manifest as 'little presents' (ibid.: 139) that are exchanges between individuals that serve to punctuate everyday life. The most conventional exchange might be the kinds of cultural products that one cannot justify purchasing for oneself. These exchanges are not only ubiquitous, but also obsequious in that they are a kind of deference that maintains social connections. Facebook is essentially driven by a broad range of informational exchange between users (Miller 2008). Users are pressured to give little presents by providing personal details, responding to wall posts or playing a third party application in order to maintain their standing in the network, as well as maintain the network itself. The bulk of lateral surveillant relations, an internalized coupling of watcher and watched, is based on this kind of exchange.

The above branding and marketing strategies are a response to a longstanding disconnect between design and use of cultural goods. This shift is tied to buzz words that denote benefits to the customer: democratic, interactive, responsive and conversational. But this shift is also a way to coerce and shape consumption, to lead and direct it. The heightened concern for and scrutiny of users runs parallel to literature on ubiquitous computing. Indeed, dominant brands organize the spatial and temporal activities of their market. This struggle seems especially important and rewarding when the market itself is ambiguously defined and delineated. Given the ambiguities that surround social media's purpose and domain, branding these services is an effective way to confer meaning upon them. Facebook deliberately seeks recognition as the key brand for a service its user base is only coming to recognize, and find the appropriate terms to describe (social networking? social utility? information brokerage?). This effort is necessary and bound to collecting users' personal information on a vast scale.

Facebook as Branding Individuals

Corporate brands are adopting new strategies because of a perceived loss of consumer trust. Facebook's growth and new features for information exchange were met with user resistance, thus pushing the web service to augment its public relations efforts through effective branding. During the news feed scandal in 2006, Mark Zuckerberg described Facebook as being 'about real connections to actual friends, so the stories coming in are of interest to the people receiving them, since they are significant to the person creating them' (Zuckerberg 2006). Thus, Facebook's founder is shaping its brand in a way that channels users' desires to see and be seen into the site itself. The above example describes the precarious relations of trust between corporations and populations. Yet individuals are also struggling with these issues on an interpersonal scale. This becomes an important development in light of the apparent loss of trust through increasingly mediated communication, leading to the desire for a new kind of mediated verification

(Lyon 2001, Ball 2002). A contemporary lack or loss of trust triggers a heightened need for verification, and new kinds of public relations.

Face-to-face sociality is complicated by interfaces, most notably the personal profile. But profiles are increasingly built to establish some degree of mediated recognition and trust. Key features do this explicitly, including eBay's feedback, LinkedIn's references, Friendster's testimonials and Facebook's friends in common. Yet the general idea of a profile is also an attempt to produce trust through visibility. Personal profile construction involves an increasingly complex set of socio-technical procedures (Hardey 2008). This is exemplified by recent concern over protocols for appropriate conduct on online dating sites. Users build profiles with specific intentions in mind, often negotiating deceit, be it theirs or a potential mate's. Online dating is a kind of self-marketing, where undesirable attributes may be smoothed out or obfuscated through deliberate self-presentation (Jagger 2005). While computer-mediated-courtship is a very specific example, trust and authenticity have a generic presence on most online services.

Social networking sites are ultimately about self-presentation (boyd and Heer 2006). They describe the profile as a body of information that stands in for the corporeal body. Indeed, through profiles the logic of brands extends to personal identities (Hearn 2008). The comparison seems apt given that both individuals and corporate brands manage their identities through web-based technologies. Yet this has important repercussions for attributes and boundaries of individual identities. Not only does collapsing individual identities and brands raise a gamut of psychological and existential issues, but the increased branding of personal identities leads to heightened relations between these and corporate brands. On the one hand, individuals are invited to build their profiles using brands, logos and other corporate content as building blocks. Facebook's activities and interests fields are a clear example of this. Content in these fields links individual identities to branded products and services, bringing the latter to life through the faces and names of their enthusiasts. The quasi-corporate branding of individuals impacts corporations. As profiles and interfaces are embedded in domestic spaces, the types of knowledge accrued grow in depth and in their level of abstractness. In particular, researchers have noted that pervasive social networking interfaces allow them to make new inferences about cultures, or at least taste patterns (Beer and Burrows 2007). A symbiotic relation between personal and corporate branding enables the former to align itself with the latter, and endows the latter with a heightened ability to know and sort the former.

Constructing profiles, whether corporate or interpersonal, is a key feature of a contemporary information economy. The profile intersects visualizing data and portraiture (Lury 2004). Profiles are used to know more about consumers. Facebook's advertising scheme is a testament to this. But profiling visible individuals is a growing process, and it seems an initial sense of comfort with information collection will lead to a more pervasive set of profiling consequences. Social media users have valid reasons to use these services, and they experience rewards of an intrinsic and extrinsic nature. Yet the growth of these services also reflects a desire in contemporary culture to invoke speech in individuals. Baudrillard (1995) describes the growth of interactive technologies as a recent strategy to harness masses, noting 'the interactive mass is still a mass, with all the characteristics of a mass, simply reflecting itself on both sides of the screen' (ibid.: 101). While self-expression is foregrounded and highly lauded in this cultural zeitgeist, it might come at the expense of our right to remain silent and invisible. The rising popularity of services like Facebook suggests that online visibility is more of a requirement than a guilty pleasure, and an absence from these dwellings is a potential liability.

Facebook Publicity in Relation to Privacy

Facebook's success rests on its visibility, which in turn rests on the visibility of users. It seeks to be the default location for self-presentation online. Indeed, the private profile is still a kind of public presence with information given-off (Goffman 1959). Facebook invites users to build public profiles using personal information. The advent of this and other web-based services for sharing this information, coupled with mobile and ubiquitously present technology, has profound repercussions in terms of the public exposure they produce.

Publicity and privacy are often treated as a zero-sum game, such that a privacy violation is a direct outcome of a public disclosure. boyd (2008) considers the impact of features like the news feed for privacy and exposure. She observes that while users may be comfortable posting this information in a specific location online, the fact that the news feed automatically broadcasts this information leads to unwanted exposure and compromised privacy. This perspective rightly identifies that users do not approach their personal information with a binary public/private framework. They may be comfortable with a modest degree of publicity offered by their personal wall, but not the exposure offered by feeds and other aggregated news services.

Yet privacy and publicity can also be thought of as two separate values that are pitted against each other. A user may value publicity as well as privacy. Indeed, both values may factor prominently in information exchange. The notion of contextual privacy is helpful here: users may be comfortable with some kind of exposure in one context, and a separate exposure in another context, but compromising the boundary between these contexts would be experienced as a core violation (Nissenbaum 2009). Thus, personal information like one's medical history could be willingly offered on a public discussion group online, but this individual may insist on maintaining privacy elsewhere by withholding this information, such as on their Facebook account. This perspective asserts that a flatly totalizing and zero-sum view of privacy and publicity is insufficient. Social convergence on Facebook complicates this. If Facebook's designers want to colonize vast swaths of interpersonal sociality, they have to be able to ensure that information can be public to one audience and private to another.

Contemporary public exposure is augmented by ICTs. As cheap storage, rapid transmission and potentially indefinite retention are heavily promoted features, the exposure offered by Facebook will often bring about a visibility not anticipated or desired by its users. While public exposure and privacy have long remained sociological concerns (Goffman 1963) the spread of this technology coupled with the interface between corporate and personal branding strategies suggests that the public representation of interpersonal identities is a heightened concern, and that the path of least resistance for personal information is that of greater and greater exposure. Andrejevic (in Roychoudhuri 2007) makes a valuable contribution to the discussion of privacy and publicity in noting that researchers need to consider an emerging kind of privacy: the privatization of public sociality. Issues of control and ownership are a pressing concern as users are increasingly invested in these sites. The relation between networked sociality and the commercial interests of growing databases is scarcely publicized.

Key Features

Concerns about publicity are incorporated into the way Facebook is typically used. These concerns are anchored around user profiles. Profiles are an assemblage of information related to the individual user. This typically includes biographical details, cultural taste preferences, photographs and status updates. However, profiles may also contain videos, lengthier text and virtually any other kind of media. By default, both the user and their peers are able to submit information on the profile. This adds a collaborative dimension to public exposure where identity management extends beyond being responsible for the self. Facebook users and their friends can routinely build their public presence by placing content on the user's profile. But tags, which serve as a link between the individual's profile and relevant content elsewhere, also augment this presence. The profile also has an indeterminate quality, such that more content can always be added.

The relation between corporate and interpersonal branding has become more intertwined with recent changes made to the profile structure. The content from key fields on user profiles, including activities, interests and locations, are now automatically linked to fan pages. Thus, if a user lists a fast food restaurant as an activity, their profile will be linked to that restaurant's corporate fan page, and vice-versa. Not only does the user's public persona contain explicitly corporate elements, but individual fans also populate those public brands.

In order to cope with its own public scrutiny, Facebook has long promoted privacy settings. These settings purport to offer users extensive control over where their public information may circulate. These settings are heavily granular, such that a particular section of a user's profile can be hidden from a specific user or group of users. Yet by default they leave profiles open to a broader public. Initially this public was the regional, academic and workplace networks to which the user belonged. Yet in 2010 this default became friends of friends. If a user had three hundred friends, and each of those friends also had three hundred friends, by following the default privacy settings their presence would be accessible to an audience of ninety thousand, most of whom would be strangers. This shift was justified by the claim that original networks were no longer relevant, giving way instead to whom the user knew as well as whom those people knew. This shift endorses the view that friends of friends are a trustworthy category of stranger, deemed to be safe by a common social tie.

In 2007 Facebook made user profiles partly available via Google searches. Thus, people who were not signed in as Facebook users were granted partial access to the site. This had the effect of pushing information beyond Facebook's border. Supposedly this is done to draw people searching onto the site, which they will explore and join. As such it is an effective strategy to promote and publicize Facebook as a brand. But the privacy that was afforded to users under a walled garden model has consequently eroded.

The above efforts encapsulate Facebook's longstanding attempts to push personal information further into the public eye. These changes to its interface have occurred alongside public statements by Facebook concerning how its users supposedly perceive privacy. In 2010 Mark Zuckerberg claimed that recent changes to make even more information searchable reflected user demand, stating that '[p]eople have really gotten comfortable not only sharing more information and different kinds, but more openly and with more people. That social norm is just something that has evolved over time' (Kirkpatrick 2010). The relation between cultural values, Facebook's user base, and Facebook itself is complex, but the above statement overlooks the way social media impose a heavily publicized usage upon individuals. Interestingly, Zuckerberg himself has been the victim of information leaks on Facebook when changes to privacy settings pushed his own private photos into the public (Tate 2009).

Facebook is a Site of Labour and Exploitation

Previous sections consider Facebook as software, as a network and as a reconfiguration of publicity and visibility. Yet these perspectives overlook corporate motivation for profit and accumulation of capital through Facebook, and the further growth of a personal information economy. In no uncertain terms, Facebook's developers want to collect as much information as possible and develop as many ways to monetize that information (Oreskovic 2010). Personal information is a kind of raw material that users willingly generate. Facebook's user-base – even those who are disillusioned with social media's offerings – do not frame their engagement with the site as one of labour and exploitation. The business of Facebook speaks to a new kind of surveillance economy that resembles a high-bandwidth information brokerage. The rapid growth of Facebook and other free services – including Google's growing assemblage – warrant critical scrutiny. Of particular concern is that a clear language based on commerce and exploitation is absent from most public discourse on the topic.

Michel de Certeau's work on everyday life speaks to the relation between social media owners and users. De Certeau (1988) maintains a distinction between those who own spaces, and those who dwell within them. Ownership is linked with the ability to shape and regulate spaces. While she may be nominally bound to municipal law, the landowner who purchases a town square has dominion over what is possible and not possible in that space. She can rename it, introduce new services and terminate less desirable or profitable ones. While she may never set foot on that quasi-public space, it is inhabited and traversed by a multitude of dwellers. The degree to which they depend on that space varies, but they are all in a precarious relation with that space. In terms of their respective arsenal of actions, de Certeau distinguishes between the owner's strategies and the dweller's tactics. The dweller is intimately familiar with the space, and can employ a number of tactics to get by: they may cut through a busy farmer's market as a shortcut, they may seek refuge in a less-visible corner, or they may set up a makeshift kiosk for an unsanctioned event. These tactics are often temporally bound and based on a ground-level knowledge of the space. Yet the owner's strategies, while potentially out-of-touch, can very quickly do away with these tactics. The dweller's tactics have empirical value: they describe how the enclosure is actually used. Yet the owner's strategy ultimately determines how the enclosure is known and experienced.

Three issues are particularly salient here. Firstly, social media services emerge from a Silicon Valley culture of deregulation and capitalist expansion. This represents an ongoing expression of a 1960s west coast counterculture, couching entrepreneurship and venture capitalism as being on par with communal living and an activist ethos. This perspective currently celebrates free services and open access, and these buzz words are conveniently left unpacked. Compared to other Fortune 500 companies, the discourse surrounding their emergence gives them a special designation for growth and accumulation. Secondly, these developments are also the latest manifestation of the information economy, specifically audience exploitation using ICTs. Targeted and prolonged engagements with an increasingly granular user base are the outcome of a knowing capitalism. Finally, the extent to which this reaches domestic everyday life has important repercussions for a rapidly growing surveillance economy. Increasingly, purchase histories, entertainment and personal disclosure are all contained within a kind of enclosure: the database. These enclosures are presented as sites of interactivity, with the increasingly active, labouring and visible user heralded as a sign of empowerment. The monetization of personal information within enclosures is part of a greater surveillance economy where watching and being watched are increasingly a kind of work.

Emergence of a Silicon Valley Ethos

Key business figures in computing have laid out an ideological landscape for digital media. These figures treat the computing industry as distinct from other commercial sectors, and therefore exempt from scrutiny and regulation. They treat the goods and services they manufacture as transcending current social issues.

Popular and academic literature on information technologies often treats them as a kind of rupture from current political economic relations. However, the history of the Internet has always been closely linked to capitalist growth (Turner 2005). The fact that information technology is always tied to a kind of revolutionary potential suggests that this is more than a consistent oversight. The popularization of technology in the past hundred years is defined by a consistent claim that emergent technologies, ranging from the telegraph to cable television, would lead to a 'technological sublime' where current constraints and social problems would be rendered obsolete (Mosco 2004). As a consequence, current market regulations are seen as fetters because of this anticipated mass change. The implication is that technological determinism and technological utopianism are used as a point of leverage for new forms of capital accumulation and deregulation. The Internet and new media have no shortage of such thinkers. John Perry Barlow and Bill Gates are longstanding figures, but more recent spokespeople like Tim O'Reilly, Don Tapscott and Clay Shirky extol the revolutionary virtues of social media services like Facebook.

The claims made by these thinkers merit further inquiry. Recurrent claims from virtual communities emerge from information technology. While a sense of community can be clearly supported by empirical research, these features are typically foregrounded, while business models and other fundamental concerns are tucked away (Kelemen and Smith 2001). For all the talk about ubiquitous computing and ubiquitous connectivity, a ubiquitous capitalism is absent from the conversation. Businesses rely on manifestos in order to carefully shape the language of emerging technologies, including the curious absence of their own monetary gain (Van Dijck and Nieborg 2009). The decision to describe the impact of new technologies through manifestos is a curious development, suggesting a paradigm shift that is long overdue. Beyond this, the authors also suggest a kind of discursive shaping of the new media economy, as any discussion of monetization or business models are avoided, at least in communications meant for mass audiences. Businesses may discuss monetization with investors. Following Tapscott and others, contemporary business models are heavily reliant on 'mass creativity' as well as 'peer production' (ibid.: 856).

These claims present a consistent account of users as creators. Moreover, all creator-users are portrayed as operating in concert towards common good. But not all users are creators, nor are all creators interested in anything beyond mere distraction or self-involvement. Further, these manifestos point to Wikipedia as a key example, but the overwhelming majority of sites relying on user input are for-profit. A critical reading of this literature suggests that the personal information economy seeks to enrol common good and community into a low-cost business platform. These developments suggest a reconfiguration of public spaces as for-profit services. Creative work will now take place anywhere, fuelled by intrinsic motivation (Shirky 2008). The exploitative nature of this configuration is obscured by the myth of open-source operations. Industry literature describes open-source and collaborative models as a return to a kind of public commons, yet all that is being shared in most cases is the programming code, and even then ownership is in the hands of very few (Borsook 2002). This shallow version of open-source substantiates industry claims that the new media economy is fundamentally different from other sectors, and as a result does not need the same kind of regulation. This is also tied to the devaluation of authorship, as information is meant to be free to circulate. This approach has profound consequences for content producers and other members of the creative economy. The ideology of free access, coupled with increasingly easy ways to exchange information, contributes to a devaluation of the creative class.

Emergence of Cyber-Capitalism

The perspective outlined above by industry leaders operates in tandem with the continued expansion of the information and information technology sector. Key features of this sector are emblematic of latest shifts in capitalism. These developments culminate in a cyber-capitalism that is rapidly growing within the information sector. This section describes its contours in a general sense, in order to demonstrate that, contrary to the industry literature described above, the Internet produces the latest manifestation - or mutation (Lazarrato 2004) - of capitalism. Political economic conditions are often overlooked amid hype as well as actual developments (Mosco 2004). But issues of ownership, labour and control are as important as ever.

Broadly speaking, work has been transformed to be less constrained and more networked, but also less stable (Boltanski and Chiapello 2005). Employers and employees are regarded as more promiscuous, such that rapid turnovers are increasingly common. For corporations this involves an accumulation of capital built on minimal infrastructure. Contrary to claims that an information revolution will neutralize class struggles, class antagonism continues through new technology, as seen for example through the heightened concentration of media ownership at the start of the twenty-first century (Dyer-Witherford 1999).

Many who study the emergence of new media underscore the continuities that exist with earlier forms of capitalism. (Mosco 2009) Commoditization of media and consolidation of ownership are increasingly salient issues following the 'digital revolution'. An especially troubling issue regarding the growth of cyber-capitalism is the increasing disentangling of labour from labourers. That is, a lot of new media business models rely on the extraction of value from non-paid labour. An example may include a tech support message board for a hardware company where users offer support to each other. While users may experience intrinsic rewards from this kind of participation and collaboration, their labour obviates the need for a full wage-earning support staff.

Value extraction is especially salient when using audience labour as a point of reference (Smythe 1977). Audience involvement, by virtue of the value it adds to broadcast media, is regarded as a kind of labour. Even if audiences do not treat their efforts as such, it is labour in its consequences: it adds value to media, and some groups are exploiting this feature. The notion of audiences as commodities is relevant for discussions of audience labour, but also for thinking of relationships between audiences, advertisers and media companies (Mosco 2009: 137). In the broadcast model, audiences provide their attention in exchange for a service, typically entertainment. Broadcast media sell audiences to advertisers. Audiences work by being trained by advertisers, and this can be considered part of the productive cycle. However with social media, audiences are directly involved in the production of content, and they are also sold to advertisers. The onus of activity is more heavily shifted to audience, with the need for professional/paid content producers heavily diminished.

This is a new kind of immaterial labour (Cote and Pybus 2007), where networked subjectivity and affect offered in social media enable users that also produce content, with the consequence that production and consumption are increasingly conflated (though it should not be assumed that all consumers are producers, or vice versa). This discussion is also enriched by recent work on the attention economy (Davenport and Beck 2001) as well as the engagement economy (McGonigal 2008). The difference between these two suggests a shift towards an active, rather than merely attentive, user base as one from which value can be extracted. Whereas an attentive audience adds value to content by watching it, an engaged audience adds value by actively contributing to content. This shift also marks the emergence of a domestic surveillance economy, as users are willing to make part of their social life visible for a business platform.

Leisure-labour and workplace-labour may be treated as distinct categories, but they are related to each other. Consider the Italian Autonomist concept of the social factory where the entirety of social life is integrated into the information economy (Terranova 2004). This is tied to a kind of disintermediation, whereby the relation between commerce and production is greatly streamlined. Immaterial labour is no longer restricted to the knowledge economy. These developments are not a matter of capitalism infiltrating a once-pure realm, but rather that it has always been an integral element. The 'cognitive surplus' that Shirky extolls (2010) 'does not exist as a free-floating post-industrial utopia but in full, mutually constituting interaction with late capitalism' (Terranova 2004: 84). The above is a timely reminder that the supposedly revolutionary character of digital capitalism is merely the latest incarnation of profit seeking and the exploitation of raw material – personal information in this case – and labour.

Reconfiguration and Commodification of Everyday Life

The previous section outlines the continued expansion of business models based on online activity. The rise of social media in particular suggests that everyday sociality is increasingly subsumed into the information economy. Business models attempt to monetize information that would otherwise be classified as personal. That this information is collected without compensation speaks to a growing mass of unpaid labour. Yet these developments rest on the heightened visibility of users within services, which are increasingly conceived of as surveillant enclosures. A significant subset of the information economy is based on interpersonal surveillance. This unpaid surveillance labour is two-pronged, in the sense that users are willing to both submit personal information as well as watch over other people's content. The relation between visibility and scrutiny has been explored in literature on reality television (Hill 2005). This connection extends to other forms of domestic surveillance, most notably social networking sites.

Understanding this shift at a conceptual and empirical level is greatly facilitated by the idea of mass customization. In response to limitations with broadcast media and Fordist production, mass customization relies on users to engage on a large scale in the development of goods and services. This is often touted as desirable for users due to a kind of interactivity, in response to the homogeneity and inflexibility of mass culture. It is also a powerful resource for market research. A notable development is that domestic life becomes 'increasingly economically productive insofar as consumers are subjected to comprehensive monitoring in exchange for the promise of customization and individuation' (Andrejevic 2003: 132).

On first pass interactivity on Facebook seems democratizing, as everyone has the potential to watch over each other. But those who manage the enclosure have a privileged view of sociality. As a result, user behaviour can be the basis of revisions to the interface/enclosure. Users may develop their own practices within an enclosure, and this can be framed as a kind of customization, or even resistance. However, owners of the enclosure can observe and either subsume or eliminate those practices. Manovich (2008) borrows from de Certeau to indicate that a user's tactics become an owner's strategies. This does not preclude further tactics, which are generally centred on disengagement. Yet visible discussions within the enclosure about disengagement from the enclosure can be used to keep users (Cohen 2008).

The increased focus on everyday life is in itself a concerning development. Mark Poster remarks that everyday life was formerly the remainder of institutional action and scrutiny (2004). However, the rapid onset of digital media in the domestic sphere means it is increasingly subject to commoditization and scrutiny. The extent to which business models rely on online sociality shapes the visibility and knowability of its user base. Users make active contributions to Facebook by providing biographical details that make the site compelling to other users. But this also has consequences for their presence on their site. It is not just a matter of providing content that attracts other people. They are increasingly living their lives through these services, and this has important consequences for their visibility. These developments suggest the emergence of a surveillance economy based on the flow and monetization of personal information. The term surveillance economy encompasses a lot of features, but the one most relevant to this study is the transformation of everyday life into a kind of enclosure where information can be extracted and turned into a brokered raw material.

Key Features

Facebook is keenly aware of the market potential of the vast amount of personal information it collects. Indeed, its 2010 valuation of 35 billion dollars US is likely more a factor of all this information rather than the software code. During its growth it has attempted to integrate the submission of personal information into commercial activity, and has repeatedly encountered a backlash.

In the fall of 2007 Facebook unveiled Beacon, through which users would publicize their commercial activity on other sites onto their profile. The intended purpose for Facebook was to 'try to help people share information with their friends about things they do on the web' (Zuckerberg 2007). This had the effect of bringing user commerce into the Facebook enclosure, with a kind of viral marketing to follow, as this news would be sent to their personal network. Users had reservations about commercial transactions being made visible to their friends, and this feature was eventually scrapped. A similar feature was introduced in 2008 under the name Facebook Connect. Facebook's claim was that Connect 'makes it easier for you to take your online identity with you all over the Web, share what you do online with your friends and stay updated on what they're doing' (Zuckerberg 2008). Connect met a similar backlash. Facebook has since attempted to monetize personal information with similar schemes like 'Instant Personalization' and 'Social Ads', marking a further push towards the commercialization and exploitation of social media dwellings.

Integrating outside transactions into personal profiles is one of a set of strategies to make Facebook commerce-friendly. Under Facebook's 'Marketing Solutions' as well as Facebook Ads, businesses are offered a prolonged engagement with users. Not only are they able to target a very specific audience based on information users submitted for unrelated reasons, but they are also presented with detailed feedback based on user response to this advertising. This suggests an increasingly granular and targeted kind of advertising. As well, it suggests a relation between users and advertisers based on an asymmetrical relation of visibility. Advertisers have a sophisticated knowledge of a target audience, yet that audience is virtually excluded from this endeavour.

While these features have known modest success, it stands to reason that Facebook's potential for monetization rests on a long-term investment. That is, its ability to exploit the productive labour of its user base will become apparent as its user base grows, as it is integrated into everyday sociality and as it is increasingly treated as a de facto service for sharing personal information. This brings an inertia whereby moving to another service will be less plausible due to traction (Nye 2006).

Conclusion: Social Media Dwellings as Digital Enclosures

The four perspectives outlined above each offer a partial account of Facebook's functioning as a social media. All four perspectives raise sociological issues pertaining to the augmented visibility of its users. These accounts underscore the need to consider surveillance practices that are emerging through social media. Taken together, these perspectives enhance our understanding of social media as a dwelling, specifically by outlining to its enclosing features. Yet by taking the above perspectives and features into account, we may consider the extent to which social media dwellings are enclosures. Mark Andrejevic refers to the digital enclosure as 'the creation of an interactive realm wherein every action, interaction, and transaction generates information about itself' (2009: 53). This description suggests an infrastructure where personal information is produced but also made meaningful insofar as it generates more information.

Individuals submit information about their consumption in order to individualize it, and by extension, themselves. This leads to a kind of visibility where users are offered a host of personal information within specific spaces, whether an online database or a reality TV set saturated with microphones and cameras. Within these enclosures, sociality is further restricted to these spaces. While the enclosure suggests a return to pre-modern sociality, the presence of surveillance technology suggests new kinds of visibility. As Andrejevic suggests: 'Interactivity promises not a return to the relative lack of anonymity of village life, but rather to a state of affairs in which producers have more information about consumers than ever before, and consumers have less knowledge about and control over how this information is being used' (2007: 27). Such asymmetrical relations of visibility may also be found between those who own social media enclosures like Facebook, and those who dwell in them.

Each of the above sections infuses some meaning regarding the kind of enclosure made possible by social media. A software studies perspective highlights not only its algorithmic functioning, but also its reliance on a variety of hardware devices. A social network perspective underscores the way its scope is augmented by social ties. Users are not providing information for Facebook's database; they provide this information for friends on their social networks. Moreover, these friends also provide information on their behalf. A publicity perspective underscores the status of visibility in this enclosure. While enclosures are used for corporate and other kinds of knowledge production, its inhabitants use it primarily to stay in touch with one another. A labour studies perspective underscores the fact that while users who routinely operate with the interface provide content, their efforts are part of a business model by the owners of the enclosure itself.

Whereas the panoptic guard tower has been a guiding imagery for Surveillance Studies, the digital enclosure speaks more directly to social media's key features for surveillance. Jeremy Bentham links the panopticon to a utilitarian context and vision, namely the management of populations within an institution. All inmates are enclosed in cells, and sociality among inmates is restricted. The prison guard can see all inmates, yet inmates cannot even see if the guard is present. Michel Foucault (1977) returns to this model to underscore its effect in terms of disciplining the soul. In particular the uncertainty about the guard's presence invokes self-discipline among inmates. Following Foucault, surveillance scholars devised updated models that account for the saturation of information technologies in late modern society (Poster 1990, Boyne 2000). Yet new technologies do not displace existing power relations. Digital enclosures are a broader kind of containment, but also allow a broader collection of information, a broader range of interests, all with great potential for convergence and coordination. They provide an elegant mechanism of control, as distributed and seemingly autonomous user activity is steadily collected, to be utilized at a later point.

This is the structure that facilitates the practices described in the following chapters. Treating social media as potential or actual enclosures also provides an important balance to perspectives that treat these services as ephemeral in use and consequence. Users do submit information with immediate and localized contexts in mind; their privileging of this context and use does not diminish long term consequences made possible by the retention of this information. There is a disjuncture between immediate use and long-term consequences of exposure in social media enclosures. People live their lives through social media, and these enclosures are the interface in relations between individuals, businesses and institutions. The mutual augmentation described in this research is the result of the increased co-existence of these groups. Facebook as an enclosure may contain information about users, but little is known about why and how users – on behalf of themselves, institutions and businesses – have an increased presence on this site. Knowing so much about Facebook's emergence but so little about its users' reasons for being on the site is a gap that the following chapters will address.

Chapter 3
Interpersonal Social Media Surveillance

Introduction

Social media surveillance is a growing concern for scholars, as well as for individuals who use services like Facebook. We know that individuals increasingly live their lives through Facebook. We know it impacts their life profoundly. We have an idea of how this affects their visibility and exposure as a result of Facebook's design as a digital enclosure. This chapter shifts its focus towards individual users. At the risk of redundancy, people matter to Facebook. It is made up of people seeking and watching over other people. This chapter addresses this concern by focusing on one axis of visibility on social media, interpersonal surveillance, using Facebook as a case study. To be clear, interpersonal surveillance is one of many kinds of surveillance that occur through social media. These purposes vary from law enforcement to marketing to institutional scrutiny, and are united by their shared use of social media. As a form of peer monitoring (Andrejevic 2005), interpersonal social media surveillance renders users visible to one another in a way that warrants a care of the virtual self (Whitson and Haggerty 2008). Yet this care is complicated by social media's rapid growth, and especially Facebook's cross-contextual information flows that publicize otherwise private information. Visibility on social media makes this care necessary, but not sufficient.

Facebook is an exemplar of social media. Its users maintain profiles, upload photographs, and share personal information with each other. Facebook's users make their lives visible to each other, and this exchange enables other kinds of visibility that users do not anticipate. What makes interpersonal surveillance interesting in the context of social media is that it is closely linked to the use of Facebook itself. Users consider interpersonal surveillance to be a product of social media, because services like Facebook encourage the asynchronous exchange of personal information. While interpersonal social media surveillance can be abusive, these incidents are on the extreme end of a continuum of social media use. Interpersonal surveillance is also normalized because users act as both watcher and watched. Unlike most kinds of peer surveillance, an individual watching over others on Facebook is typically also exposed to those peers. Users experience interpersonal surveillance as a violation, but also come to see it as a pervasive condition of social media use, suggesting a further normalization of surveillance (Murakami Wood and Webster 2009). This chapter uses ethnographic accounts to describe interpersonal surveillance made possible through Facebook. The findings below present interpersonal surveillance as a matter of users being both the subject and the agent of surveillance. The intervisibility (Brighenti 2010) that these individuals exhibit and exploit is an increasing feature of contemporary sociality. Through their prolonged engagement with Facebook, users contribute to and are affected by a growing regime of visibility in social media enclosures.

Facebook's first users were university students, mainly undergraduates engaging in peer-to-peer relationships. This is where it began, but other agents and other kinds of watching have joined social media sociality. The interviews discussed below occurred at a time when family, employers and others were increasingly involved with Facebook. Social media sites are a new kind of public dwelling that scholars and users scarcely understand. Facebook in particular promotes the networked and public dissemination of personal information, all while developing increasingly granular privacy settings. In connecting over half a billion users, Facebook has grown beyond student populations to a more generic social network that crosscuts contextual barriers.

We may ask what kinds of surveillance are present on Facebook. Not all forms of surveillance are alike. Police investigations are clearly different from an undergraduate student making sure her parents do not upload any embarrassing photographs. But these different kinds of scrutiny are occurring in the same interface, feeding into and drawing from the same body of information. Conventional surveillance practices are augmented by user-generated knowledge. In particular, marketers recognize the 'value-added' aspect of the types of information that are authored and circulated through social media and thus eagerly seek access to those data through Facebook and others. In recognition that several kinds of surveillance occur on Facebook, users will come to watch over themselves as well as their peers, scrutinizing the content of their profiles with yardsticks like 'employability' and 'liability' in mind. Some types of scrutiny are more visible to users than others, and therefore are more influential in shaping their behaviour. Peers and parents shape student visibility and watching in a more immediate sense than employers and marketers, at least at this stage in their lives.

Identities and Communal Living on Social Media

Before focusing on how the students interviewed have come to live on Facebook, we may situate this in the broader context of individuals migrating to social media, and the impact this has had on their identities and communities. As these are sites where users share personal details in a quasi-public environment, their impact on identity is apparent. Social media profiles display a vast range of descriptors, ranging from cultural markers to favourite movies. The rich vocabulary produced on profiles is a standard form of self-expression. Users are explicitly displaying cultural taste patterns, and that this information can be tied to the larger body of personal information found on these networks (Liu and Maes 2005). Not only do social media make users visible and identifiable, but this information can also provide more insight than anticipated by the user. User profiles go beyond the immediate identity, offering a predictive insight not unlike the recommendation systems found on sites like Amazon. For now this is primarily used to recommend new friends and upcoming events to users. This suggests that a seemingly autonomous personal identity is an interconnected project on social networks.

One of the striking features of identities on social networking is that they are invariably a communal process. Personal self-expression is tied to an audience of peers that not only receives this information, but is also involved in its production. A lot of scholarly literature on social media has addressed its consequences for community formation and maintenance. Contrary to popular criticisms that sites like Facebook erode social ties, researchers have found that they contribute to their maintenance. Consider the maintenance of social capital through sites like Facebook (Steinfeld et al. 2008). Online services are especially well suited for the needs of young adults who are struggling with the transition to university life. Not only do these sites facilitate the creation of new, close friendships, but they also enable the maintenance of long-distance ties. This suggests a flexible model of community building where geographic proximity loses importance. This treatment of social capital lends support to the idea that this is becoming an explicitly valuable resource in that it is increasingly visible and measurable.

If community is important in identity construction, it stands to reason that community building adopts an increasingly egocentric premise (boyd 2006). Users are centrally located on their list of contacts, and this results in the formation of a specific kind of community. Rather than speaking of a cohesive community whose parameters are agreed upon, social media resemble a series of individualized networks built around the user. Communities are based on friendship, and an egocentric view of group formation locates and contextualizes both the individual user and their collective of friends. The fact that communities now take on increasingly personalized dimensions is a curious development. The tension between networked individualism and community values is especially pronounced in countries that embrace collectivist values. User activity on the Korean social networking site CyWorld is split between network maintenance and self-reflection (Kim and Yun 2007). This suggests a longstanding tension between autonomy and connectivity. Furthermore, online relations are a direct extension of offline values. Future research should consider how societies that emphasize greater openness and transparency between citizens would adapt to online services that prioritize the open exchange of personal information.

While the above features can arguably be found across social media, not all sites are homogenous in terms of the kinds of communities they foster. By being relatively accessible in membership and in content as well as having a flexible interface, Facebook has a relatively loose set of norms, leaving the construction of a community to its users (Papacharissi 2009). In comparison, sites like the professional LinkedIn and exclusive ASmallWorld provide a more readymade community by having tighter restrictions on access, content and form. While most social media services have the kind of public/private balance found on Facebook, it is important to remember that more exclusive communities remain, and that the kinds of capital that are tied to these communities are associated with longstanding disparities.

Complicating Privacy and Domesticating Exposure

A dramaturgical approach to new media suggests that some forms of identity expression are meant to be more public than others. Yet the supposed distinction between front and back stages is complicated on social media (Pearson 2009). Indeed, seemingly intimate moments may occur in plain sight, while public displays go unnoticed. The abundance of privacy settings and heterogeneous spaces (private inbox messages versus a posting in a public group) suggest that designers and users are actively reconstructing some degree of comfort and appropriateness. The maintenance of private and public displays speaks to the novelty of these sites as locations for identity construction. The active and deliberate construction of one's identity leaves room for playful negotiation. Photographs as identity markers are framed and edited deliberately and often strategically. While this speaks to a playful and empowering potential for identity construction on social media, this self-presentation involves specific protocols that are upheld by peer scrutiny (Sessions 2009). There is a heightened concern about deception on social media, specifically a discrepancy between photographs on a profile and the user's actual physical appearance. This hints at a normative climate on sites like Facebook, where accurate embodied representation is required and actively policed by other users.

Communal living on Facebook complicates privacy. As we have seen in the previous chapters, scholars are moving beyond a dichotomous understanding of privacy and living in public. Scholars and users both approach social media surveillance by way of privacy, yet sites like Facebook underscore the complexity of understanding as well as maintaining privacy (Nippert-Eng 2010). Users are reconsidering privacy as a concept alongside managing their own privacy on social media. Facebook might contribute to an erosion of privacy, yet young users in particular develop a nuanced understanding of privacy and publicity within Facebook (boyd 2008, West, Lewis and Currie 2009). These users were experienced in maintaining a degree of privacy from parents prior to social media, and these experiences inform their use of sites like Facebook. But users do not just hide information from some users; they actively share it with others. Users maintain a trade-off between ensuring privacy and achieving public exposure (Tufekci 2008, boyd and Hargittai 2010). The public nature of information on social networks is more than a default setting. It is also tied to cultural values that may be deliberately espoused by users.

Using social networking involves information that is considered both public and private. Not only do users adopt tactics to publicize some information while obscuring others, but sites like Facebook perpetually revise their settings to accommodate a more granular understanding of privacy. Some users go so far as to maintain separate profiles for private and public purposes. Yet even a typically private profile will have content intended for public consumption, including profile pictures and contact information. Social media complicate a public/private binary, and this is no more evident than when users attempt to bifurcate private from public content.

Yet many social media users have a paradoxical understanding of privacy where the connections between everyday use and longstanding consequences are scarcely understood (Barnes 2006). This speaks to the limitations of an embodied and situated approach to privacy and exposure. Ideally this produces an online presence that is contextually appropriate in that the user is as visible as desired at that moment. Yet sites like Facebook are not just fleeting moments of expression: they are cumulative archives of personal information. While users do take measures to protect personal details, this often happens though boundary mechanisms like privacy settings rather than the deliberate withholding of information. Consider the user backlash against Facebook's 2006 decision to publicize interpersonal activity on the site as news feeds and mini feeds (Sanchez 2009). The fact that much of this backlash took place on Facebook itself suggests that users have a significant investment in using the site. They did not simply condemn Facebook as a substandard service and stop using it. In addition to sharing outrage, users are publicizing the kind of social networking service they want. If these suggestions do not interfere with the site's business model, this protest actually benefits the site's designers.

The public nature of information on social networks is more than a default setting. It is also tied to cultural values that may be deliberately espoused by users. As discussed in Chapter 2, applying the concept of the brand to personal identity suggests that users are actively involved in their public image on social networks and other new media venues. While self-presentation is a longstanding social concern, its current manifestation online suggests a further blurring between 'notions of the self and capitalist processes of production and consumption' (Hearn 2008: 198, cf. Beer and Burrows 2007). Thus, publicity is a desirable outcome, albeit one that is increasingly difficult, in part because of the social convergence associated with these sites. Facebook is synonymous with privacy violations, but there is more going on than moments of exposure. Surveillance on social media is more pervasive than a series of incidents. It is increasingly a lived condition: a product of ubiquitous mobile technology and a rapidly growing user base. In light of these developments, scholarly research needs to interrogate the conditions surrounding peer visibility on sites like Facebook. To be specific: what compels users to engage in Facebook surveillance, how do they perceive these conditions of visibility and how do they manage their online presence?

Silverstone and Haddon's work on domestication (1996) provides insight when it comes to user adoption of social media. In the context of increased information and communication technologies in the household, they recognize that users – far from being passive – inscribe meaning and values into technology. Technology is a lived experience, and so their framework anticipates a qualitative focus on user reception of social media for interpersonal surveillance. Domestication addresses how information and communication technologies are integrated into everyday life, with a focus on the struggles that emerge in consequence. From a domestication standpoint, the continued migration of everyday life onto social media dwellings leads to specific tensions. The struggle between privacy and public exposure is a concern, as is the tension between the familiar and the strange when interpersonal relations are mediated (ibid.). The fact must also be considered that although reputations on social media are treated as an individual's responsibility, in reality this creation is a much more collective and complex process.

Although social media trigger privacy violations, sites like Facebook are more than a hit-and-run location for information exposure. Users have built extensive presences on social media, and privacy concerns are only one factor that influences how they use these services. In order to understand how users perceive and manage their visibility on Facebook, it is incumbent to focus on a broader range of activity, attitudes and interactions. Rather than approaching Facebook surveillance as a series of incidents, it should be framed as a more long-term engagement. Users have a broad and extended presence on these sites, and they are responsible and committed to this presence. Their attitudes and behaviours are guided by a care of the virtual self that compels them to manage their reputation online. The Internet has long played a central role in identity construction and maintenance (Turkle 1995, Miller and Slater 2000), but the growth of sites like Facebook means that users' reputations are increasingly monopolized. It is a common sense assumption that potential employers will look up a candidate on social media, along with searching their name on Google. This is clearly not an exceptional practice, as virtually everyone can turn to these services to gather information about their peers. Users are told that they need to manage their digital reputation, and that they need to be vigilant when uploading personal information. But it is precisely the social aspects of the social media enclosure that complicates these efforts.

Privacy as a value is being reconfigured through users' familiarity with social media. They may experience privacy violations, but these violations are part of an increased normalization of social media visibility. For this reason, this book not only positions privacy concerns alongside publicity, but also situates these values alongside users' broader experiences with Facebook. Findings in this book are thematically presented along a narrative charting exposure to, use of and familiarity with Facebook. Through pressure and convenience, joining Facebook becomes the path of least resistance. Users then come to realize that surveillance and visibility are at the heart of the interpersonal use of Facebook. Meanings are constructed around these practices through terms like 'creeping' and 'stalking'. These experiences also lead to a reconsideration of privacy and publicity. Users then develop a set of tactics to manage more problematic forms of exposure. They also regard users as being responsible for managing their own online identity, while acknowledging the difficulties involved in this task.

About the Student Interviews

I conducted semi-structured, in-depth interviews focused on how users coped with peer-to-peer surveillance. Thirty undergraduate students who use Facebook were selected for study. Participants were all enrolled at the same mid-sized Canadian university at the time of study. These students were selected from all faculties at this university through a series of posters on campus as well as by notices sent by email to undergraduate listservs. Of the thirty students interviewed, twenty-three were women and seven were men. Seven were in the first year of their studies, eight were in their second year, five were in their third year, seven were in their fourth year and three were in their fifth year. Twenty-six students were in the faculty of arts and sciences (or 'artsci'), three were in health sciences and one student was in the faculty of education. Twenty-seven students checked their Facebook account at least once a day. The three that did not check it once a day instead received email notifications of Facebook activity. When quoted below, respondents are anonymized using pseudonyms.

The interviews took place in a face-to-face setting, either at the participant's place of residence or at an office on campus. Interviews ranged from forty-five to ninety minutes in length. All interviews were documented using a digital audio recorder. Prior to recording, these interviews began by having the participant sign onto their Facebook account and demonstrate how they would typically navigate the site. If using the interviewer's laptop, the respondent would use a browser with cookies and history disabled, such that no personal information would be retained. They would then be asked to browse through the site as they typically would, responding to a few preliminary questions about their use, including how many times a day they visit the site, how much time they spend per visit and what kind of content do they browse on the site. This activity helped contextualize the interview questions as well as provide information on the rooted practices surrounding social networking. While participants were asked questions and some notes were taken regarding actions performed on the website, at no point was any personal information recorded.

Students were incredibly eager to talk about Facebook. When I put my notifications out via email and posters, it took mere hours for enough participants to contact me. Though I was there to gather findings from these students, they arrived with questions of their own. These questions pointed to a mix of befuddlement as well as enthusiasm concerning the very recent growth of Facebook in their lives. Many students use Facebook to maintain social relations with friends and family elsewhere, as well as foster new relations with other students. Yet they are also entering adulthood as well as the job market or postgraduate studies. For these reasons they become increasingly concerned with their public exposure. Interviews focused on a set of general themes, including describing their Facebook usage over time, the types of personal information made available to others and reasons for doing so, types of personal information acquired from others through Facebook and reasons for doing so as well as their perceptions of information exchange on

Facebook. While these were my principal themes, students were enthusiastic to discuss related and often unexpected aspects of living on Facebook. Consequently, these interviews were semi-structured, and I brought extra batteries to make sure that we were able to explore these aspects.

Ties that Bind: Peer Pressure and Convenience

Many respondents felt compelled to join Facebook due to peer pressure. This pressure was felt either from high school classmates or from new friends at university. Peer pressure on social media went beyond recommendation or prescription. Some respondents reported that their friends would construct profiles on their behalf, and then transfer control of this nascent profile to them. In more extreme cases, would-be users learned that Facebook contained photos and other content about them, even in the absence of them having an official profile. This was especially perplexing for people who were not familiar with the kinds of visibility in which they were implicated. Chloe, a second year artsci student, offers the following:

> I was like, "How can pictures of me be on the Internet?" They would show me and they'd show a picture of me with other people and they'd show comments that other people had made and, like, "How are people making comments on this photo of me and I don't even know it's there? I should be involved in this. I should know what's going on".

Chloe's confusion stems from the fact that she was already fully active on Facebook. Her friends, and even complete strangers, are able to upload photos of her for other users to see. Indeed, many respondents realized that they already had a presence on Facebook, even if they never intended to join the site. This presence was only manageable by becoming a Facebook user.

Respondents join Facebook because of peer pressure, but they stick around because of its social convenience. Facebook is often used for on-campus coordination, like broadcasting one's presence in the library, or requesting class notes. In other cases, it is used for a more spectacular kind of visibility, such as uploading photographs from a recent vacation. Facebook is a mix of memorable events coupled with mundane details, and is recognized as a resource for sociality. It is particularly convenient because it allows users to be visible without needing a context or justification. The way that information can be uploaded without being directed at any particular individual or group enables a passive visibility that is ideal for impression management (Goffman 1959). Respondents give the impression that they do not care about being visible to their peers, and this indifference generates a valuable social capital for digital youth. Gregory, a third year health sciences student, describes using Facebook as 'all very calculated to look the coolest and getting the most attention without seeming like you want it'. By allowing users to upload content for no explicit reason, Facebook enables a visibility between users that extends beyond what they would typically know about each other. For Katelyn, a third year artsci student, this provides 'a general feeling of how your life is going … it might not be things that would like merit a whole email'. As submitting personal information is a pervasive activity, Facebook produces a visibility that is akin to a 'general feeling' of individuals.

A lot of student users also actively dislike Facebook. Many offered detailed diatribes that cast the site in a critical light. Some of them went so far as to deactivate their profiles. These students invariably returned to Facebook, though their absence has only strengthened their admittedly mixed and occasionally contradictory criticism of the site. Their return to a service they dislike is fuelled by the perceived need to stay online. Not being on Facebook is equated with being cut off from their colleagues, especially for social events. This is the soft coercion typical of social media. People first join at the behest of their friends. Nobody directly prevents them from leaving, but there are clear costs associated with doing so. Respondents cite losing contact with particular sets of friends as a reason not to leave the site. Even when respondents question most of their friendships on Facebook, they state that leaving the site would mean losing enough valuable social ties to make them reconsider this decision. Likewise, key social events on campus necessitate a presence on the site. Peter, a fourth year artsci student offers the following:

> It's my damn friends, man. Like, there's Homecoming and there's a bunch of people coming up to Homecoming and [for] a lot of my friends, Facebook is the only reliable way to get a hold of them. Which is annoying. It's really annoying. Because I don't really want to be on it and I probably – like, after university's done, I probably won't be. But I don't know, right now it's just – it's almost too convenient not to have it.

Social media increasingly monopolize events like Homecoming. Social coordination is easy on Facebook, but this is tied to the risk of unwanted exposure. Staying on Facebook is seen as too convenient, and leaving it is too costly. Even when staying in touch with people is generally desirable, these ties pose risks on an everyday basis and as such require heightened vigilance *vis-à-vis* offline sociality.

Facebook Visibility as Surveillance

Respondents are fully aware of why Facebook would be used for surveillance, and they describe the site as a vast resource for personal information. Respondents cite the fact that they can access this information in a low-cost, low-risk manner as facilitating peer surveillance. As well, Facebook is seen as having unique searching abilities. Instead of looking for an email address or screen name, searching is typically based on actual names, facilitating interpersonal monitoring.

Respondents described interpersonal surveillance on Facebook in terms of them being watched by others. They were aware of instances where other users would watch over them on Facebook. In addition to former and current romantic partners, respondents were concerned with parental scrutiny. Parental access to profiles led to a convergence between social contexts that respondents typically wanted to avoid (boyd 2008). Facebook also provides a distorted representation of the person. Ralph, a third year artsci student, describes how Facebook misrepresents him to his father:

> My dad is on Facebook. He knows what I'm up to. He knows the shenanigans
> that happen. But at the same time, he doesn't see that I put in like twenty hours
> a week at the library along with fifteen hours a week of classes. He doesn't see
> that I'm working every weekend on essays and stuff. He sees the guy holding
> the red plastic beer cup.

Being visible on Facebook is risky because it gives other users' access to personal information that is misrepresentative. In particular, alcohol features more prominently than lengthy study sessions at the library. It may also publicize information that respondents would simply prefer to keep to themselves. For these reasons respondents have some ambivalence about their presence on the site.

Interpersonal surveillance on Facebook is also mutual, as watching and being watched both feature prominently. Respondents turned to Facebook to discover more about people who were of interest to their romantic lives. This is justified by the availability of relevant information on profiles, including sexual orientation, relationship status, the kind of relation the user wishes to pursue and material for small talk. Respondents describe their own exposure as a distinct concern from watching their peers. They typically hold different standards between what they want to expose about themselves and what they want to find out about others. When discussing concepts like privacy, stalking and personal information, they easily switch from one to another. Yet when considering their own visibility, their ability to access their peers' personal information is the most accessible yardstick. Andrea, a fourth year artsci student, frames her own visibility on Facebook by way of her ability to see her boyfriend's ex-girlfriend:

> I find it kind of weird that I have such insight into her life and I can, like,
> basically judge her, like I don't know, it's really weird to me. That's why I don't
> really use it that much, because I feel like all these people can do the same thing.

From this perspective, surveillance on Facebook is treated as a mixed engagement where the benefits and detractions of watching and being watched are traded off against each other. In Andrea's words, a user's presence on Facebook provides a kind of insight that lends itself too easily to making judgements. The kinds of insights she could glean from others' profiles forced her to reconsider her own presence.

While the logic that 'everyone is doing it' appears to put respondents at ease, the above quote suggests that peer visibility often compels respondents to guard their own information. This adds an important dimension to social media surveillance: that peer visibility triggers greater self-scrutiny. They come to watch over themselves, using imagined audiences as yardsticks for appropriate content on the site. Knowing that they are being watched and knowing the extent to which they can watch others compels respondents to monitor their online presence for content they believe that others will find objectionable. This kind of self-scrutiny triggers the strategies for impression management detailed later in this chapter.

'Creeping' and 'Stalking' on Facebook

The terms associated with Facebook surveillance warrant exploration. Social media's discursive formation sheds light on how contemporary information exchange and related forms of visibility are framed. Two terms were predominant in these discussions: stalking and creeping. Both terms were used to describe problematic ways of getting information on Facebook. Creeping was seen as a milder version of stalking, which in turn is meant to reflect more negatively on the user: 'It's all a matter of degree. I mean, if you were looking to assign either Facebook stalking or Facebook creeping to one person's activities, I'd think you would have to do it on a case-by-case basis' (Gregory). Creeping is a more involved and targeted way of using Facebook, though respondents treat this as a matter of circumstance. Creeping involves perusing somewhat extensively through that person's Facebook content: a few pages of wall posts, or a photo album. This will happen for a several reasons. Users may wish to see what events and news they have missed. They may want to see what content a particular person has recently uploaded: 'If there is like a definition of Facebook creeping it means looking at someone's profile a lot – then I've done it for sure to like, probably … well, what is creeping? I look at people's profiles every now and again, but like what is the creep aspect of it?' (Mary). Mary treats creeping as a function of using Facebook, as using the site in the way it was intended leads to the prolonged scrutiny of others' information. Creeping can also be brought on due to boredom, or simply because content on the user's news feed – the content that first greets people when they sign on – caught their attention. Andrea contrasts a conventional definition of creeping based on 'actively searching' against a more mundane understanding where 'you're just bored and you're just looking at people's profiles and you don't have an active interest or motive to look at it'. The fact that so much personal information is so accessible arguably makes this a more routine activity, brought on more by boredom than an active interest.

Stalking resembles creeping, although it is a more pronounced way of collecting information. If a user consistently returned to another user's profile, this would be framed in terms of stalking. Facebook stalking refers to all behaviour that could potentially be or has become actual stalking. As Facebook stalking is not restricted to actual stalkers, respondents suggest that the site facilitates this kind of behaviour from its users. Much as Clay Shirky (2008) suggests that emergent media lowers the threshold on group activity, Facebook appears to have the same effect on interpersonal stalking. While stalking is treated as problematic, Claudia, a fourth year artsci student, also acknowledges that it is an extreme version of creeping, which is bound to the manner in which Facebook is designed.

> I think creeping, from what I've heard, is more of a friendly way of being like 'I was so bored that I was just kind of clicking on people's profiles and looking at what was going up'. I think stalking is a little bit more aggressive, maybe? And a little bit more – like, it might be somebody who you haven't added as a friend who keeps requesting being a friend? Or somebody who keeps posting messages on your wall? (Claudia)

Terms like creeping and stalking imply that some forms of exposure on Facebook are more troubling than others. Yet this is measured in increments, as the threshold between creeping and stalking is 'a little bit' of aggression. And users generally grow accustomed to this range of visibility, leading to a normalization of interpersonal surveillance on social media. Clancy, a first year artsci student, states that having his personal information accessible to a network of peers has consequences that he is only beginning to realize and accept: 'I've had like a few people phone me and I'd say, "How'd you get my phone number?" "Oh, yeah I got it from Facebook, sorry." "Okay, yeah, no that's totally fine." Because I put it up there, right? I put it up there for a reason' (Clancy). Through their experiences with creeping and stalking, respondents learn what kind of visibility they should expect from the site. These incidents lead to greater self-scrutiny and management of their presence, but also a level of comfort with their exposure. They understand the fact that they are putting information 'up there for a reason' when those reasons emerge in consequence. Creeping and stalking are not necessarily seen as negative, simply because users do it themselves. Surveillance between users ranges from casually discovering what a close friend did over the weekend, to the targeted and prolonged monitoring of strangers. The consequences vary from everyday identity maintenance to criminal harassment. This range of surveillance practices is unique in that it emerges seamlessly from the everyday use of social media. For this reason many respondents suspect that Facebook was designed specifically for activities like 'stalking' and 'creeping', verbs that have since become synonymous with the site.

Making Sense of the Private/Public Distinction

Student respondents frequently used the terms private and public when describing Facebook. From these discussions it is apparent that not only was a public/private binary insufficient to describe Facebook, but it seemed that Facebook was a catalyst to reconsider these values. Facebook represents a kind of blurring of private and public, at least as generally understood in North America prior to the advent of social media. In addition, the term 'personal' typically crosscuts this discussion, such that personal information appears in public spaces, private spaces or both.

One can speak of Facebook as a public presence in that users report an ostensible comfort with sharing personal details with an extended audience of 'friends'. Here, public seems to be synonymous with an audience-based exposure. Users share their information with a public. This is a public that they have wilfully shaped by choosing their friends. Some respondents, especially those in their first year of studies like Rachel, drew parallels between their exposure on Facebook and the kind of publicity sought by reality TV stars. Clearly one of the key motivations for using Facebook was to share specific information with a somewhat amorphous (though occasionally specific) audience:

> It's pretty much all about attention, as far as pictures; taking pictures, things like that – because everyone can see that. … It's almost as if we're in a world where we watch a lot of reality TV and there's TV shows like *The Hills* and things like that, Facebook is our own little form of entertainment where we can get a glimpse of everyone's life. (Rachel)

Rachel's description underscores the desirable aspect of publicity on Facebook, but also the fact that this is a two-way engagement where users enjoy watching each other. Some respondents approach the kind of publicity offered by Facebook with a degree of trepidation. Often they would make comparisons to real-life exposure in order to underscore its novelty, and the difficulty of adjusting to the service. Peter likened the circulation of photos on Facebook as if 'I had a photo album at my house and somebody came and copied it and then put it in their photo album'. Another student claimed that the wall was modelled after the whiteboard on students' doors in residence, making it a kind of public space. Students also drew comparisons between putting content on Facebook and being visible outdoors. However, the implications of this imagery were not unanimous. While some believed being outside legitimated scrutiny by the public, others using this imagery believed that they still had reasonable expectations against monitoring and harassment, especially in the form of creeping and stalking.

Privacy also matters to respondents, especially when personal information leaks in unanticipated or undesirable ways. Mary, a first year health sciences student, described Facebook as private because of its extensive privacy controls, yet also acknowledged a public element insofar as the site itself is open to all:

I'd say it's private in the sense that like your own profile is like, your own profile and you can control what's on it because even if somebody writes on your wall, you can make it invisible kind of thing. So, it's totally private because you can have as much information as you want or as little information as you want, but then it's public in the sense that anyone can use it.

Although some respondents – especially those nearing graduation – value privacy more than others, most respondents managed their privacy and publicity simultaneously. Samantha, a fourth year artsci student, referred to Facebook as 'a completely public expression of private and personal matters'. This statement suggests not only that competing values coexist on the site, but also that using Facebook is contradictory. It suggests that by default users are taking information and putting it in a context that is more public than desired or necessary. The fact that this is typically a deliberate and wilful act is especially perplexing for respondents. Samantha comments on this confusion: 'It's supposed to be personal information but Facebook makes it very public and you're supposed to be, I guess, with every post you make, keeping in mind the fact that everyone can see this and that this is a public sphere for, I guess, private communication.' While conversations about public and private on Facebook are messy, it is clearly not a matter of simply having a boundary that separates private from public, even though some spaces are designated as more private than others. Private information may become public in consequence later. Respondents treat social media as a cross-contextual public, and respond to this transparency with a deliberate performance of public exposure. As Gregory notes, Facebook is ultimately 'a tool to remind people you're there'.

Managing Online Presences

Although social media like Facebook offer new opportunities for public exposure, respondents have a range of tactics at their disposal to manage their presence. Caring for the virtual self (Whitson and Haggerty 2008) involves restricting information flows, and exceeds the range of privacy features offered by Facebook. In general student users make extensive use of privacy settings. They do this to restrict information from a general public, but also for more targeted purposes like hiding a particular photo album from specific individuals. The majority of respondents are familiar with privacy settings. Others find them confusing, but maintain a commitment to mastering these settings. Based on prior experiences, respondents periodically return to their settings to ensure that they are still in order. Upon joining her school's academic network, Rachel noticed that her personal information had gone public to a degree that she did not anticipate. Following this incident, she appraises her privacy settings 'every so often … to make sure that only my friends can see my profile'. Other respondents set their privacy controls such that other users cannot seek them out. In effect, they have to initiate contact with others.

Another tactic employed by respondents is to maintain dynamic and contextual privacy settings. Students often augment their privacy during job interviews, such that potential employers cannot locate their personal content. One respondent keeps her profile fairly private by default, but lowers it on her birthday to receive well wishes. Zachary, a second year artsci student, went so far as to cancel his Facebook account temporarily in recognition of how his position as a political leader could be compromised by his online presence:

> I cancelled Facebook for a little while; it was for quite a long period of time. It was because I was vice-president of the [youth political group]. And, that was for all of [province] and there was something like six to eight thousand people who were under me. ... I had that leadership position too and, that's when I realized that you know, this is my personal life but, it's publicly ... like my public personal life, that could reflect negatively on the [youth political group].

Other respondents would log onto their friends' accounts in order to see the extent to which they were visible. By looking at their presence from another user's perspective, they were able to get a better sense of how their online presence was perceived. Interestingly, this is a feature that Facebook later integrated into their privacy offerings. During the interview many respondents stated their intention to revise their settings, with one respondent doing this mid-interview.

Respondents also manage their online presence by deliberately choosing not to upload certain information. This self-censorship is described along very common-sense lines. Respondents describe a process where they simply do not share photos and thoughts that do not reflect well on their reputation, or are otherwise discomforting.

> Anything I put out there on the Internet – if I'm afraid of it ever coming back to haunt me, I won't put it out there. And I consciously make that decision for every piece of information that I put out. So I'm not really worried about stalking or creeping because anything out there on me is kind of what I've already put out. (Madeline)

> Anything that you wouldn't want your parents to know isn't something that should be on the Internet. (Andrea)

Madeline and Andrea claim that they retain control over their online reputation by virtue of their ability to omit or remove damaging content. Here the spectre of parents and stalkers is invoked to justify this degree of self-censorship. Self-censorship includes not uploading information, but also not behaving in a way that could be photographed or otherwise documented:

> For me to be caught on photo doing something stupid, I had to be doing
> something stupid in the first place. And if I avoid that, which I have been hit or
> miss about in the past, then it's a non-issue. They can't post photos of me that
> didn't happen. (Gregory)

Facebook users are not only able to control what they upload, but they are also able
to control their behaviour in public. Not doing anything 'stupid' is an appealing
common-sense recommendation, but it also lends itself to complications when
others take control of one's presence, or when otherwise 'smart' behaviours are
misconstrued and taken out of context.

Many respondents monitor the kind of content that their friends will post about
them. These respondents have taken exception to some wall posts and photos
authored by their friends. These posts have been deleted, and the culprits are now
under increased scrutiny. Here respondents watch over their more problematic
friends, recognizing that others are watching the kind of content that is exchanged
with these friends. Yet some respondents also suggest that they might not know
all that is out there about them, acknowledging that their efforts to manage their
reputation may be insufficient. In some cases respondents will also prune their
social network by removing people from their friend lists. This is done as a last
resort when these friends are deemed to be a liability, but also occurs when a
respondent feels they accumulated too many friends. In the latter case, respondents
target friends with whom they maintain weak ties.

Respondents also manage their personal network of friends by appraising
individual friendship ties. These respondents draw parallels to common-sense
assessments of friends beyond social media. That is, they hesitate to become
Facebook friends with someone who lacks discretion in face-to-face settings.
Beyond this scrutiny respondents develop more general guidelines to determine
whether or not they add someone as a Facebook friend. As Katelyn offers:

> I'm not going to Facebook friend someone after the first meeting, unless
> someone expressly jokes about Facebook and is like "oh, I'll add you". I've
> decided that I'm not going to Facebook friend someone until the second or the
> third meeting because; otherwise you get a lot of like excessive friends, who
> you'll never see again.

Katelyn's concern about never seeing Facebook friends again is noteworthy,
because their lives will still be visible to one another. This speaks to the paradox of
visibility on Facebook: an absence of real life visibility is coupled with an ongoing
and intimate kind of visibility.

Responsibility and Futility

Respondents feel responsible for the outcome of their exposure on social media, and extend this responsibility to others. In the event of privacy violations or other unwanted consequences, respondents report that users only have themselves to blame. This suggests a perceived locus of control when users upload information to Facebook. That is, if they did not want information to end up on their profile, they would have chosen not to upload it.

> I've never been an enormous personal information-panic person. It's not a big deal to me if someone knows where I am or what I'm doing, for the most part. Especially when you can exercise so much control over what's visible, it's boggling to me, honestly. If I didn't want people to see my profile, I'd make it private, and that would be that. (Gregory)

Because of this perceived sense of agency, the idea of other users encountering trouble with their online presence is met with little sympathy, as respondents feel these users should simply know better. In particular, respondents claim that by uploading information onto their profiles, users are 'inviting people to look into their life' (Rachel). Here users are seen as deliberately uploading information about themselves in a public setting, and then complaining about consequences that they clearly should have anticipated. Respondents do treat their own creeping and stalking as problematic, but self-judgement is tempered by the perception that users are responsible for their own visibility. As a result users like Andrea justify their own stalking of others by citing the other user's decision to upload this information, or their failure to use more stringent privacy settings: 'If I'm looking at it, I feel like if she has it public, then I can just look at it and I don't feel bad.' Thus, users have nobody to blame but themselves when others take advantage of their unwanted exposure.

Respondents feel responsible for managing their online visibility. Yet they also acknowledge that managing this visibility can be difficult. Attempts to manage privacy are often case-based; that is, to stop specific information at a specific point in time. Many respondents acknowledge that information will still 'leak' (Lyon 2001) beyond an intended audience. The sheer volume of information as well as social ties for any user means that managing an online presence is challenging. Respondents acknowledge that simply having information on a profile, whether public or private, leaves users open to considerable risk because of the sheer volume of people who will have access to that information: 'I guess we all tend to forget is that what we put on Facebook isn't personal or private in any means because of the hundreds and sometimes thousands of people that you allow to see your profile' (Samantha). This respondent compares this unexpected exposure to the 'reply all' button on email interfaces, where users will accidentally send a message meant for one person to an entire community.

Respondents also describe the non-friend friend (a Facebook friend but a stranger otherwise) as a potential vulnerability:

> Everything that I've put up, I know that somebody's probably looking at it. Like, there's probably somebody on my friends list who I don't really know that well who has actively taken an interest in my life because they think – maybe they think I'm an interesting person or, like, I don't know that they don't like me. (Andrea)

> I think just the people who you kind of add, maybe two or three years ago, who you've kind of forgotten about. They're still on your friends list but you may not actually be friends with them in real life and you may not see them ever or talk to them ever, but you still have access to their profile and they still have access to yours. (Claudia)

Here, the quantity of seemingly trusted friends means that it is near impossible for a user to manage their entire audience. Even when respondents place the locus of control – and blame – on individual users, they are quick to acknowledge that Facebook is primarily a public domain, and that attempts to limit exposure are futile. Respondents also acknowledge that privacy measures are far from perfect. They do not have full confidence in the site's ability to keep contextual information in that specific context. Respondents are aware that proper conduct on Facebook is based on a contradiction: individual users are expected to be vigilant, but this vigilance will not offset all potential risk. Safe use is necessary, but not sufficient on social media.

The above suggests an acknowledgement of partial futility: if information is uploaded it will most likely leak. Facebook surveillance is a product of information convergence, as so many people are using it. The challenges for visibility and exposure posed by Facebook are augmented as more people join it, and as it takes on a greater presence in different social contexts: 'Like, Facebook is so new, like, we don't know what kind of social implications it's going to have. And it's becoming such a momentous force that I don't think, like, it's like people jumped on board before they knew where it was going' (Peter). Much as interpersonal surveillance is rooted in the everyday use of social media, mitigating the risks of unwanted exposure is embedded in mundane practices like un-tagging photos and choosing not to upload damaging content. As these risks are tied to information flows between previously distinct contexts, students use privacy settings extensively to ensure that these leaks are kept to a minimum. Some respondents like Samantha are overwhelmed by Facebook's opportunities for public exposure, and cite this as a reason to not be diligent:

> I'm pretty sure all my private information is already long gone. There's no sense of privacy in this modern world and because everything I do is basically online

these days, I feel like there's little or no safety and, therefore, I don't need to curb what I'm doing on Facebook.

Samantha presents a kind of ambivalence in terms of her comfort with Facebook. She has grown accustomed to being visible on the site, but this is in response to the overwhelming amounts of exposure offered by the site. She is actively participating in her visibility, but this is not necessarily the kind of social media that she wanted. In considering the negative outcomes associated with Facebook, respondents describe them as a mix of outrage from undue risks coupled with an acceptance of these vulnerabilities based on individual responsibility and agency. Respondents understand that the complexity of social ties on Facebook means that there will be unexpected and undesirable forms of visibility that arise. For respondents, it all comes down to the idea that users are choosing to be on Facebook, even when this is only in response to peer pressure. In Zachary's words: '[i]t's designed to do that but at the same time we're not forced to do it, I feel. Yeah, so we get desensitized to the fact that how many people can have access to it, but at the same time we're choosing to put it up there.' Zachary identifies a key tension of social media: users lose track of the extent of their visibility, but are ultimately responsible for this visibility.

Discussion

Student use of social media follows a general trajectory: initially enthusiastic users come to learn the consequences of their visibility, namely that information that is constructive among friends has socially destructive consequences in other spheres. Facebook endeavours to make everyone's information accessible to everyone else, and students learn that this leads to humiliation, harassment and further sanctions from parents, employers and other watchers. As a result, they become cautious and many students anticipate cleaning up or shutting down their Facebook account upon graduation. Young users get more conservative with age, especially in the transition from the first to the fourth year of their undergraduate degree:

> I don't really have a strictly professional life that's why my profile is, I believe it's completely open. I don't think I've set limits or anything but yeah, in the future once I do move on from being an undergraduate I am gonna start locking down stuff right away. Like if I'm going to apply to do a Masters or a PhD, I don't want people browsing my page to see if I'm a worthy candidate, it should be based on academics. Same thing in a professional world, I'm not going to allow it to prevent me. (Ralph)

At the time Ralph did not consider his life to be 'professional', but entering graduate school or the work force would warrant greater privacy. Students recognize that what is desirable in their current context will not be desirable upon graduation, and anticipate a shift from publicity to privacy-based concerns:

> I think it might be because I'm eighteen and I never look at the big picture. I never look at consequences, so as of right now it's not a concern. I think as like later on ... I would never post wedding photos, I would never post baby photos. ... I think as far as university goes, it's fun and it's functional but, I wouldn't want – as soon as I'm done university, I wouldn't want people knowing anything else about my life. I wouldn't want them to know my grandkids and things like that. (Rachel)

Rachel describes her Facebook use as a gradual accumulation of information. The vast amount of photographs she would have in ten years is justification for an eventual rupture:

> I mean if I were to continue to have Facebook for the next ten years, I'd probably have over a thousand photos albums. So, I don't know if I could go into ... say I was a high school teacher, and then once some of my students graduated they added me on Facebook, I don't know if I'd want them to see pictures of me all the way back from my high school days. Like, I don't think that's appropriate.

Rachel's concern here is emblematic of friendly surveillance on Facebook: an online presence is built from small contributions by users and their friends. No single act seems malicious, but when taken together over time they can have damaging consequences. This is especially true at a time when Facebook's user population is sharply increasing, with a consequential increase of contributors to any user's visibility, audiences of that visibility, and social contexts in which that visibility will have consequences.

In this chapter, three issues emerged that characterize social media surveillance among university-aged users. The first issue is users' relations to other kinds of surveillance. Surveillance concerns for student-users are primarily individualistic. They report and anticipate surveillant relations with family, friends, romantic interests and classmates. They are generally concerned with situated and immediate forms of surveillance. Users do not want parents to find out about their social life, nor do they want ex-boyfriends to know the details of their friendship network. They want to maintain boundaries that separate different social contexts. Potential consequences range from social embarrassment to forgoing life plans, notably careers and further education. From their perspective these concerns eclipse government, institutional and market-led scrutiny conducted through Facebook. Yet peer-based surveillance does not follow a specific diagram. Users will attempt to keep in touch and maintain visibility with one audience while hiding from others. Users typically make use of increasingly granular privacy settings, but also go beyond Facebook's privacy offerings when they provide a false name, manage multiple profiles for different audiences, or temporarily deactivate their profile.

In general users do not believe that state- or institution-led surveillance will happen to them. Yet upon some reflection, they will acknowledge specific concerns. While downplaying the general threat of government-based surveillance, Katelyn concedes that she could be subject to complications entering China as a result of politically-themed content on her profile. These risks are less tangible, but clearly still present when users consider their visibility on Facebook. Users focus on relations with individuals because these are the relations that are most visible in social media enclosures. Users are rendered visible to each other, and interact with each other more often than with other parties. It stands to reason that this exposure is the more tangible concern.

Second, interpersonal surveillance is mutual, as watching and being watched are interchangeable. Users were able to describe their own exposure as a distinct concern from watching their peers. They typically hold different standards between what they want to expose about themselves and what they want to find out about others. Yet when discussing concepts like privacy, stalking and personal information, they easily switch from one to another. When considering their own visibility, their ability to access their peers' personal information is the most accessible comparison. From this perspective, surveillance on Facebook is treated as a mixed engagement where watching and being watched are traded off against each other. This applies to more extreme cases of Facebook scrutiny like creeping and stalking, but respondents also understand their own visibility by way of others. Users seek comfort in the fact that others engage in social media surveillance. Yet the fact that 'everyone is doing it' is also reason for them to perform greater self-monitoring. Surveillance is thus mutually augmented, as visibility and scrutiny are conditions that justify further visibility and scrutiny.

Peer scrutiny marks a convergence between care for the self and care for others. In Chapter 1, the balance between care and control was shown to govern surveillant relations with others. When users are in the same enclosure as loved ones, their care will be manifest as scrutiny of their online presence. Similarly, the self-care necessary for proper identity management is at least partly informed by relations with others. Not only do close peers provide an imagined audience, but witnessing their gaffes fuels an individual's vigilant self-scrutiny.

The third issue pertains to users' perceptions of agency and responsibility. Even novice users are aware of Facebook's extensive privacy controls. As a result users feel responsible for the outcome of their social media experience, and extend this responsibility to others. In the event of privacy violations or other unwanted consequences, respondents believe that users only have themselves to blame. Yet users also acknowledge that managing an online identity is complex and laborious. This is because managing a presence on Facebook means managing an extensive set of peers, an ever-changing interface and a variety of pathways in which seemingly protected information can leak. This apparent lack of control pushed Peter to contemplate quitting for a second time. He was quick to acknowledge that he will not regain control by deactivating his profile. Even if he leaves, he will still be there. Facebook retains his information, and other users can still post information about him: 'I don't want anybody to have anything on me, you know what I mean? So, once again, like, it will, like – I mean, it just gives me another reason to even get off Facebook. Deactivate, sorry – you can't leave Facebook.' The observation that you cannot leave Facebook speaks to its features as an enclosure. Users describe their behaviour – and that of their peers – in terms of free will and agency. They have the option to act as they please, and are fully responsible when they misbehave. Yet they also report that Facebook's owners have made it remarkably difficult to remove one's self from the enclosure. Even if an individual deactivates their profile, they still have a presence, and Facebook still retains their information. Ultimately, this compels users to maintain their vigilance on the site.

Respondents have a growing familiarity with interpersonal surveillance on Facebook, but this familiarity is mixed with some uncertainties and tensions. Users join at the behest of their friends, and maintain visibility because of these friends. The kind of visibility required for surveillance from Facebook is borne out of everyday practice, with users maintaining relations with their colleagues. Peer pressure notwithstanding, users willingly supply information about themselves to this enclosure, making it suitable for interpersonal scrutiny. An ever-growing friendship network means that unanticipated risks come up, but choice and responsibility are placed on users themselves despite this complexity. Tensions between individual control and greater complexity on social media, much like tensions between private life and public exposure, are indicative of the further growth and domestication of social media (Silverstone and Haddon 1996). As an increasingly central feature of everyday life, social media surveillance between users is framed not so much as a violation than a condition that users need to manage. Visibility and exposure on Facebook is normalized. Exposure is not limited to any specific instance, but rather is a pervasive condition of social life on social media.

Users express some ambivalence in their responses. They grow accustomed to Facebook visibility, yet its effects remain chilling. These developments complicate efforts to manage their online presence. Users feel responsible for their presence, but are aware that managing this presence is beyond their control. They perceive online reputations as being a personal responsibility, even while acknowledging that vigilant self-scrutiny is not enough. Student users are aware that different audiences and social contexts intersect on the site, but they still construct a visible profile for close friends. Moreover, the continued growth of Facebook – in terms of audience, contexts and features – augments the importance of content on the site. This is especially true at a time when Facebook's user population is sharply increasing, with a consequential increase of contributors to any user's visibility, audiences of that visibility and social contexts in which that visibility will have consequences. A photograph that was uploaded when there were a million Facebook users becomes all the more important when its potential audience reaches one billion users.

This chapter has focused exclusively on interpersonal social media surveillance. While this provides specific context for user concerns, subsequent research should focus on how a more diverse population is settling into Facebook and its conditions of intervisibility. As a partial study of the mutual augmentation that exists on Facebook, this chapter indicates that this surveillance ranges from interpersonal scrutiny to an awareness of other kinds of watching. Chapter 4 further considers these dynamics by shifting focus towards university watchers.

Chapter 4
Institutional Social Media Surveillance

Introduction

Chapter 3 focused on students living on Facebook. These students are coping with uncertainties about their visibility and broader social consequences but they are generally comfortable with their presence on social media. If migrating to Facebook is inevitable, we may ask who else dwells there. This chapter also focuses on the university sector, but shifts its attention to institutions instead of individuals. Facebook began as a social networking service for undergraduate students at select universities in the United States, allowing these students to author and distribute information about their personal identity, interpersonal connections and social activities. Today, a broader demographic from different social spheres has converged on the medium. Facebook claims that it is used 'to give people the power to share' (FB About 2011), suggesting comfort and control for users. Yet like so many electronic media, Facebook is a 'leaky container' (Lyon 2001) and both seeping and stronger outflows are common occurrences. By virtue of using Facebook, students make themselves visible to a large population of individuals, primarily friends and colleagues. And while there has been considerable analysis of the type of peer-to-peer visibility afforded by Facebook, institutions also access this site. Here, institutions refer to formal organizations that provide services to, or otherwise manage, a specific population.

A cursory search of news media suggests that social media impact nearly all aspects of organized social life (Dodd 2010, Roper 2010, Sweney 2010a, Sweney 2010b). Facebook and other social media are increasingly interlaced with a host of institutional functions. This prevalence is a by-product of the site's popularity among users. As a rapidly growing user base volunteers information about themselves, their peers and their social world, corporate bodies have become particularly eager to capitalize on this valuable commodity, with designers and businesses attempting to exploit this informational goldmine.

This chapter explores how institutions, focusing particularly on universities, are adopting social media. While Facebook has expanded its scope beyond universities, student life remains a heavily 'Facebooked' phenomenon. Facebook contains a wealth of content that various organizational units within a university are keen to explore and exploit. Their presence on sites like Facebook entail distinct types of surveillance that focus on a set of individuals, increasing the institutional visibility of personal information. This institutional presence on Facebook marks the latest attempt by schools and universities (Monahan and Torres 2010), to watch over and control their populations. Students that make themselves visible to one another on social media unintentionally augment institutional surveillance. This relates to what danah boyd (2007) identifies as invisible audiences in social networking, such that users do not know who can access their personal information.

Focusing on universities helps clarify Facebook's status for institutions. The fact that the site offers unprecedented access to personal information suggests that it is a valuable institutional resource. Yet it can also be a liability to universities and other institutions in that it augments their own visibility in ways that are difficult to manage. Users openly criticize schools, workplaces and corporations, and these criticisms are retained and easily accessible through the site's search function as well as through external search engines like Google. Institutions and individuals may be mutually transparent, as both are made visible through social media. Yet institutions develop practices to manage risks on social media, while exploiting the visibility of individual users.

This chapter is arranged into sections that chronologically depict how universities have adopted social media. It returns to the students from Chapter 3 to consider their opinions about being watched by their school on Facebook. It then looks at the emergence of institutional use from interpersonal experience. It then addresses the perceived appropriateness of using Facebook on behalf of the university and the prescription of a complaints-driven approach to social media. The visibility of the university on social media, with its reputation in student hands, triggers a task force to determine official guidelines. Social media like Facebook are also used to publicize security incidents. Finally, respondents contemplate their future involvement with social media.

At the time of this research no guidelines existed at a university level to shape employee conduct, with protocols and best practices still in negotiation. Hence, part of the appeal of this analysis is precisely the fact that norms and protocols for such institutional monitoring are currently emerging. Surveillance Studies benefits from considering how surveillance-related institutional policies develop, with user-initiated, bottom-up practices informing official mandates. This chapter points to instances where institutional scrutiny assumes a more categorical approach, namely in targeting student parties that risk tarnishing the school's reputation. Facebook's recently enhanced search feature makes it easier for the university to target what they consider to be relevant content.

Domestic Technology Refit for Institutions

Social media have an increasing impact on relations between institutions and individuals, and the nature of that impact requires abstraction. For all the discussion of social networking sites and social media, there is no consensus regarding what 'social' means. We may unpack this term using a Weberian understanding of social action. Social media's growth lies in their ability to foster communication, as they facilitate a networked sociality made up of exchanges between social actors, institutions and social contexts. We may return to Chapter 2, specifically

Wittel's (2001) theoretical implications of such a networked sociality. His work is less concerned with these networks as it is with underlying social dynamics. In particular, networking as a contemporary practice in the Western world marks a fusion of labour and leisure. The information sector relies on 'barcamps', happy hours and other non-work work practices where leisurely sociality becomes a means to enhance capital. Everyday life is further colonized by work, notably through the cultivation, commodification and exploitation of social ties. Wittel's work predates social media, but he identifies the boundaries between social realms – work and play, public and private – as compromised by the promotion of corporate networking. Such theoretical grounding underscores that social media can be distinguished from other online technologies through their emphasis on pre-existing, offline social ties.

The notion that private lives are increasingly exploited and scrutinized is also anticipated by material on the domestication of technology. Domestication scholars note that audiences play an active role in adding meaning – and value – through consumption. This focus underscores the importance of the situated context in media studies. It produces a more robust social science, enriching academic but also corporate understandings of information and communication technologies. Silverstone's treatment of users' communicative efforts anticipates the emergence of social media, and its emphasis on user-to-user communication to generate value. And while the domestic sphere often refers to the homestead, Silverstone was careful to point out that the domestic is in fact a broader concept. Everyday domestic life, once the overlooked remainder of capitalist production, is made visible through new media (Poster 2004). Recent scholarship using Silverstone's approach has turned to mobile technology, and how its domestication leads to contested boundaries between public and private life (Ling 2004). Ward (2005) furthers this approach by focusing on what she calls the second generation Internet, and its emphasis on flexible, user-driven content.

Both academics and industries have a growing interest in the domestication of technology. That is, user activity is increasingly under scrutiny. Users are treated as a source of innovation, but also a potential liability. Watching over them is entirely in line with state and institution-led attempts to control populations (Scott 1998). Indeed, information technologies have long been central to institutional surveillance (Dandeker 1990). But what is unique with social media and universities is that an institution is utilizing a domestic technology. The domestication of technology is a growing concern for Surveillance Studies. Lyon (2001) rightly observes that the rapid uptake of mobile devices marks a progressive creeping of surveillance into everyday life by enabling users to be located and tracked in a pervasive manner. Despite the expansion of new forms of surveillance and visibility in a wireless world, the effects of this visibility are far from obvious. Webcams (Koskela 2006) and social media (Albrectslund 2008) enable an empowered visibility, such that their users control how they present themselves. Yet the voluntary use of these technologies augments surveillance enclosures where the totality of everyday life is visible to businesses and governments (Andrejevic 2007). Both perspectives hold empirical purchase. But the domestication of surveillance has grown too vast, and so this research will focus on the university sector.

Institutional surveillance on Facebook fits in a broader history of keeping order in schools. Control and discipline have been attempted through a variety of architectural, pedagogical and technological approaches. In the United Kingdom, a national database tracks student activity (Lyon 2010). Other technical solutions for managing and monitoring students include x-rays at entrances and drug testing for athletes. At universities smart cards are pervasive, tracking and regulating the movement of students on campuses. These technologies exert control over students by focusing on their physical presence. Social media complicate this focus by offering a new terrain for disorder to occur.

Social media first emerged as services for individuals – students in this case – before being adopted as tools for institutions. Beer and Burrows (2007) offer an early account of the consequences of social media in the university. The initial effect is the heightened visibility of faculty and teaching staff online in a searchable and editable format. This is experienced as an upset to staff and faculty under scrutiny, yet the full consequences of social media in the academy remain to be seen. Students are increasingly making themselves visible; all the while other watchers are taking an increased interest in sites like Facebook. When Beer and Burrows published their article, Facebook was only recently established beyond the Ivy League network. While their study uncovers how universities are subject to exposure, these institutions are responding by turning to social media themselves. Universities are still scrutinized by students using social media, but they are increasingly able to manage their own visibility as well as to take advantage of the visibility of students. Social media further compromise the boundaries between everyday sociality and institutional scrutiny. Not only are universities able to manage their reputation online, but doing so affords them scrutiny and control of student population, by virtue of that population's increasingly public presence. They capitalize on the augmented visibility of students on cross-contextual platforms, which in turn augments the surveillance and control of that population.

Recent scholarship has also documented how these sites play an increasing role in a range of social spheres. Although Facebook began as a university tool, since 2006 the site has gradually spread to other populations, as the initial users moved beyond campus and access has been granted to non-students. Its rapid uptake by others suggests that social media are now shaping social milieus that were at least partly sheltered from online activity. Within the academic sector, the rising presence of faculty users raises some challenges for personal disclosure and professionalism in the classroom. While trade literature suggests an explicitly preventative approach (Young 2009), a degree of openness on teachers' profiles could facilitate learning in the classroom by enabling students to identify with their instructors (Mazer et al. 2007). While student-teacher relations are a longstanding issue in academia, social media are dwellings where these relations can be publicized. The professional boundary between instructors and students remains, but a degree of porousness and transparency requires a reappraisal of old norms.

Within the classroom, social media have arguably become part of professional development. As students make the transition from campus to career, their public image is a substantial concern and can even become a liability. For instance, medical students and residents treat their presence on social media as part of their professional competency, especially when it comes to the public disclosure of private information (Ferdig et al. 2008). It stands to reason that concerns over professionalism and codes of conduct can be extended to other careers. Beyond risk and liability, Indian university students use social media to gather information about career prospects and generally familiarize themselves with the business environment (Agarwal and Mital 2009). This suggests that student conduct online is indicative of a new kind of virtual professionalism, and that labour struggles among emerging professionals will be shaped by social networking.

Students and University Monitoring on Facebook

Students have a comparatively lengthy history of using social media. They have experience with Facebook, are privy to stories and anecdotes, and have developed opinions about their school potentially watching over them. Student respondents had some awareness of the kinds of surveillance issues raised by other students. In almost every interview these issues were framed by a controversial event that was unfolding at the time.

The president of an undergraduate student society had made a racially charged comment on a friend's photo on Facebook. Because of his prominence on campus, news of this comment spread quickly. Someone took a screen capture of the comment before it could be removed, leaking it beyond its original privacy settings. While respondents framed this incident in terms of university-led surveillance, it bears noting that the university only responded to content when students brought it to their attention. Debate ensued over whether or not the president should resign from his duties. This story was relevant for two reasons. First, it was only the latest of a series of racially charged incidents on campus. The university has long struggled with its reputation as unwelcoming. The fact that this behaviour was now taking place on a quasi-public medium, and by a public figure, added to the embarrassment. This leads to the second source of controversy: comments that would otherwise remain private and bound to a particular context now transcend privacy settings as well as social contexts.

There was no consensus about whether the blowback that the student experienced was appropriate. Some respondents, while condemning the comment itself, felt that the president should not be held accountable to what they said in a non-professional setting. Peter claimed that '[i]f it wasn't on Facebook, and he just said that to his friend in passing and somebody's walking by, they wouldn't be like "Oh my God, I demand your resignation!"' Others felt that Facebook was an extension of the president's public image, and that similar standards would apply online as on campus: '[H]e posted it on someone else's wall and anyone who is his friend can see this wall. It wasn't like a private message that we managed to steal' (Katelyn).

The fact that the student president placed content onto someone else's profile is given as reason to consider that content public. Here, public designates a condition whereby the author loses some control over the flow and circulation of that information. Following last chapter's discussion on taking responsibility, many students believe that individuals caught in this kind of situation have nobody to blame but themselves:

> If your profile's public and you make a public comment that is inappropriate like that then by all means. If you've chosen to put yourself out there and become a public figure – like, I wouldn't be so keen on a university just checking out what students are doing who aren't in public positions like that. But I guess, like, you just kind of have to be conscious of what you're doing and you shouldn't be making comments like that anyway. (Andrea)

The controversy surrounding this issue suggests that concepts like private, public, personal and professional are routinely used to describe Facebook. The site, as well as appropriate conduct and retaliation, is contested terrain. Regardless of what respondents felt was appropriate, they generally agreed that university-led monitoring was a possibility, especially for students who held some kind of prominence. Consequently, students felt that they were not likely to be targeted by university staff or administration:

> He's been targeted because he's in that position of power and he is representing everybody else whereas, like, if I said something like that, which I wouldn't, to one of my friends, it probably wouldn't be picked up – and people might see it, but it wouldn't be made into such a big deal (Claudia).

> I guess the only reason I can think of is like, [the university] wanting to make sure there is no negative image of themselves being portrayed somewhere on the Internet. (Mary)

Student respondents struggled to imagine a situation where content they uploaded on Facebook would be of interest to the university. This is partly because they considered their lives to be less interesting than that of a racially insensitive student politician. Yet the tangibility of peer-led monitoring also eclipsed less overt forms of scrutiny. One exception to this perception is when students would organize house parties. The university also struggled with a reputation as a 'party school', which damaged relations with alumni as well as with non-university residents of their town. Students like Mary recognized this issue as motivation for the university to watch over student activity on Facebook: 'The institution might want to bust up crazy sounding events before they happen. Stuff like massive parties that might get the police involved and [the university] doesn't want any more of that exposure I know, so that's probably a good motivation why they would want to know that information.'

Other students, like Claudia, believed that parties were targets of university as well as police intervention: 'And I'm sure, like, the [municipality] police and [the university] have some kind of alliance together so, in that sense, the police could find out who's having a pancake kegger and who's going to be on [street name] even though it's not Homecoming.' Regarding these risks, students would take precautionary measures like removing an event posting in the days leading up to a party. This was treated as a compromise between generating publicity for the event and maintaining some privacy from unwanted visitors. Given the media exposure that homecoming and similar events received, it stands to reason that these parties would be subject to university surveillance. Generally students believed that the university actively searched Facebook for evidence of these events.

When asked why the university would collect information on Facebook, students generally cited the school's reputation as motivation. This presents a novel development in terms of surveillance and social media: that the post-secondary institution was also subject to heightened visibility and scrutiny. Gregory suggested that the university was in a more precarious position than any of its students: 'It reflects pretty negatively, I think, and it makes sense to me that they're interested about knowing more, at the very least. I don't know what they plan to do with that information, but I don't blame them at all for being interested.' The perception of university-based surveillance adds another dimension to the friendly strain of surveillance described in the last chapter. While users are generally not concerned with being visible to administrators, this risk pushes them to scrutinize their presence as well as their peers. These findings occurred when the university was increasingly present on social media. This illustrates why there are grey areas for appropriate conduct by universities. As university administrations continue to migrate to social media, student users are only beginning to develop a language to describe this use. It is reasonable to expect a shift from students not seeing themselves as targets of university monitoring to one that takes this kind of scrutiny for granted. These interviews document a turning point in terms of university presence on social media, which is followed up below.

Students felt that the university has legitimate reasons to watch over them. Based on this knowledge they would assess whether or not they fit their perceived criteria for targeting, namely if they were public figures or hosting a student party. Knowledge of these criteria extends from offline sociality in the university setting. The migration of these criteria onto Facebook is a key feature of the convergence that fuels the mutual augmentation of surveillance on social media. Because academics and social life overlap on Facebook, students feel obliged to consider the former when using the site for the latter. This overlap is the reason that universities, but also other institutions, are taking an increased interest in these services.

About the Institutional Interviews

The findings below draw on a series of fourteen semi-structured, face-to-face interviews with employees at a mid-sized Canadian university. Of the fourteen participants, two respondents worked for campus security, two for marketing and communications, four were employed by residence life, two were tenure-track professors, two were human rights advisors and two worked for the registrar's office. The university in question maintains strong relations with alumni and other donors. However, recent incidents have raised concerns about its reputation as a 'party school', which the administration is struggling to manage. This coincides with a rapid uptake of social media like Facebook by undergraduates. The university is currently coming to terms with how to manage its own involvement on this site. Much like the students, university respondents were especially eager to discuss the challenges they faced with the growing popularity of social media. While some employees had informal experience with these services, the professional integration – including the decision to integrate these into professional functions – was a matter of individual discretion. They had anecdotes and anxieties that they wanted to share.

Interviews with participants addressed four themes. The first theme considered relevant policies at the time of Facebook's emergence. This clarified how the university first framed social media as well as the gaps and challenges posed by this approach. The second theme considered practices, notably how social media are used in a professional setting. As social media are not conventional institutional services, it is appropriate to focus on how employees first approached them and in what capacity they were used as part of their work. The third theme examined the perceived validity of information found on social media as well as the perceived appropriateness of obtaining information in this manner. Again, because Facebook was rooted in interpersonal exchanges, respondents negotiated their position among themselves but also with students. The fourth theme considered experiences using social media, both in a personal and professional setting. The novelty of this subject means that respondents raised additional issues. As much as possible respondents were able to address these issues during the interviews.

Genesis of Facebook as a Professional Tool

Given Facebook's interpersonal origins, its emergence as an institutional service warrants exploration. Here, Facebook emerged organically. Instead of a mandate from above, respondents reported a ground-level realization among employees that relevant information could be retrieved on the site. Many key operators were already Facebook users, or worked with someone who used the service. In the majority of cases personal accounts were used to access information. One exception is the case of a human rights advisor who previously abstained from Facebook and created an account strictly for professional duties. In addition to harnessing a pre-existing familiarity with the site, these employees blurred the line between professional and personal presence by using the latter to augment the former.

As there were no guidelines for using Facebook, professional practices first emerged to facilitate minor tasks. Respondents used Facebook to identify students by putting a face to a name. Howard, a coordinator for campus security, reports:

> Facebook in the past has allowed us to confirm identities of people. It has allowed us to – and when I say confirm identities, I really do mean simply in an anecdotal way, more along the lines of confirming for the people in the office that we're talk about the same person, not so much as institutionally identifying someone.

Howard describes an innocuous entry for the professionalization of Facebook by noting its quasi-official use to confirm an identity during a conversation. Using Facebook in a professional setting does not mark a rupture from personal usage. Rather, it resembles personal usage extensively, as employees rely on personal accounts as well as navigation skills gained from personal experience. While it was used to identify persons of interest, the consequences and appropriateness of that identification are not obvious to respondents, and for that reason employees used Facebook casually.

These findings present a diagram of institutional surveillance that fuses user-initiated practices into a larger structure. Institutions take advantage of information that individuals – students in this case – submit online. In this case they do not initiate, but rather exploit the heightened scrutiny afforded by social media. Moreover, the university's ability to watch over students on Facebook is facilitated by employees' familiarity with the site in an interpersonal context. Many of these employees were Facebook users first, and this experience is leveraged to monitor students on behalf of the university. The employees who usher social media like Facebook into the institution are a hybrid category. They operate on behalf of the academic institution, acting as its eyes and ears. Yet this is only possible through their presence on Facebook as individual users. This personal-professional hybrid facilitates the institutional adoption of an otherwise domestic technology. Not only can employees access Facebook content with their personal accounts, but their experience as users also allows them to navigate the site. This is a key feature of the augmentation of institutional surveillance by the interpersonal use of social media. The skills gained by users watching over users directly translate to the university being better suited to scrutinize their students.

At the time of the interviews nobody had the specific task of managing social media on behalf of the university. Instead, employees already working for the university were put in charge of social media because of their knowledge and enthusiasm for these services. Respondents were generally passionate about this topic. Cindy, a coordinator from marketing and communications states:

> I sort of do this in addition to my regular job because I have a love for it. And so,
> a lot of the time, most of the stuff that I do is outside of work hours because I'm
> on these places anyways and I like researching them, it's just a passion of mine.

The decision to put enthusiasts in charge of social media is sound, although it
also has important labour implications. Because of their passion for social media,
these employees assume added responsibility with no financial compensation.
This echoes what Shirky (2008) has said about decentralized organizing: that
corporations benefit from input provided by individuals who use social media for
intrinsic rewards. From a labour studies perspective new media augment what is
already expected of workers (Dyer-Witherford 1999).

The majority of interviewees report that social media have greatly complicated
their duties. This counters the perception that social media facilitate the management
of student populations. Indeed, the sheer volume of information now accessible
is staggering. Christine, a marketing and communication employee states: 'It's
almost impossible to find out what everybody is doing at [the university]. ... It's
very explosive, this use of social media that it's pretty hard to keep on top of, there's
no one person that can control or audit everything that's happening.' Not only does
Facebook grant access to a vast body of personal information, but the absence of
explicit guidelines from the site and from the university greatly complicate what
can be done with this information. A residence employee reports that instead of
witnessing events as they unfold, incidents discovered through Facebook occur at
an undisclosed point in time. Likewise, Howard reports on its mainstream status,
noting that Facebook is a burden because of the vast access to information that it
offers campus security:

> It's so widely used and has become such an accepted staple in people's daily
> routines that if there is harassment that is going to take place, there is a good
> chance that it will find its way onto Facebook as well. ... It's more of a bone
> of contention for most people in our service and I mean that along, broadly
> speaking. Generally speaking, we will all tell you that it has created more work
> for us than it has ever solved.

Facebook augments the visibility of university life, such that employees struggle
to make use of all that is made visible. This suggests a kind of institutional
growing pain in regards to Facebook. While it is currently treated as a burden,
this is because the institution has not yet developed proper strategies to cope with
social media.

Perceived Appropriateness of Monitoring Facebook

Facebook offers universities unprecedented access to student information with
no guidelines for appropriate usage. This has led to uncertainty among university

officials. Facebook is recognized as a source of relevant information, and is accessed by universities for this reason. But employees and students are ambivalent about whether or not this information should be used for institutional purposes. Respondents report that content found on the site has been uploaded in an interpersonal context, and that they felt uncertain about using it for other reasons. This uncertainty is also exemplified in situations where the university might intervene in student conversations online. Louise, an admissions coordinator, offers that she does not 'feel comfortable in us jumping in. I don't think it's our place, they don't think it's our place'. Employees and students oppose the university having a visible presence on Facebook. A residence employee conducted a survey to screen student attitudes, finding that they were overwhelmingly opposed to the university's presence on the site. In particular actively seeking out information on Facebook was deemed to be inappropriate. Not only did the survey confirm the admissions coordinator's suggestion that the university should not visibly intervene on Facebook, but also that they should not patrol the site for objectionable content.

Most respondents were quick to point out that they did not actively scour the site. They provided both ethical and logistical reasons to explain this approach. From an ethical standpoint they did not consider actively monitoring the site to be appropriate, which is compounded on top of their uncertainty about acting on Facebook content. However, logistical reasons carried more weight. Respondents claim that navigating the site to find information was incredibly time consuming, especially when users perpetually cope with a changing interface. Louise states: 'on a really basic level, now that I'm thinking about morals and ethics, we just don't have the manpower at the time'. Other security and residence employees echo this claim, citing time and workload as reasons not to patrol Facebook for relevant content. Despite these constraints, many of the respondents felt entirely justified having a professional presence on Facebook. This was partly based on the accessibility of Facebook's content. Howard prioritized logistical reasons over ethical ones, citing the semi-public nature of information on Facebook as justification to act:

> I definitely don't have enough hours in the day to spend surfing. And ethics … I don't know so much that it's really ever been questioned if we do visit a Facebook site, I don't think we have ever found ourselves in a position where someone says that it's unethical for you to visit that website. … If my ten year old can see it at home, then I don't see any problem with me pulling it up on my computer at work.

Student reactions indicate a clash between a contextual approach to privacy (Nissenbaum 2009) and one based on mere access. Employees acknowledge that contextual boundaries are a concern, but also that personal information will likely transcend these boundaries. While students may want others to disregard information found on Facebook, one residence coordinator asserts that students themselves disregard the ease with which this information is accessible and the extent to which it is made public:

> I think it's funny when people feel like it's private, but again I feel like it's only when it's convenient for them they'll call that and they'll say "that's private, don't comment on that", or "that's none of your business" or "don't use that against me". Well, this is the image, this is the story you are telling about yourself without you being there to explain yourself. (Holly)

Yves, another residence employee, claims that students are complicit in their own visibility, citing that students are uploading content that is made accessible through its association with Facebook's university networks:

> If you're part of the [university] network, you basically have access to pictures of anyone. It's like a database that people have helped create. I can find pictures of anyone on campus, anyone who goes to [the university]. So of course, that's useful. If that's a tool that's available to help keep the community safe, we'll exploit it.

As well, employees describe the inability to ignore information found on the site, and framed this as being hard-wired into all users. Howard describes the impossibility of not reacting to information found on Facebook, noting that humans are 'creatures of judgement'. The ease with which personal information is found on Facebook, especially when it is the only information available to investigators, strengthens this reactive judgement.

The issues raised by these employees highlight the effects of an increasingly visible social life. Facebook makes personal information accessible, but accessing and acting on this information is controversial. The act of deliberately looking over individuals is especially problematic for employees. Debates over what is public and what is private on Facebook – as well as the meanings held by these terms – spread from interpersonal concerns to relations between institutions and individuals. These tensions are an effect of the domestication of technology, as familiar information exchange is reconfigured in strange ways (Silverstone and Haddon 1996). Despite this uncertainty it is clear that Facebook is a new location for institutional problems. Conversely, it is also a tool to identify and manage these issues.

Complaint-Driven Activity Versus Patrolling Facebook

Campus security, human rights and residence employees were quick to point out that they took a complaints-driven approach to Facebook. That is, if an incident were brought to their attention from a complainant, they would investigate the site. But they claimed that they would not actively search Facebook, and certainly would not wander aimlessly for suspicious content. Daryl, the director of campus security, presents the investigative approach as an alternative to the complaints-driven approach, and criticized the former for the ethical as well as practical reasons listed above: 'We're not looking at it as an investigative tool. You've probably noticed the whole time we've been talking, that's the first time that I've ever used the term investigative. We don't investigate, we follow up.' This decision is informed by protocols pre-dating Facebook, and Howard also reports an avoidance of a 'quasi-investigative role at the best of times'. Following up, instead of investigating, suggests a reactive rather than proactive approach. Given the vast amount of information that could warrant investigation, employees prioritize material that others brought to them. Sarah, a residence employee, echoes this sentiment:

> If there's a complaint or something and then it comes up in the information that we've gathered that there's actually pictures on, or it's a harassment issue and someone comes to us and says it's happening on Facebook then part of the information gathering will then be going to Facebook to see if that is. But it's reactive, it's not a proactive "go and scour Facebook for information" ever.

By focusing on outside complaints, these employees rely on non-employees – typically students and local residents – to direct them to persons and incidents of interest. This approach facilitates their duties because external agents are informally enlisted to scrutinize the site. Their own ability to monitor student activity is augmented by their connection to the greater community. Holly from residence claims that they 'don't ever go seek out things on Facebook but if it's bought to my attention we don't ignore it'. The university's ability to watch over its student population is augmented by relying on other users to watch over each other online. Not only is this an effective labour-saving strategy, but it also enables a more penetrating gaze. Having friends watch over friends on Facebook enables the university to side-step privacy settings employed by users. Institutions thus capitalize on domestic technologies and the interpersonal visibility that these technologies generate.

Despite endorsing a reactive, complaints-driven approach, respondents conceded that they proactively search and scrutinize Facebook in particular situations. Leading up to events like the annual homecoming celebration, Cindy describes how marketing and communications searched and monitored Facebook events and groups: 'When homecoming, the debate happened, yes, there were people in my office who sort of went in and sort of printed or took an inventory of the kinds of things that were being said.' Louise from admissions states that senior members of the university's administration have employed this proactive scrutiny: 'It was the Dean of Student Affairs monitoring Facebook and let the police know about all these keggers that were going on. ... And the police contacted these people beforehand and said, "nope, not happening. Good luck".' Employees generally describe their Facebook monitoring in terms of responding to complaints about specific individuals. Yet categorical suspicion emerges based on homecoming events and a student party culture. This suspicion emerged in the interest of the school's reputation, a point that is further explored below. Proactive searching on Facebook accompanies this suspicion. This is a contradiction of employees' own best practices. Despite claims that patrolling is not an adopted strategy, it is logistically sound when searching for information about student parties. The ethical implications remain to be sorted out. This development marks a shift from the surveillance of individuals to something distinctly categorical. In other words, Facebook is now used to watch over abstract problems, not just student biographies. Yet the focus on categories still implicates students and their personal information.

The balance between reactive and proactive approaches to social media warrants further exploration, especially as different branches of academic and other institutions connect with sites like Facebook. Likewise, Facebook's changing features and privacy settings suggest that new conditions of visibility will arise. The site's search function has recently augmented its scope (Wable 2009), which affects the kinds of information that can be quickly accessed as well as what is made visible to non-users.

University Reputation and Mutual Transparency

Although the principal focus of this study was students' heightened visibility in the wake of social media, administration and staff were also concerned with the way their university was made visible through social media. The marketing and communications department is especially concerned with virtually everybody shaping the university's reputation in a public forum. These concerns amplify longstanding practices where potential students learn about the school from upper-year students. Often these students post harmful or inaccurate descriptions of the university on Facebook. This is especially concerning when high-school students and their parents are weighing their options for post-secondary education. In other instances students hosting a party or making inflammatory comments reflect poorly on the university when they publically confirm its reputation as a party school, or as one that struggles with racial insensitivity. Employees in the registrar's office confirm that students on Facebook publicize the school's reputation. This is used as a justification for an institutional effort to monitor the site. Cindy, a marketing coordinator, likens Facebook to a kind of feedback mechanism that the university should harness, stating that '[u]nless you sort of gauge what's going on, you can't just adjust what's going on in your real presence'. A wealth of consultants and public speakers stress the importance of managing an institution's reputation online. Cindy is no stranger to these services:

> There are a whole new bunch of businesses that are now saying: "for a fee, we will tell you what is going on in all these different social media platforms".

There's one called [business name] and I've got a free account. And so you can put in search terms ... and they'll churn this report and they'll search blogs, social networking sites, for what is being said.

Christine was especially struck by a consultant's recommendation that 'you basically have to go there because you're already there'. These services rest on the claim that universities are already present and visible on social media regardless of their actual involvement. This supports Beer and Burrows' (2007) work on social media surveillance. The multi-contextual nature of social media conversations coupled with a growing user population means that the university is subject to unprecedented exposure.

In light of these concerns, the marketing and communications department monitors university-themed groups for discussion. Respondents claimed that they do not conspire to monitor individuals, but simply seek out false information. While they felt tempted to intervene on these spaces, they did not think that this would be well received by students. Posting a response in a student-led discussion would make their presence visible, and be subject to pushback by student users. Instead, they rely on the university's own website to provide accurate information. Yet this was regarded as futile since students do not always visit official sites for information. Employees may attempt to create their own Facebook group, but these would remain nearly indistinguishable from other content on Facebook. This issue raises a key dilemma that became central to subsequent policy recommendations: should universities establish an institutional presence on these sites, converse with students in student-led spaces or covertly watch over students? These different strategies reflect differing degrees of visibility of the university, which is seen by marketing and communications as a liability due to student perceptions that the university should not have a presence on Facebook.

This dilemma also gets at the heart of privacy issues on Facebook. Students are clearly comfortable sharing information with one another in a public forum. Yet they regard university administrators' presence as a violation of privacy. This reaction supports a contextual view of privacy, as the content they share is meant for their peers, and not a broader audience. Moreover, this is a barrier that employees are only encountering now that their involvement on the site is directly linked to their service to the school.

Emergence of a Social Media Task Force

In response to these concerns, the university created a task force that attempted to make sense of social media's function in the academic sector. Led by the department of marketing and communications, the task force drafted a report for staff, faculty and students who use social media on behalf of the university. This report featured guidelines that resemble the early stages of an official policy vis-à-vis social media. This task force emerged in a climate where little knowledge or consensus exists concerning appropriate conduct for universities on Facebook. Respondents note that existing guidelines were drafted prior to social media and are insufficient to cope with emerging risks. As stated above, social media strategies have long been left to employee discretion and have led to conflicting approaches.

While institutional monitoring on Facebook began with individual employees' practices, the fact that it remained up to their discretion troubles respondents. Discretionary measures, coupled with the growth of social media within and beyond the academic sector, led to growing pressure for the university to provide some kind of policy response. Yves from residence suggests the university is reaching a tipping point: 'It's become more pervasive. It must change. The university cannot ignore its bearing on university life now. From the type of groups people can have, all that stuff. It's only a matter of time before some kind of policy comes out, or something to do with online usage.' Employees in other departments agreed with this statement, and added that they were waiting to operate within proposed guidelines. The task force's report included a description of social media for academic purposes, a description of social media usage in general and at the university, as well as guidelines for using social media within the university. Regarding student-led discussions, the report recommends that employees '[m]onitor, but not attempt to control what's being said in social media' and also to 'not become involved in the dialogues in student-administered groups' (Social Media Report 2009). This recommendation reflects admission coordinator Louise's usage, who states that her department is 'monitoring Facebook' and that they 'never jump in'.

Social media can potentially foster conditions of mutual transparency. Facebook allows any user to view as well as speak on behalf of any other user, brand or institution. Yet the task force's report recommends the scrutiny of the university's reputation on social media, as well as not adding to this visibility through any further engagement on social media. The university's strategy restores an asymmetrical relation of visibility between students and institutions by watching over sites like Facebook without acknowledging its own presence. The task force enables institutional control of a target population by authoring protocols to manage domestic technology.

The task force struggles to obtain a full understanding of the university's social media presence. Different branches of the university use sites like Facebook for varying purposes, and many do so independently of the administration. The fact that new services emerge while older ones adopt new features complicates attempts to speak authoritatively about social media. The task force accounts for these challenges:

> The guidelines had to be such that you couldn't get that specific, and we're talking about something so big and something that's still not totally understood

that we wanted to make it enough for people when they phone and say: "I want to set up a blog, what can you tell me?", we'll give them these guidelines. (Christine)

The university wants to pre-empt emerging technologies and practices by drafting an open-ended set of guidelines. This suggests that policy follows technology, and relations with students follow suit. Social media extend new possibilities for the university to watch over students, and related policies are intentionally vague to include these possibilities. Given that these services emerge from interpersonal usage, anticipating innovations is a complex task. Louise echoes this approach: 'That's one of the challenges we discussed, is that it's got to be, even though it's a policy, it's got to be open ended enough to deal with the challenge of a media that's ever-changing.' Here, flexible policies are presented as a remedy to volatile media.

Other Functions: Emergency Communications

Although Facebook and other social media were first received by the university as a vast source of information about students and university issues, some departments have contemplated other purposes. Campus security considered using Facebook and microblogging service Twitter to communicate to students and staff:

> The one thing that we're taking a look at in our job currently with Facebook is using it in the future as platform for disseminating information. ... I feel that the social networking sites are an excellent opportunity to disseminate information but we have to ensure that information that's getting disseminated through a third party is trusted, is going to be used appropriately, because the type of platform that we would be looking at is how we disseminate personal safety tips, personal safety information, possibly even campus security alerts during a critical incident. (Daryl)

While these services would be used to advance knowledge about safety, Daryl presents another important surveillance implication. By broadcasting real-time security alerts campus security is able to exponentially augment their scope when it comes to tracking suspects. Social media's coupling with mobile technology means that students and staff receive notifications about ongoing incidents and can observe and report on behalf of campus security. Here social media amplify pre-existing social networks. In particular, word of mouth dissemination of information is seen as a quick and effective way to communicate security-based issues. Daryl presents enrolling the community as antithetical to an Orwellian vision of surveillance:

> I always find it very interesting that when people talk about Facebook and then the next word is security, automatically they have the George Orwell kind of *1984*,

Big Brother's watching. In our department, it's the exact opposite, right? We're all about sharing information. Our philosophy here is security is everybody's responsibility. Our philosophy here is giving you all the information that you need to make informed decisions about your own safety. So the first thing that when we look at Facebook is getting that information to our community. So letting them know what's occurring on their campus and how to react.

The director of campus security claims that sharing information provides a useful service to the university. Yet student and staff return the favour when they receive, disseminate and submit information about ongoing incidents on campus. Students not only make themselves visible in a way that augments institutional surveillance, but also directly contribute to this watching on behalf of the university. Social media offer multiple avenues for individuals to augment institutional scrutiny.

Looking to the Future: Uncertainty and Commitment

The initiatives described above suggest that universities are paying more attention to social media. When asked about their future involvement, Yves from residence suggested that hate speech is an obvious and appropriate entry point for regulating student content on Facebook:

I guess something I would want the administration to take into consideration when they're making a new policy of whatever, if they choose to, is the fact that you can join any kind of group on Facebook. It can be racist. It can be anything. That's something the university should take into consideration. That if they were to try and attempt to control people's usage, like regular students' usage, that's probably where they would have to start.

The above suggestion furthers the use of social media for categorical suspicion. Monitoring hate speech on campus is an uncontroversial justification for this scrutiny. In that this is an issue that already concerns the university, it stands to reason that they will search for this content.

In general, respondents were reluctant to speculate about what Facebook would look like in the immediate future, nor were they willing to consider how their engagement with social media would evolve. Despite this uncertainty, everyone was confident that they would have an ongoing presence on the site:

I think it's going to continue to grow. I can't really say ... who can predict that unless you're in there? Yeah, I really can't predict. I really don't know, but I do know we're going to continue to be part of it, whatever it is. ... And we can't not use social media, we have to be there, we have to be involved, because that's where our target audience is. (Christine)

Their certainty about being involved with Facebook is based on its predominance. As social spheres migrate to social media, the amount of information generated on these sites will continue to be of interest to the university. Yves claims that 'everything is happening' on Facebook, from students signing leases to selling furniture, and that it was only a 'matter of time before the university sees the need to have some sort of control' over relevant content. In anticipation of student protest against this development, Cindy from communications claims that they fail to understand Facebook's privacy affordances: 'You'd think that they would know these things but I think they're under this perception that Facebook is hidden from the Internet. Like, for some reason, it's their own little community and no adults are going to come in here, they're not going to look at this.' Facebook's continued growth means that the information it hosts is increasingly accessible to the university, and this will impact students' values and expectations. It was more private before, but only because fewer people had access to it. As universities assume greater control over information found on Facebook, respondents suggest that students will need to scale back their expectations of privacy.

Discussion

This chapter presents Facebook as a tool for institution-led surveillance. Social media in general and Facebook in particular have gained an unprecedented user base. These users, many of whom are students or employees in the academic sector, generate an ever-growing body of information that has become accessible and easily searchable. Universities and other institutions are using the information located on Facebook in their administrative duties. These practices began with employees bridging pre-existing knowledge about Facebook with institutional tasks, yet their involvement with sites like Facebook become more formal with time. In addition to individuals, institutions are also dwelling within the enclosure. They are in a position to watch over individual users, such as their students. But they too are made visible as a result of information about them that circulates online. Employees working on behalf of the university have experience managing the school's reputation, as well as experience locating and monitoring students of interest. Nevertheless, the migration to social media is a challenging and disorienting process.

Social media's use by universities is a recent emergence, but even at this stage some features are observable. First, Facebook's origin as a domestic technology is a unique development for Surveillance Studies. Facebook and other social media were first used by individuals for interpersonal purposes. Yet individual users employed by post-secondary institutions also enable institutional surveillance through social media. This suggests that universities and other institutions harness interpersonal relations in order to further the institutional control of target populations. In particular, they are using the site to identify relevant categories, such as student parties and hate speech. Domestic technology can compromise the private realm, such as when television reconfigures the homestead (Silverstone and Haddon 1996). Yet social media is a technology that was exclusively used in a domestic setting, and is now adopted by institutions. This is an unusual kind of diffusion, and the fact that it is spreading so aggressively is doubly strange. Starting in university dormitories, it now encapsulates institutions and workplaces. As enclosures, Facebook and other social media have an expansive social reach.

Second, social media are both a means for the university to watch over the student population, as well as an enclosure for the university to be made visible. Individual users were initially more familiar with social media, and thus able to use them to the detriment of the academy (Beer and Burrows 2007). The university was exposed, and some of its less desirable features were put onto a searchable and archived enclosure. This was especially a concern for the university described in this chapter because of its reputation for riotous parties and overt racism. Yet such concerns can be extended to other institutions, as we will see in the Chapter 5. This speaks to the nature of visibility on social media enclosures like Facebook. While they were initially designed to make individuals visible, they are also capable of pushing an institution's reputation into the public eye. Moreover, institutions have little control over the fact that they now dwell on social media. Much like students whose friends uploaded information about them to Facebook, respondents above discovered that their institution's reputation was subject to public debate and scrutiny. Social media exposure is not just a problem for any single group, or a means to make one population visible. It is a mixed risk enclosure as it makes everyone visible to everyone else. However when focusing on students and university administrators, we see discrepancies in how they act in the enclosure. Universities and other institutions develop mandates, and are also courted by consultants to help develop explicit strategies. We can speculate that marketers and investigators in Chapters 5 and 6 will have even greater means to manage their presence, and exploit the presence of students and other individuals.

Finally, social media are a remarkably plastic service for institutions. They are able to quickly adopt and exploit it, for example, by locating specific individuals. Following a Surveillance Studies perspective, social media are used as an extension of institutional mechanisms to locate and identify its population. This is an obvious application of social media. But social media have less obvious functions like emergency communications. This plasticity is made possible by its expansion. The fact that Facebook attracts so much attention – and enrols so many users – means that it is potentially fruitful for any task that involves the public. As a digital enclosure, Facebook will continue to perform these functions. However, services like Facebook are deeply volatile and unpredictable. This means that it will likely be a slightly – or perhaps dramatically – different enclosure in the near future. The employees interviewed in this chapter are not sure what to expect from Facebook in the short term. As a stakeholder, the above university was able to leverage some advantage over students, for instance, by anticipating illegal parties. But this is done by using a tool that they rent, rather than one they own. Potentially, these employees could show up to work one morning to find they have lost their access to Facebook. This risk speaks to the relation between individuals, institutions and social media. Institutions may be in an advantageous position vis-a-vis individuals on social media, but they are both vulnerable when it comes to maintaining a long-term presence on social media enclosures like Facebook.

So far individuals have to cope with institutions getting comfortable in a dwelling that individuals call home. This is a cause for concern. Some treat this as a violation of privacy, and others change their behaviour on the site. But they also know why this is happening. Students recognize how their university benefits from using Facebook, and treat this migration as inevitable. The university's adoption of Facebook provides insight about social media surveillance and mutual augmentation. Individual scrutiny and sociality amplify the kinds of watching that institutions can perform. The people doing this watching often have dual citizenship on Facebook: they started as individual users, and their knowledge of interpersonal surveillance helped them watch over students on behalf of the university. Students also actively contribute to institutional surveillance when they submit complaints involving Facebook and when they respond to security bulletins. Facebook allows institutions to take advantage of individual usage to watch over those individuals. Institutional surveillance on Facebook combines interpersonal features of everyday scrutiny with emerging categories that are easily searched. Institutional control is facilitated through the continued growth of domestic information exchange.

Labour for the above respondents is increasingly centred on Facebook. It is presented as a helpful tool, but gradually is revealed to be a complicated mess. Facebook is also presented as something you 'have' to be on, even though this presence is also problematized and framed in terms of uncertainty. This echoes what we already know about work and technology, namely that seemingly time-saving devices and services do little to lighten workers' burdens. But by virtue of its social convergence, social media raise unique dilemmas for work. Their lack of ownership puts respondents like Howard and Louise on an uneasy footing. How will other employees and future employees cope with careers intersecting on social media? It may possibly cost them a job, either because of a controversial presence, or even because of an anemic one. Moreover, services like Facebook will certainly complicate whatever job they manage to secure.

Social media are a domestic technology that has spread to institutions and other realms. Privacy and visibility on Facebook are transforming, and this is the principal tension facing users. Content on Facebook that was previously treated as confidential is now subject to greater exposure. Employees believe that students can no longer consider the site to be private. Insofar as its reputation is implicated in student activity, the university sees Facebook as part of its jurisdiction. Yet recommendations to avoid detection on the site mitigate student opposition. With new features added on a monthly basis, Facebook is an ever-shifting mediascape. Increased scrutiny as well as privacy concerns mean that relations between individuals and institutions are also shifting. It stands to reason that these developments occur in other institutions, including workplaces, law enforcement agencies and government branches. Chapters 5 and 6 further consider these developments by looking at social media's applications as a business tool as well as an investigative tool, respectively.

Chapter 5
Market Social Media Surveillance

Introduction

This chapter describes in detail a new kind of visibility that is made available to businesses on social media enclosures. A broad set of organizational tasks – including market research, recruitment and customer service – is augmented through a growing body of searchable personal information. Sites like Facebook have undergone a tremendous diffusion into the business world, the effects of which are only now becoming apparent. These developments extend from marketplace surveillance of consumers' personal information. The large scale of information offered by Facebook, as well as its rapid spread to different social spheres, suggests new possibilities for market surveillance, including monitoring social relations as well as a broad range of transactional data.

By mapping key sites through which a personal information economy emerges on Facebook, this chapter illustrates how organizations utilize new relations of information exchange. It offers findings from a series of thirteen semi-structured interviews with professionals who use Facebook as a business tool, including marketers, brand managers, community builders and communications officers. As the emergence of business strategies for Facebook is an ongoing development, a key task will be to move from industry literature on these practices towards a rich description of how these services are actually being used. In particular, this chapter will supplement terms like 'listening' and 'conversations' that are meant to describe the way businesses collect personal information from a growing user base and deliver targeted content to those users.

The students we met in Chapter 3 have made Facebook their home. Many have left their geographic homes to come to university, and social media has been a remarkably good replacement. Universities took note of this migration, and are now strategizing and building a presence on this site. Students are watching over each other, and universities are watching over their students. This development has attracted public attention, and now many businesses are wondering about the kind of presence they should have on social media. Whereas individual surveillance concerns the known acquaintance, and institutional surveillance sets its gaze on the members of a fixed organization, market surveillance is the collection and processing of information of all Facebook users. This chapter will consider the unique properties of the third type of practice. This chapter also considers the emergence of a political economy of personal information (Gandy 1993, cf. 2009) through social media. It does so by exploring key developments in a variety of sectors that are adopting social media services like Facebook and Twitter as part of their business platform. The research involved is aligned with the study of audience labour (Smythe 1977), political economic concerns in the age of new media (Dyer-Witherford 1999), as well as social media in particular (Andrejevic 2007, Fuchs 2010).

Popular literature highlights the revolutionary potential of new media. By treating the range of online services and mobile devices as a landscape of information exchange, some authors claim that they enable 'organizing without organizations' (Shirky 2008). Yet instead of redundancy, organizations face new opportunities by taking advantage of sites like Facebook. The rise of social media means an exponential increase in visibility for both individuals and organizations. Disgruntled clients and co-workers may broadcast compromising information on Facebook and Twitter, yet their own personal lives are also made transparent through their prolonged engagement with these sites. The risks and opportunities associated with social media cannot be decoupled. We saw this in Chapter 4, where students as well as their host institution exposed themselves to public scrutiny.

So-called experts, 'gurus', and 'rockstars' present social media as a kind of cure-all for businesses. Indeed, most technologies are ushered into the public through a series of promotional efforts. Facebook and other social media are no exception. Advocates claim that social media will benefit businesses by making it easier for them to communicate with and listen to their markets. Organizations are taking proactive measures to exploit these sites. In recognition of the heightened visibility of their brands, many companies are actively searching social media for conversations between users about their brands and products. They are especially concerned about complaints and other damaging statements. Beyond this strategy, companies are also using these services to gain new insights about their market. The open-ended nature of sites like Facebook also allows for other possibilities for use and engagement, which are considered below. The promises and celebration surrounding social media run parallel to the global economic downturn. A lot of people lost their jobs and fortunes, and a lot of companies search for efficiencies and innovation. At the individual level, people flocked to sites like LinkedIn and other social media to promote their skills and tap into their social networks. Those fortunate enough to remain employed also jumped to social media under the assumption that it was a new skill to master and market in order to justify their employment.

By looking at these issues and responses, this chapter foregrounds the intersection of labour and visibility in social media. Labour refers to two distinct contexts: the labour of those hired by businesses to manage their online engagement, and the labour of social media users whose personal information is the raw material for social media business strategies. Both cases benefit from employee as well as user comfort and familiarity with social media services. Employees are typically passionate about the work they do, and also use these services in their free time. Likewise, social media users are unlikely to think of their engagement as labour, but rather in terms of interpersonal activity.

These developments are not unrelated to the previous chapter on institutional surveillance. Both cases look at how organizations relate to a key population using social media. Yet market surveillance marks a further shift toward categorical searching from scrutinizing individual profiles. This is a shift from a key institution that has a longstanding involvement with social media to a loosely organized group of institutions that are incorporating these services into their functioning. However, this also marks a more subtle shift from one institution coping with and managing its online presence to a range of consultants and industries deliberately engaging with social media for purposes of growth and revenue.

Market surveillance on Facebook extends from previous attempts by businesses to gather data on a large scale (Elmer 2004). This area has grown through a number of initiatives, including the use of geodemographic information to locate markets (Burrows and Gane 2006). Market surveillance on social media intersects purchase habits with personal information, but also with relational information. These sites are spaces where users socialize with others, yet they are privately owned and subject to market-led scrutiny, searching and sorting. This kind of monitoring is important when considering surveillance through markets more generally. In this light social media go hand-in-hand with market power. They allow businesses that own or purchase this data to know their market at a greater resolution, extract value from it, and manage their own publicity (Winseck 2003). The growth of market scrutiny is facilitated by Facebook's push towards relational searching. In contrast to conventional, 'Google-style' analytics, Facebook searches what users are saying and doing (Vogelstein 2009). This approach pulls categorical content out of social media information. Brands are visible, but this data is always bound to individual profiles. Relational searching scours personal information to yield insight about brands, markets and categories that are relevant to businesses.

This chapter begins by returning to the students from Chapter 3 to interrogate their views on this growing branch of social media surveillance. It then describes how people employed in this field began working with social media. It then focuses on how respondents describe their own professional relation with Facebook. The following three sections then focus on three business strategies involving social media: radical transparency, listening and watching and finally conversations. Based on respondent accounts and popular literature, these strategies are positioned from least to most effective in terms of exploiting social media. This chapter concludes by re-appraising the term 'social' in social media in light of these findings.

Students, Workplace Surveillance and Market Surveillance

Students are a target population for many businesses. Not only are they future employees, but they are also current customers. Student respondents were less accepting of surveillance led by employers than they were of university administrators. While post-secondary institutions had a reputation seemingly tied to students' private lives, respondents cited a personal-professional barrier that was ruptured by employer-led scrutiny on social media. Curiously, almost all students acknowledged that workplace-based scrutiny occurs. Regardless of their views on the matter, it seemed reasonable to them that an employer would access the social media service to find information about their employees. Here, ethical concerns are trumped by the sheer ease-of-access associated with sites like Facebook. Not only is it a matter of Facebook information not fitting in a workplace context, but passing judgement based on the site augments the legitimacy and authority given to information on Facebook, which Peter feels is problematic. This is an important dynamic for mutual augmentation: that the increased use of Facebook by different agents only augments the legitimacy of the information the site hosts. While acknowledging moral as well as practical issues with employers using Facebook data, students are inclined to believe that it is criteria for employees. Student users also report a struggle between a contextual sense of privacy and privileging sheer access. Users have the right to treat Facebook as a context that is separate from the workplace, but employers can often access it and form judgements about users. Andrea elaborates on this point:

> I don't think that there's really any measure of appropriateness. There's not really any etiquette when it comes to the Internet, because it's so new and there aren't any real privacy laws when it comes to that. So it's kind of just information that's floating around, so employers and institutions have kind of taken this as like: "Well, if they're putting this out there, then it's for your information, you can just access it and it just is another tool that lets us judge people's integrity."

Andrea's notion that personal information on Facebook is 'floating around' suggests that even though it is not intended to be used in a workplace context, it is very accessible. Gregory speculates that employers would know that information on Facebook would not determine workplace performance, but go on to use it as criteria simply to thin out a candidate pool, stating that 'they've got to start somewhere'. The sheer ease-of-access offered by Facebook makes it an obvious starting point. Some users justify Facebook scrutiny based on the nature of work, which may ask for more of a personal engagement. For instance, Katelyn suggests that an employee at a queer-positive workplace may be scrutinized for homophobic content on their profile.

As with earlier instances, users are accorded with a degree of control, and thus held accountable for negative outcomes. Claudia states that the only way employees could access incriminating information is if the user has 'privacy settings that are incredibly minimal and open to everybody'. Samantha echoes this sentiment:

> Employers have every right to sort of type in your name and if they see fit and see if you're there and see if there's anything incriminating on first glance because you have the ability to make it more private and because you have the

ability to completely control what people see. And if you were smart enough, I guess you wouldn't put up photographs that are incriminating or make posts that are incriminating.

Here, failing to conceal incriminating details is tied to a lack of intelligence. Yet much of this judgement is speculative. As the majority of respondents had little experience with full time work, their attitudes towards workplace surveillance and Facebook were usually not based on their own ordeals. Among respondents lacking workplace experience, many anticipate that social media scrutiny would be a concern later on. This was especially true when applying for jobs and when attending interviews:

> Because now most of my friends are in fourth year and they're going to graduate and get jobs and that kind of thing, they're learning the hard way that, you know, everyone looks at Facebook and there's a necessity to defend yourself or prevent people from really seeing problematic behaviours such as drinking or, you know, embarrassing photos that have a tendency to get up on Facebook even when you don't want them to. (Samantha)

While it may seem common sense to restrict damaging content, many people are 'learning the hard way' when they experience unanticipated leaks. In anticipation of these risks, respondents state that they would deactivate their profile while searching for a job. Others intend to open a more public profile. By this they mean that this profile would have fewer privacy restrictions, but also content that would be more suitable to a general public, including potential employers. Peter learned this technique from a colleague:

> I have one friend, she's twenty-four and out of high school she went to become a realtor and so she has two Facebook pages – one that's of her as a realtor and one that's her, like, with her friends, which is interesting, you know what I mean? Kind of living a dual life on Facebook.

The above example shows how doubling one's presence on social media, instead of abstaining, can potentially help maintain privacy. Yet restrictive moves were also employed in anticipation of summer jobs. For Gregory, this involved the removal of problematic content, and increased self-censorship:

> During the lead up to the end of the school year, I remove things like "Gears of War 2" as my religious views and Favourite Movies … it's just stuff like that, you know. I remove all my … basically, all my information that isn't my profile picture or contact. Or I change it to something that's very palatable. My political views are now moderate and I have no religious views, or whatever.

When compared to peer-based scrutiny, student respondents have little experience or awareness with workplace surveillance. This trend is furthered when speaking about market surveillance. At the time of interviews, respondents are generally not concerned with the possibility that marketers, advertisers or third-party developers could access their personal information. Student respondents acknowledge that Facebook would use their content in order to generate feedback regarding the site's services. When discussing third-party applications, respondents are not aware of the access these had to profiles. Rather, they based their criticism on the claim that these applications were a waste of time and cluttered up profiles and news feeds. In terms of Facebook itself, some users speculate that Facebook is not taking a unique approach to personal information when compared to other web services. Mary states that if anything, Facebook would be apathetic about all this data. Here the interpersonal use and value of the site is seen as taking precedent over any viable business strategy. Many users speculate that Facebook was adopting a business model based on selling personal information to businesses, as well as through targeted advertising and profiling users:

> They're selling it to advertisers. Advertisers will know what people at [the university] are interested in or what a certain age group is doing. Basically I don't think that they have any sinister motives – they're not personally collecting my information and looking at it, they're just interested in money. Like, what they can do, selling it to advertisers, selling it to interested parties. (Andrea)

Peter takes a perspective based on indeterminacy of use. While he speculates that it is being sold to interested parties, he also suspects that key uses – and related business models – have yet to be established. This speaks to the potential value of the service:

> Sell it to the highest bidder, I guess, maybe? Because, yeah, I don't know, you can use – I mean, we've barely even scratched the surface with how much you can determine from, like, so little information. And whether you determine things that are real or not, you're still drawing conclusions, right? I don't know. I can see corporations loving that shit, right?

Gregory focuses on feedback mechanisms in Facebook's advertising services as using personal information for gain. He treats this as a lesser of two evils (the more evil option being untargeted advertising), but borrows some Orwellian imagery to describe the scheme:

> And, if you can target your advertising – you know, they even have your little "More ads", "Did you like this?" ad. They're making a very deliberate effort to make more money off you, which is fine, I mean, this is free and I don't have to look at the ads if I don't feel like it. It seems like a trade to me. Totally, the idea is to maximize their output from advertising. … I approve of the fact that

> I'm seeing an ad for something that might interest me rather than something that has nothing to do with me. There's a certain "Big Brother" aspect to it, which is kind of uncomfortable, but, uh, honestly, I prefer targeted advertising rather than having to sit through some dumb ad about a coffee machine on TV, for instance.

Interestingly, he later positions a heavily surveillant approach to Facebook as detrimental to its business model: 'And I can't see Facebook being used as a Big Brother tool just because that would limit its potential for profit, and it's so profitable. So yeah, anything you do to decrease the audience limits the amount of capital you can generate from it.' In terms of surveillant perceptions, this suggests that targeted advertising is seen as a relatively mild form of scrutiny when compared to police or government surveillance. The consequences of targeted advertising for this user are relatively benign, especially when juxtaposed against more popular surveillance imagery. Other users, while acknowledging that their information is being used for these purposes, treat it as a reasonable price to pay for a service they use so extensively:

> It doesn't bother me about that. That's just part of using the free service. It's a free service that I wholeheartedly take advantage of, and that's something they ask me for and I don't mind that they see that I'm using ... I'm browsing pictures a lot. That's fine with me, I don't mind. (Zachary)

Student perceptions of market-based surveillance are linked to their use of Facebook. Because it is free, many students willingly consent to Facebook-led scrutiny in exchange for this service. While students do not explicitly describe these practices in terms of surveillance, the idea that they consent to being monitored by the site in order to watch over each other suggests that monitoring is fundamental to using the site.

About the Business Interviews

Businesses were rapidly adopting social media at the time this research was completed. What started as a small group of readily identifiable workers has now spread to the extent that social media are establishing a ubiquity in the corporate world. For this reason, these interviews were arranged and conducted in an exploratory manner. While the participants below come from diffuse backgrounds and perform different duties, roughly half of them do consulting work for clients while the others are fully employed by a corporation.

Susan is employed at a digital marketing agency, where she develops marketing strategies for clients. She assesses whether social media services are a useful addition to these campaigns, and offers clients guidance in terms of how to exploit services. Wade is employed at a venture capital firm where he is developing a web-based application that relies on the labour of online communities. He is also a digital strategist who consults with organizations to help them connect with stakeholder groups through Facebook. Ben is a co-founding partner at a search engine optimization (SEO) company. He manages his clients' online reputations through social media services. Damien is the president of a software development company specializing in cloud computing for businesses. He develops software for managing web content on sites like Facebook, and also uses these services to promote this company. Liane is a self-employed consultant who focuses primarily on organizational development. She helps clients develop appropriate social media strategies. Corey is the president of a new media marketing agency. He works with large and mid-sized companies to develop marketing and public relations strategies on social media.

Matthew manages the technical support network for a transnational consumer electronics company. He scrutinizes social media to identify consumer feedback, but also to recruit employees. Martin works for an independent gaming company that produces third-party applications for Facebook. In addition to developing applications, he manages a growing community of users on Facebook. Janine is a brand manager for a major food producer. She promotes new products on Facebook, scrutinizes the site for user feedback, and recruits Facebook users for viral marketing campaigns. Jared is the director of new media at a radio station in a mid-sized city. His manages a Facebook fan page by promoting the station and interacting with the station's online fan base. Joana is a marketing and communications manager for a major paint producer. She describes her work as a mix of advertising and public relations. Marc is a sales representative for a software company focusing on game-based learning for the academic market. He uses Facebook primarily to research and contact prospective clients. James is a communications officer with a public health organization funded by provincial and municipal governments. He uses Facebook to coordinate advertising and public relation strategies.

Given the divergence of affiliations and experiences, not all respondents share the same attitude. Paying attention to commonalities as well as differences among respondents provides a preliminary understanding of this growing sector. Understanding these nuances is important, as subsequent research will examine diverging strategies regarding social media as professional tools, especially as they pertain to surveillance and visibility. Not all of the above participants are doing the same work, but all are directly involved in business development. Even if they are not situated in the information sector, their actual duties intersect with the personal information economy.

The context in which these interviews took place is similar to Chapters 3 and 4. Businesses were partly concerned with managing their reputation, but they were also eager to find new sources of relevant information. Respondents experience some degree of precariousness on Facebook as they do not have full control over their online reputation, nor the enclosures that augment the visibility of that reputation. Yet they are also taking advantage of user activity on Facebook and other social networking sites. Overall they described their engagement with social media as a kind of personal information frontier. These interviews were semi-structured in order to account for variance among respondents' line of work. Yet all interviews were broadly structured along the following three themes:

First, respondents were asked to describe the work they perform as well as when and how Facebook and other social media impact their work. Related topics included the kinds of skills necessary for working with social media, whether they used social media in a personal context, and how that might have shaped their professional use. This provides a base understanding of how social media has crept into the business world, as well as how this is potentially located at the intersection of personal and professional engagements.

The second theme considered how respondents approach and make use of personal information found on Facebook. This included describing the kinds of information they seek out on Facebook, the perceived advantages of collecting information in this manner, and what Facebook can tell respondents about their clients or market. Given the lack of protocols and best practices surrounding this activity, these questions sought a rich description of how these services are currently used on a case-by-case basis.

The third theme considered respondents' perceptions and uses of other social media offerings. Social media augment the visibility of its user base, but are dynamic enough to produce other effects. This theme considered how a decentralized social network like Facebook affords other possibilities for businesses. This included advertising and viral marketing within Facebook, but also mitigating against risks associated with personal networks.

What Kind of Workers and Work are Involved?

Facebook's genesis as a business tool is one of many examples of the shifting conditions of contemporary labour. This is a product of the rise of the information economy as well as the digitization of other forms of labour. As Facebook emerged as a multi-purpose service, its exact function for businesses is unclear. Not only does the interface consist of numerous applications, but each individual feature can also be used for different purposes. Corey cites the wall feature on fan pages as a site for 'customer service, research and development, and product management interaction'. As this feature is increasingly a means for businesses to interface with their market, businesses are finding multiple ways to exploit it. Others refer to the fan page feature as a multipurpose space, depending on the intentions of the business. Wade states:

> For some brands, it's pretty much market research. For some organizations
> it's the ability to have another channel to push offerings through. For some
> companies it's the ability to build more long lasting relationships with their
> stakeholder groups, with their audiences. All the same reasons that any company

might market in any particular way, be it conversational or transactional, but just
depending on the goals of the organization.

Considering that business practices surrounding Facebook are still in formation,
Wade suggests that the service, and its fan page feature in particular, offer a range
of opportunities to businesses that revolve around the exchange and collection of
information from its user base.

The presence of businesses on Facebook is noteworthy, in that Facebook now
exceeds university culture. This shift is tied to Facebook's increased popularity
among older users. Several respondents claim that its fastest growing demographic
was forty to fifty year olds. Marc sees this growth as evidence that Facebook
was entering financial maturity. Wade supports this view, stating that this kind of
demographic shift was found with other commercially viable media:

> So you see the same thing happens with movies and video games and iPods and
> those sorts of things, so I think it's natural that if a product is very successful in
> the way that Facebook has been in that demographic, it's likely that it's going to
> move out into other demographics if it's well suited to that as well.

Facebook's appeal to businesses goes beyond exploiting the university-age
demographic. Yet Facebook still allows businesses to target this population in
ways that were previously not possible. Wade elaborates on how the biographical
information on Facebook allows for more precise market analysis: 'If you're
looking to sell Coke to more college students, which college campuses are the
most receptive? Does messaging X or Y work better for boys or girls? Or freshmen
or seniors? Or undergrads or graduate students?' Much like university employees
in Chapter 4, respondents cite that Facebook was more likely to create work than
it was to resolve any longstanding issues. This was partly attributed to the lack of
clear guidelines in terms of how to use it. Not only does Facebook offer a variety
of application and 'business solutions' but it is only one of a host of social media
services currently used by companies. Determining the most appropriate tools is
itself a time consuming process. As well, Facebook's origin as an interpersonal
service means that it is also a potential threat to productivity, and many traditional
businesses are reluctant to adopt it for this reason. Even maintaining a corporate
presence on the site is a time-consuming process, as businesses are expected
to provide new content on a regular basis. This underscores the complexity of
being visible on social media, and that a more effective strategy is simply to take
advantage of the visibility of others.

The above findings suggest new possibilities as well as severe challenges for
businesses that want to utilize social media. Many respondents believe businesses
should not automatically rush into social media, but instead first determine what,
if anything, they seek to get out of their engagement. Liane, a consultant, asks her
clients: 'Why are they using Facebook, because that's not always clear. Are they
actually looking for business, are they looking for another place to channel a blog

or a website through? Are they looking just to raise awareness?' Many clients approach social media out of a perceived sense of obligation, and as a result do not know what they want to get out of it, nor do they know how they would achieve those goals.

For this reason there is an abundance of social media consultants. Joana, who was beginning to work with social media, suggests that they were actively looking outside their organization for help. Not only was her organization looking for an outside expert to manage their social media presence, but they were also looking for an additional outside expert to provide content for the space that the first expert created. James refers to a reliance on outside labour that provides content in a public health context, noting that former smokers can provide invaluable experience to current smokers through social media.

As this is an emerging field, there are not yet any clear criteria for who is eligible and capable to work as a social media professional. While respondents acknowledge that a lot of people claim social media expertise, they are reluctant to endorse these credentials. Damien describes his own professional engagement with social media as a very tentative, trial-and-error process, and for that reason states: 'I can't tell you that this is all based on hard science, I think anybody who thinks they are an expert in this is a bit flaky at the moment – I think people are still trying to figure it out.' This suggests that enthusiasm and prior experience are prerequisites for social media expertise, but are by no means sufficient criteria. Interestingly, some users also feel that their expertise was questioned on the basis of their age. While acknowledging that people of his age were historically less willing to adopt social media, Ben notes: 'I'm 53 shortly. So, when I go to see people and I talk about social media, they look at me like I'm off my rocker.' Opting for younger people as social media experts is based on assumptions about their experience with online sociality. While they may not have the same organizational experience as their elders, they are assumed to be familiar with living their lives online.

Other respondents endorse a perceived generational shift, stating that young people are 'expecting a work environment where it's free and open and it's an open exchange of information and ideas' (Susan). This response assumes that recent graduates are prepared for work conditions that optimize a free flow of information. Although a changing work environment can be attributed to generation-based expectations, it also involves increased demands placed on workers in terms of the depth of their engagement with work, as well as how this shapes their personal and professional boundaries.

Many respondents describe that their involvement with social media work emerged from their experience as university students. Martin, a software developer, first started developing applications on Facebook as a result of a student co-op project. It stands to reason that businesses would turn to students to do this work, given their familiarity with social media. Other respondents echo earlier statements about Facebook being a liability for students applying for work. However, those who were familiar with this hiring process added that Facebook could also benefit prospective candidates:

> I've had a really good first-hand knowledge on what companies are looking for when they're recruiting. And one thing I can honestly say that is they are going online, and they are looking at your Facebook, they're Googling you as well, and they're going to see what comes up, because they're looking for something that's going to, obviously, turn them off or turn them on. (Marc)

Marc also claims that Facebook, in comparison to more professional social media like LinkedIn, enables users to make their personal lives visible. Their ability to manage a visible personal life was seen as a potential asset to those working in social media.

Businesses' emphasis on younger employees suggests a reliance on people who are familiar with student culture. As these students are well represented on services like Facebook, having younger people doing this work connects them to these sites, as well as to a university-age demographic. Not only are these employees expected to leverage their experience with these sites to make themselves and their business visible, but they are also expected to watch over other users. Thus social media users augment market-based surveillance on social media, whether or not these users are employed by the business in question.

Relations with Facebook

While Facebook explicitly offers 'business solutions' for advertisers and marketers, it frequently makes changes to the interface that benefits its own growth at the expense of others engaged with the site. Users may assume that Facebook and businesses are engaged in a kind of partnership, yet businesses describe their relation to Facebook in terms of them coping with decisions that Facebook makes unilaterally. Third party application developers are required by Facebook to comply with its terms of service, which some respondents describe as a struggle. Their relation to Facebook resembles de Certeau's (1988) distinction between tactics and strategies. Developers and other businesses dwell in the space that Facebook owns. They grow familiar with the features offered by the site, and develop unanticipated ways to exploit them. Yet their status as renters – and not owners – of this site is made apparent when Facebook alters its interface without regard to consequences for businesses. Following Martin: 'We're in it just like the user. We have access to using the space but for how long? That's up to Facebook. They create the rules so they can make the decisions to box us out or let us continue at any point.' This struggle is especially salient for businesses that develop applications for Facebook's application programming interface (API):

> Facebook is constantly changing how applications interact with Facebook itself from a technical standpoint and without informing us so that they change it to shut our games down, and then we have to go in to figure out what happened to bring them live again. There's not a really amazing conversation that's going on between developers from medium and small gaming houses to Facebook proper. (Martin)

Facebook makes changes to which developers have to adapt, although this respondent adds that some larger companies have closer relations to Facebook and are better suited to cope with these revisions. Employing tactics to take advantage of being on Facebook is difficult, as business activity is rendered completely visible to Facebook. Martin is willing to operate within terms of service because others have been shut down for similar infractions. He states that being shut down 'would be enormously bad, painful and if you lose your customer's attention span for even a day or two, they'll move on to another game and never return. Any sort of outage whatsoever is a big fear for us'. He goes on to justify Facebook's restrictive approach. Given that these changes are typically not well received by users, Facebook chooses to prioritize its own interests, often to the detriment of businesses that will invest in their presence on the site: 'Facebook has not figured out how to perfectly monetize what they have. The goal is to build their customer base still and then figure that out later, again, trying to keep in mind the lessons they've learned by watching other social networking platforms starting to tank, you know' (Martin). Respondents who are not directly involved in creating applications for Facebook also describe their engagement as being uncertain. Wade cites the shift from groups to pages and from the API to Facebook Connect as rendering one option redundant in comparison to the other, at the expense to those who invest in older services:

> Facebook has made major changes several times to their offering to business without notice and significant changes that largely nullify the investments that businesses have made to date. Facebook put a lot of emphasis on groups and was charging for groups and all of a sudden, pages are more important. And then they open up an API so a lot of companies welcome Facebook applications, and then the focus moves from the API to Facebook Connect, which is about bringing Facebook into the site, into your own web application, your own technology.

Once again, respondents position Facebook's long-term interests against those of businesses and others who may invest in a presence on the site. Wade, who considers Facebook a low-cost service for businesses, regards this volatility as a risk that is often overlooked when migrating to social media enclosures. In terms of surveillance, businesses have to manage their visibility online just like individuals and institutions. Yet application developers are also visible in the sense that their software is subject to Facebook's scrutiny to ensure compliance. These developers are watching over users as Facebook is watching over them.

Corporate Self-Presentation Alongside Self-Branding

Many businesses feel compelled to maintain some kind of visibility on social media. This involves not only the visibility of products and services, but also the visibility of people representing an organization. An interpersonal style of self-presentation is often adopted as a corporate strategy for social media. This makes sense given that these companies are promoting their brands and products in an enclosure that was first tailored for interpersonal exchanges. At the same time, many individuals who are working in these organizations are adopting branding strategies to promote themselves individually within this sector. These developments suggest a growing conflation between individual and corporate visibility on social media, leading to a selective visibility of key representatives on behalf of corporations. Being visible is a form of labour performed by people formally hired by companies as well as by people enrolled informally through social media. Visibility is key to marketing and public relations, especially with the advent of social media. Recent literature in the industry calls for 'radical transparency' on the part of corporations (Tapscott and Ticoll 2003, Li and Bernoff 2008). This material overstates privacy's irrelevance by treating transparency as a best practice:

> Secrecy is dying. It's probably already dead. In a world where Eli Lilly's internal drug-development memos, Paris Hilton's phonecam images, Enron's emails, and even the governor of California's private conversations can be instantly forwarded across the planet, trying to hide something illicit – trying to hide anything, really – is an unwise gamble. (Thompson 2007)

Underlying this literature is the belief that the executive class will gain a competitive advantage by baring their insecurities and dirty laundry to the world. Augmenting a brand's visibility through social media requires the involvement of employees and consultants. Individuals who are already good at making themselves visible are predisposed to this labour. While most industry literature calls for top brass to make themselves visible, respondents suggest that a comfort with visibility among workers is also highly valued.

Respondents use personal branding to secure employment in social media. In terms of navigating one's career, personal advancement was seen as a result of effective branding strategies. Here, they draw parallels between corporate branding and personal branding within a corporation. This implies a broad range of identity management tactics, ranging from managing information online to dressing appropriately. Susan is quick to point out that the deliberate management of a personal identity brand should not come at the expense of authenticity:

> You can create your image the same way you would create your company's brand. You are a brand, you're potato chips basically. And you know, you can make sure that you have a strategy in terms of what you post, and you know how you present yourself online, the same way that you would have a strategy

in terms of what you wear when you get up in the morning and how you present yourself offline.

For Susan, the self-presentation involved in these branding strategies is a concern that pervades every personal and corporate engagement. This strategy is not meant to compromise authenticity, but rather 'telling [a] consistent story' as a strategy should be prioritized. Some businesses see the combined desire for effective branding and personal authenticity as a product of the heightened visibility created by social media. As a result, networking and building relationships is seen as a factor of a kind of passive communication via one's online presence:

> You have to communicate your brand, your self brand, and you have to be aware of what's out there about you because information is becoming more public and public, privacy is becoming less and less, ... that's going to create channels of success and failure for you. Whether it's making sales, or creating relationships on the business side, or even just trying to get a job, right? It's all about communicating the right message. (Marc)

Coping with this visibility is treated as a requirement to ascend in a career, in terms of self-promotion and building ties with others. But in a more general sense, people who work with social media cope with a pervasive visibility to their market. This is because Facebook obliges businesses to have a personal identity tethered to a corporate presence. The conflation of personal and professional is especially concerning for smaller organizations:

> That's just the nature of the space. Facebook itself, you are you; you're not anonymous, for one, in general. And when you're dealing with people, we're also ourselves. Facebook doesn't allow you to create fake accounts as a corporation. I'm me on the account that I'm responding to players, for instance. And our relationship, and this us, this is not every company, there's sharks out there and there are medium to small sized fish like us who decide to do things in a certain way. (Martin)

Business users are able to cope with these conditions by using privacy settings to restrict what details are publicly available. Despite this, the connection between their personal presence and corporate endeavours is seen as obligatory and overwhelming. Martin changed his setting to prevent strangers from adding him as a friend, stating that he 'just got overwhelmed by people I didn't know in Louisiana wanting to be my friend on Facebook'. Other respondents have enabled limited profiles for similar reasons. Managing a fan page also leads to the visibility of one's profile such that those fans can choose to add the respondent as a friend:

> Because the fan pages are actually linked through my profile, a lot of the people ... who are within those fan pages also end up seeing my name, associating my

name and invite me as a friend. Most of them I have as a limited profile so it still allows me to see what they're saying without them knowing that I just got married or my daughter just turned two, or any of that personal stuff that I don't necessarily want to share with the general public. (Jared)

Using personal branding and self-presentation online is regarded as an effective strategy, though it is not appropriate for all businesses.

Some small businesses benefit more from a personal engagement of social media than others. Liane offers a comparison between a divorce counsellor and a debt counsellor, stating that the former is better suited to render their personal life transparent:

> Because divorces are very personal and coaching is very personal, it's a great point of entry to join a group and say, "I am also divorced, I've been divorced for however many years and as part of my healing process from that divorce which was very acrimonious, I decided to become a coach and help other people and so, let me tell you a little bit about my journey and I'm always willing to talk with other people". That's a very nice point of entry. If you have someone who is running a debt counselling service … if they have been in debt it might not be something that they really want to disclose. So, I'm not sure if it works for all business.

According to Liane, certain professions will be associated with particular personal details that may or may not be fit for public consumption. This suggests an emerging politics of career visibility, where personal disclosure can be an asset or liability. Returning to the recommendation for CEOs to bare their souls to the world, many respondents suggest that this is not an easy or likely outcome. Wade reports that transparency requires a particular skill-set, and that a CEO who is otherwise shielded from public scrutiny is not going to benefit from this approach:

> If you're the CEO of a start-up company and you've always largely been a transparent person and that's your general nature, these tools are probably going to help you facilitate that. If you are an old school CEO of a Fortune 500, global company, and you're not used to a world of a great degree of transparency, it may not help you become more personally transparent. … Aside from the entertainment value, largely customers don't care if the CEO of the company just bought a computer, what he had for lunch today, or that he's suffering from depression. The investors might want to know that. But on average, the average consumer does not.

In the case of the executive class of a large corporation, Wade also suggests that the audience to this transparency may be quite specific. To be sure, a CEO living transparently to investors is a different relationship. Other respondents suggest that while transparency is a valuable approach, the executive class can avoid this whereas smaller businesses are not exempt from calls to transparency.

Many companies are moving towards 'radical transparency' whether or not it is an effective strategy. Respondents refer to success stories like Dell's attempt to publicize complaints about its products. Yet others like Marc are sceptical of the outcome of this approach:

> A lot of what I've heard about has been just more of a success story with this transparent visibility, you know, than a negative. But I can foresee how that can be a problem, especially if you don't have solutions to the problem, right? It's a risky business with that, it's very risky to post things public, but what's funny, and you'll find this with a lot of businesses, their culture is moving towards that direction. Their culture is moving towards a transparent visibility that allows everyone to see what they're doing, when they're doing it, because they want to seem like they have nothing to hide.

Marc suggests that the appearance of transparency is much more important than actual transparency. For this reason, having workers bare their lives on behalf of the company, or work to construct a visible, responsible brand like Dell is a more viable approach. As with most social media strategies, this relies on user-generated content, complaints in this case. Again, like most social media, this enables corporations to take advantage of decentralized content, all while exercising censure if deemed necessary. Marc cites Research In Motion's approach as an example:

> Even with the Crackberry website, I think I heard some examples where some things were kind of filtered, because they still have complete control over the website, of course, right? It's user-generated, but at the same time they can control what user generates and if they want, delete them when they can. And I think there were a few instances I heard in the past where they did eliminate things, maybe because they didn't have solutions to the problem or maybe because it was just too negative a comment that may have turned off a few users.

Certain corporations may combine the appearance of transparency with a selective presentation of the self, omitting negative information and emphasizing positive features.

Nevertheless, respondents suggest that those not employed in large corporations will struggle with selective self-presentation. Ben uses a disgraced social media consultant as an example of personal branding gone wrong. At the time this consultant had an audience of over one hundred and fifty thousand followers on Twitter. At a public event he claimed that these followers pressured entertainer P. Diddy to agree to meet with him. Yet this was entirely false:

By Monday there was such a backlash, because the story he told wasn't true. He made it up. So, I guess out of fifteen hundred people in the audience, there must have been a few of them who didn't believe him and tried to find out if it was true or not. And they did and it wasn't true. He had to apologize online to everybody that it wasn't true. That's how fast people can find you out if you're not 100 per cent out there.

This incident cost the consultant his career, and was the result of the scrutiny of a large audience. This suggests that independent and smaller businesses may not be as predisposed to undergo a strategic transparency. Personal and professional claims they make will be subject to a scrutiny they will be less capable of managing. This comes back to the idea of the personal and professional image being conflated through branding. Damien treats this as an ongoing endeavour that is shaped by all visible aspects of one's career and life:

The personal brand and the corporate brand, the fact of the matter is, every time you open your mouth or every time you publish a photo or a video or whatever, some kind of connection to you, you are creating your brand. I think the challenge that we are going to learn from all of these tools – any technological advances have always been abused on the way. … I think with these social media pieces, we all need to understand that every time we open our mouths, we are creating a personal brand.

Transparency – through social media in particular – is touted as a best practice. Yet this overlooks those that benefit from a low profile: 'I hear reports of, you know, companies that are more transparent that are doing better than their competitors, but at the same time, you know, Blackwater doesn't seem to be going bankrupt any time soon' (Wade). Self-presentation implicates businesses as they increasingly build a presence on social media. This is either done proactively, or reactively when responding to already being made visible by their customers. Their self-directed visibility is augmented in reaction to information provided by individuals. As individual use is the template for engaging with social media, businesses' own visibility is modelled in terms of personal information, profiling and routine updates.

Watching and Listening to Users

While maintaining transparency on social media is presented as an effective strategy, it is also an approach that must be performed tactfully for the sake of maintaining a good reputation. Another key strategy for social media – one with fewer opportunities for downfalls – is to watch over users. As Facebook and other social media are a vast and easily accessible source of personal information, a lot of industry literature recommends that businesses pay attention to this. Following

Li and Bernoff: 'Consumers in the groundswell are leaving clues about their opinions, positive and negative, on a daily or hourly basis' (2008: 81). These authors go on to describe six reasons for businesses to 'listen' to social media: finding out how customers interpret their brands, obtaining a high-resolution and constantly updated understanding of the market, investing less capital in order to receive better feedback, identifying key influencers in social media, effectively identifying and managing public relation crises and generating new product and marketing ideas (ibid.: 93–5).

Depending on user privacy settings, businesses can access user content like anybody else. They may also choose to develop a page that not only centralizes relevant content, but also provides additional analytics. They may also rely on detailed feedback offered by Facebook's advertising services. Finally, they may also rely on external social media services like Radian6. Based on the access that any of these entry points offers to over half a billion users, Marc goes so far as to describe Facebook as a source of 'unlimited information'.

Returning to the idea of strategies and tactics, many respondents described their engagement on Facebook as if they were dwelling in these spaces rather than owning them. This makes sense as business users do not have more claim to much of Facebook than individual users. Yet this is not to suggest that businesses are identical to de Certeau's tacticians, who dwell precariously in borrowed spaces and have only marginal control over these spaces. Susan suggests that Facebook should be used as a site for tactics rather than strategies. When asked to elaborate on her definitions of these terms, she offers the following: 'The strategy is the overall plan, what are you trying to do. And the tactic is how are you going to go about doing it.' While businesses may experience some precariousness by not having complete control and ownership on social media, their presence on these spaces is used to augment brands and products that they do own and control. The lack of immediate control over Facebook is offset by the ability to have a more pointed engagement with the site. Businesses may employ tactics based on watching and listening to users without any responsibility towards this group.

When asked why they chose to collect information through Facebook, respondents point to its methodological advantages. Jared cites that their audience would provide personal information online that would not come up in the context of other demographic services, for instance if they were coping with a death in the family. While the immediate market value of this information is difficult to ascertain, it supplements a conventional way of understanding their audience in a risk-free manner.

Other respondents suggest that collecting information through Facebook is a lot cheaper than its alternatives. Market research in particular is seen as prohibitive and lengthy compared to social media:

> Market research is very, very expensive, so for us to get an Ipsos study done costs a lot of money and involves a lot of lengthy phone calls and interviews

and a lot of compilation of data and this would be just another avenue of hearing consumers' comments and, you know, first hand really. (Joana)

Not only is market research riddled with logistical issues of cost and time, but Joana also describes that process as troublesome when compared to first hand accounts. She believes that Facebook leads to more authentic information, as it does not rely on leading questions. This is a fair assessment when considering that its users do not conceive of Facebook itself as a questionnaire. Wade cites the fact that it is not an explicit site of inquiry, and complains that human subjects are poor at self-reporting:

> What I think even more important than where the criticism happens is being able to observe the actual behaviour. So, you know, it's often true that people will tell you that they want one thing, or they do something one way but they do it another. As subjects, humans are actually poor at self-reporting. … I think if you own the social network, or the social application, and you have good measures and analytics on the back end, you've really got this amazing tool set because you can look at not just what people say but what they do and where the delta is between those two things.

This suggests that while Facebook provides invaluable information, the real value lies in emerging analytics to process it. Facebook's potential for behavioural assessment is unclear. However, this has been a key ambition for market surveillance (Elmer 2004). Behavioural scrutiny profiles users based on their engagement with brands, purchase histories and other transactional data. By generating data about social ties as well as operating in a prolonged engagement with users, Facebook is seen as offering better insight into consumer behaviour. Wade underscores the importance of ownership of new media (Winseck 2003), including social media databases more recently. Facebook expands on this tradition by not only collecting information about behaviour in a wide range of social contexts, but also through a series of interactive gestures (including adding friends, tagging photos, liking products and brands) that are treated as behaviour.

For respondents developing applications for Facebook, their software enables a rich set of opportunities to watch over users. On the one hand, they are able to monitor user activity within the application. This allows developers to see what features are popular as well as manage vulnerabilities and potential exploits. But they also benefit from discussion groups elsewhere on the site. This suggests that developers not only have access to opinions voiced by users, but also to their behaviour on these services:

> If we watch them play our game and we know they're spending, you know, on a certain stage, we're like, "Ok, Stage 5 seems to be where a higher percentage of people spend. Why is that?" And then we'll look into their behaviour on the

game itself but that's not, that has nothing to do with their Facebook accounts. That just has to do with how they're playing our game as a player. (Martin)

The reliance on user-generated content is also regarded as a way to side-step methodological tools in order to reach user perspectives. Jared describes how Facebook enabled them to access photos their listeners would take at events that the radio station would host. These photos allowed him to 'understand what they're looking at' and 'allows us to see it from their eyes too'. While Facebook is clearly a mediating link between businesses and users, the fact that it is not an explicit service for this end suggests that it can provide a more intimate connection to a user base. The fact that businesses can collect information before engaging with users suggests that it provides the former with a tactical advantage over the later. Marc describes this in terms of gaining leverage over potential clients:

> The more information you have, the more leverage you have when it comes to making your pitch. That's one thing I've realized. And that's what I like about the social networks, it's because it's a gateway for me to, kind of, look into their lives and figure out what they like and we have in common, you know, things I can bring up to build rapport when it comes to our phone conversation.

Here data is valued for its ability to help businesses understand markets and generate sales. This is not a new feature of marketplace surveillance, yet Facebook's ability to effortlessly locate a broad range of biographical and relational details about any single person is noteworthy. Indeed, it marks a more precise resolution, where marketers and sales staff can search both abstract categories and key individuals. This also suggests that Facebook can be used to establish trust with clients in a way that may be perceived as a violation of personal boundaries. This is not surprising, given the fact that the violation of such boundaries remains a pressing concern for social media users.

While the above suggests that polling and market research services are being made redundant by Facebook, Liane believes that it is more likely that the two would enter into a partnership that would enhance the scope of the former while providing a way for the latter to monetize their content. On the heels of an announcement that Facebook developed analytics that track moods and emotions online, she states: 'Maybe a better way of monetizing Facebook is to go out, speak and share your research with research organizations. I'm sure Gallup would enter into an interesting partnership and Gallup sure figured out how to get money out of research.' The strategy described above allows businesses to easily collect information about their clients through their online presence. User visibility in this context is often motivated by reasons external to the business, such as peer-to-peer sociality. Yet businesses gain from interpersonal scrutiny by covertly accessing that information. While users may be aware that this is going on, they are never aware what information is being collected, leading to what is regarded as more authentic information. Jared suggests that users benefit from this visibility, in that it helps people voice their opinion. Yet he also acknowledges the purposive nature of their own engagement on Facebook, citing that it helps his company grow, online and offline. While users may enjoy intrinsic rewards through social media, it is increasingly apparent that businesses are enjoying extrinsic rewards. Even in the absence of a multitude of ways to monetize Facebook, the costs associated are so low that listening on social media seems like a low-risk strategy.

Conversations with Users

The previous two sections examined how Facebook is used by businesses to augment their own visibility as well as take advantage of the visibility of users. A third approach fuses these two in a way that facilitates a long-term engagement with the site's user base. Some businesses dovetail their own visibility with that of users as part of a larger social media strategy. Industry literature touts this approach as a paradigm shift in terms of market relations. Internet business guru Don Tapscott suggests to businesses: 'Don't focus on your customers – engage them. Turn them into prosumers of your goods and services. Young people want to co-innovate with you. Let them customize your value' (2009: 217). As social media have historically not been used to this end, research on this topic needs to examine the kinds of relations businesses are seeking with clients/users as well as how personal information on social networking sites contributes to this.

Both industry literature and respondents emphasize two-way communication and engagement as opposed to shouting and broadcasting. This resonates with Andrejevic's (2007) description of mass customization, where user input is presented as empowering consumers, but clearly benefiting telecoms and other businesses. Yet the kinds of engagements imagined and attempted through social media are numerous and diffuse. These developments could bring a levelling of visibility. But they could also bring about a kind of one-two punch for businesses based on listening and promoting. Popular literature describes this as empowering for individuals in their relation to businesses. Authors like Shirky (2008) claim that these tools allow users to voice their complaints, make suggestions and be less removed from production process. These features are not inherently problematic, but they can be configured by businesses to maintain an exploitative relation vis-à-vis their user base. In particular, they can incorporate unpaid labour by extracting further value from users.

A conversation-based engagement presupposes that users want to directly engage with businesses on Facebook. Sometimes users welcome a corporate presence on Facebook. In other instances their presence is seen as a violation of privacy. Joana, who is developing a Facebook presence for a brand she represents, is concerned with whether or not she should announce herself as officially tied to that brand. For these reasons, some businesses prefer to remain covert on Facebook. Yet sometimes users want to be visible and able to converse with businesses. This strategy is deemed effective when coping with negative feedback about a brand or product: 'I think people just want to be heard and if you are prepared to listen to people and if again ... [m]ost people will stop at that point. At that point, people will be like "You know what, okay. At least they are trying"' (Ben). Activity on social media often has multiple benefits. Joana describes the returns she was experiencing when building a significant presence on Facebook: 'We're getting really marketplace information, like we're getting consumer feedback pretty much first hand if we can see those comments and also it becomes really word of mouth marketing at some point when people are reading each other's comments and commenting on each other.' This suggests that an optimized social media space combines the collection of market information as well as disseminating advertisements in a viral manner.

Respondents note that Facebook in particular is optimized towards maintaining connections with users, especially when users are careful about promoting business content. Corey favours a conversation-based approach to Facebook, noting that those who bombard their social ties with content will suffer by losing network connections. Instead, he suggests that businesses need to learn about their market by watching and strategically engaging with it online. Marc echoes the idea that Facebook is best used to foster long-term relations, stating that users will find that kind of mutual visibility to be less intrusive, thus leading to a richer engagement on their part.

The conversational approach resonates with the way application developers build their products. Developers make perpetual revisions to their products based on in-game and external feedback garnered by their users. They watch over and listen to users, and respond to this information by adding value to their product. Likewise, businesses are revising their strategies and approaches based on information garnered from users. In terms of how Facebook shapes the production process, several respondents cite that it allows for the integration of user labour. By targeting key populations and maintaining a lasting engagement with them, Facebook allows businesses to channel user input at an early stage, and frequently return to these users. Damien cites that user activity in public discussions is directly exploited to add value when developing and revising products. This approach harnesses user input to the benefit of the company. Martin states:

> We often launch an application before it's completely perfect, and then fix it as it goes. We have an "always in beta" kind of mindset. Again, spending two years developing an application and then releasing it, it's better to just get something out there, watch your customers, talk to them about how to make the game more fun, and then bring those changes in as it goes. It's pretty interesting and fun that way. Sort of a ready-fire-aim approach.

This suggests a development cycle modelled after Facebook's own way of operating, notably in the sense that ongoing revisions are based on user visibility.

Both Facebook and developers are able to closely watch user behaviour on the site, as well as complaints and recommendations that they broadcast.

They are able to modify their services based on what they know about users. These respondents suggest that the optimal way to use social media for some businesses is to selectively target a group or population, gather information that they broadcast and eventually converse with them in a strategic manner. In particular respondents will encourage users to think of social media spaces like fan pages and groups as belonging to users themselves. In the case of application developers, maintaining close relations with users enables them to receive feedback to improve their products, all while giving the impression that they are committed to keeping users satisfied:

> But players have really helped us to develop the games. They're saying, "oh my god, wouldn't it be cool if you did this?" And we're like, "wow, that would be really cool". And then we do it and players like it. So they are actually helping to design the games themselves and what better way to get people's interest and potentially to get them to spend than have them as a co-designer? (Martin)

Businesses on Facebook are able to exploit users by collecting feedback from them. This relates to the idea that Facebook is more like an enclosure than a conventional database, and that it is able to gather a wider range of input, including suggestions to make products and services more valuable. This is a consequence of users increasingly living their lives in these enclosures. Respondents favour the visibility of users, citing that identifying and locating them leads to a more disciplined consumer and more useful information. Damien states that this is 'the flip side of getting rid of the anonymity: the quality of conversation goes up'. When exploiting social media content, anonymity is a barrier that inhibits monetization.

A conversational approach to market surveillance is informed by users' familiarity with friendly surveillance. It is based on many of the same tenets explored in previous chapters, especially a sense of mutual transparency. Users are more comfortable making their lives public to businesses if they feel a sense of reciprocation. The corporate presence on Facebook is typically managed by actual Facebook users who use that peer-to-peer sociality to foster these ties. Based on the descriptions offered above this approach resembles Dallas Smythe's understanding of audience labour (1977). As some authors describe a shift from an attention economy to an engagement economy (McGonigal 2008), audience labour increasingly involves a more active shaping of goods and services by unpaid labourers. This suggests that a personal information economy goes beyond surveillance in taking advantage of this connection to enrol users into the production process. When it works this resembles a contemporary version of rampant Taylorism. Users are providing free immaterial labour. Not only is their labour rendered entirely visible, but their social lives and personal information on Facebook remain visible as well, especially when using applications or visiting fan pages.

Discussion

Businesses are migrating to Facebook with some trepidation. They are reluctant and partly unwelcome housemates in this ever-growing dwelling. The 'business' of social media itself is complicated, with workers concerned about how their job will be impacted. It is not just users who are affected by business shift to social media. Employees are forced to rethink their strategies, and are largely left in the dark when it comes to best practices. This resonates with earlier discussions of social media enclosures. On the one hand, social media are not as revolutionary as first thought, as they fail to level the playing field between individuals, institutions and businesses. The latter two are still in an advantageous position given pre-existing strategies as well as services and consultants that cater to their visibility. Yet relations between these groups have changed as a result of their cohabitation on social media enclosures. They all share a risk of exposure. Three main findings stand out:

First, market surveillance extends from personal use and university demographics. The fact that university students are the first to adopt social media means that they are not only a well-represented population on sites like Facebook, but that they are presented as a kind of ambassador to businesses looking to migrate to these platforms. The skills involved with effectively harnessing social media are tied to youth in general. This is not a novel development. Framing contemporary youth as digital and social media natives lines up with previous instances where young people were thought to be especially capable of using and adapting to new technologies (Mosco 2004). Yet there are also practical reasons for this designation, as students have the experience and skill sets to capitalize on social media. The fact that an interpersonal service is now used to bridge into careers is a consequence of the social convergence found on social media enclosures.

Second, most businesses are not colluding with Facebook. Smaller application developers and companies are as unaware of Facebook's future as users. They too are on rented land. While they might have greater access to personal information when compared to individual users, they are equally unsure of their future on the site. They have the ability to watch over users, whether these users are members of a fan community, or have installed a third-party application. But they also cope with sudden changes, as in the case of Martin who had to reactively maintain compliance with Facebook's terms of service. Within a social media enclosure, they do not have complete control of their visibility. They do not have full control over what others say about them, nor are they able to completely manage their own streams of information. This leaves them in a position to consider new strategies and approaches, which leads us to the third finding.

Third, transparency is promoted, but with exceptions. Personal branding marks a mix between personal and corporate strategies. Rhetoric surrounding this area recommends that businesses get used to new conditions of visibility. This approach frames visibility as a kind of publicity, such that even unflattering details can yield positive exposure and profit. However, in practice, companies are already looking to exploit the visibility of others while giving up as little as possible about themselves. This suggests that visibility is a zero-sum game on social media. All parties involved share potential for exposure, but are still competitive with each other. A conversational approach is lauded as a kind of best practice, but unpacking this term reveals that companies want to exploit the conditions of visibility within the social media enclosure, even though they are merely dwelling in it.

Businesses are turning to social media to scrutinize personal information as well as provide targeted content to users. An emerging personal information economy relies not only on personal details submitted by users, but also on a prolonged engagement with these users in social networks. Social ties are increasingly valued as part of emerging monetization strategies on social media. These developments suggest two possibilities, or two visions that are not mutually exclusive. On the one hand, industry literature emphasizes the importance of community building online (Li and Bernoff 2008; Tapscott 2009). This implies the creation of an enduring space that prioritizes ongoing relations between brand enthusiasts and representatives. This kind of space is deliberately themed by the brand, but this does not exclude other opportunities for monetization. Yet all that is being described here resonates with Andrejevic's digital enclosures. Social media services present themselves as sharing free content. Yet ownership of this content is crucial (Wineseck 2003), especially because these enclosures are used for a broad range of scrutiny and social sorting. Following the discussion in Chapter 2, the enclosure is a space, but also a process with 'a variety of strategies for privatizing, controlling, and commodifying information and intellectual property' (Andrejevic 2009: 54). This suggests an ongoing development where practices are fluid and emerging, and where users may grow accustomed to living under pervasive scrutiny.

While respondents and industry literature offer a more positive description, they are advocating for a situation where users have a prolonged engagement with businesses, giving up personal information in exchange for targeted content. The extent to which these two perspectives overlap remains an ongoing topic of inquiry, and insight can be obtained by looking at the role that the term 'social' plays in these conversations. The term 'social' is notoriously difficult to isolate in sociological research. The question 'what's the meaning of "social" in social media?' underlies this research. Based on Chapter 3, it might mean convergence of social contexts. Users cannot keep personal information in one frame. Based on Chapter 4, it might mean something similar. In terms of liability and domain, both are extended beyond the university campus. The 'social' in social media denotes a reconfiguration of information flows. Wade claims that they become socialized insofar as 'now these streams are about the people who you know or the people you care about, friends, family, people who you follow for professional reasons as thought leaders'. Here, 'social' refers to social ties. This chapter suggests that social ties are growing from the basis of an emergent media to a vital component in emergent business models. Damien highlights the social value of social media, claiming that: 'Technology is finally beginning to deliver social value from the standpoint of allowing you to control your destiny, your voice, the way you are published, who you interact with, how things are protected or not, as you conduct those interactions.' Damien presents Facebook's social functionality in terms of affordances to users, but also businesses that engage with the site. He goes on to describe a conflation of the two:

> Social media users are increasingly becoming developers because your ability to go into Facebook, add new applications to it you know, create a fan page and connect with many other people in your customer eco-system. All of those things used to require software developers, they are now things that you or I can do ourselves. So, when we talk about power – not only the tool and the user gets more powerful, the ability to manipulate that tool and connect it to other platforms and tools is now becoming ... in the hand of you and I, as opposed to in the hands of developers.

This is described as a kind of empowerment where users can operate while unfettered by corporations, but this also benefits businesses that take advantage of the labour and feedback of users. In either case, these are being treated as spaces for long-term engagement. While it may be too soon to ascertain, social media are positioned at the intersection of interpersonal sociality and corporate monetization.

The above interviews highlight the complexity of market-based surveillance on social media. Businesses are taking several approaches with social media, and using sites like Facebook for different ends. Various kinds of work are now situated on social media, including brand management, market research and customer service. Yet at this stage some patterns are emerging. Through Facebook businesses have access to a host of personal information pertaining to their brands, products and markets. Much of this information is generated from people making themselves visible to each other. Sharing the same interface and information that is used for interpersonal exchanges augments their scope. In addition, respondents describe mimicking interpersonal surveillance in order to engage with users. Here, a conversational approach with users is deemed to be effective to maintain these relations. Businesses are employing friendly surveillance tactics to augment market surveillance.

Chapter 6
Policing Social Media

Introduction

This chapter considers policing and other kinds of investigations on social media. This type of surveillance is shaped by established populations and practices on social media. Yet it also extends from a separate history of investigative scrutiny by police. Moreover, social media policing is complicated by ongoing technological, socio-cultural and legislative developments. For this reason our focus shifts to a more anticipatory and analytic direction.

Winter 2009: Craig Lynch, Facebook Fugitive

> YES YES i fuckin made it to Xmas i beat their fuckin system and i love it.
> (Lynch, in Henley 2010)

On Christmas Day 2009, Craig Lynch uploaded the above message to his Facebook profile. A recent escapee from Suffolk's Hollesley Bay prison, Lynch was able to maintain a precarious balance of visibility and invisibility through the social networking service. He was able to evade the police while remaining in the public gaze. During the holidays Lynch uploaded a series of photos and statements not only indicating that he was still at large, but also going so far as to speculate on future travel plans. Indeed, his profile focused on the more mundane details of his fugitive status, including visiting a shopping centre with his daughter and enjoying Christmas dinner. Through this public engagement, Lynch rapidly generated a following of supporters and detractors. Furthermore, this audience was able to know him through his everyday visibility. Lynch's fugue, both spectacular and mundane, shows that even a convict evading police scrutiny could live his everyday life online.

The Facebook fugitive is a commentary on the changing nature of visibility offered by social media. Online visibility by way of personal information is a condition of contemporary sociality. Before his capture in January 2010, Lynch was able to maintain control of his visibility to the public. Regardless of the public's sympathies towards escaped convicts, his use of Facebook speaks to the empowering potential of social media for its users. This ordeal resembles a crime-based reality program that asks its audience to locate fugitives, except that the fugitives are now harnessing surveillance technology. Whether or not his presence on the site contributed to his eventual capture, social media is clearly amplifying the possibility for public visibility. Users are making their private lives visible to others, entrusting them with personal information that would otherwise be shielded from public scrutiny.

At this point even criminal life has a presence on social media. This should come as no surprise, as so much social life has a presence on social media. Online fugitives mark the end game for Facebook: all social processes are represented on the site, including criminal events. Lynch's escape is an exceptional anecdote, as most users will not willingly incriminate themselves on social media. His presence is deliberate, and it can be framed in terms of an empowering kind of visibility. The same can be said of the students who manage a booze-fuelled or otherwise obscene presence on social media. In this context empowerment refers to having some control over how someone presents herself, as well as having a manageable audience for that presence. People turn to Facebook for these processes. At the same time as sites like Facebook increasingly monopolize interpersonal security, they become an increasingly targeted site of investigative scrutiny. For users who make these sites a routine part of their lives, having police and other investigators online changes the kind of dwelling they inhabit.

In its early days, college students discovered that Facebook could be used as a source of evidence. Lynch was playing with this possibility when uploading photographs and travel plans. Social media is a means for communication, but it is increasingly a source of information for police. The distinction between communication and information in this context is noteworthy. Communication implies networking through social ties. Through communication, individuals that belong to a network maintain relations with each other, and perform social acts. On the other hand, information refers merely to the flow and collection of data, including personal information. Information flows also operate through networks, but an investigative way of using social media is concerned less with dwelling and sociality, and more on gathering evidence.

Facebook is a default location for social life. It increasingly monopolizes attention, such that getting away from it as a targeted user is difficult. Moreover, police are increasingly presumed to watch over its content through a variety of means. As a result of mutual augmentation, social media enables a diffuse kind of visibility for police work. This new visibility is not based on social media's technological sophistication, but simply its broad and enduring saturation in social life. One single software is embedded in so many social relations. It is diffuse and distributed, yet it is centrally accessible. Police have relied on other techniques and technologies to watch over social life. But never has so much social life been accessible in a single enclosure. Moreover, the social convergence and mutual augmentation detailed in earlier chapters complicates – but ultimately enhances – police scrutiny. This forces a reconsideration of policing techniques like community policing, undercover work and the use of criminal informants. The prospect in many countries that police could access this content without a warrant (Geist 2011) implies that social media could enable a pervasive kind of wiretapping.

Social media are a distributed technology, in that dispersed users actively contribute to their content, and coordinate amongst themselves through the site. This marks a contrast from more centralized media like broadcast television. But as we will see in this chapter, distributed technologies do not preclude unequal power relations (Galloway and Thacker 2007). Early adopters have invested much time and effort in their dwelling on Facebook, which contributes to a perception of the Internet as a site of individual control. This is part of the cultural imagination surrounding the Internet and empowerment. But recent state activity has showed that top-down activity is just as easy as ever. In 2011, we saw the Egyptian government shut down their country's telecommunications network, curbing the empowering potential otherwise linked to those technologies (Glanz and Markoff 2011). Likewise, the United Kingdom government is alleged to have ordered the removal of protest videos from YouTube (Travis 2011). In both cases, technology developers were willing to comply with state power.

Yet state control of social media goes beyond repression. States and other institutions are increasingly able to harness positive control over decentralized technologies, taking advantage of the way they make social life visible. We are beginning to see police and other investigators use it in ways that suggest unequal access and unequal relations of visibility. Police will increasingly be able to access private information with little effort, and without interacting with users on the site. Indeed, if individuals, institutions and businesses are dwelling on Facebook, it was only a matter of time before police established a presence as well. What is remarkable is the gradual shift towards asymmetrical relations of visibility between police and public on social media. Police are able to know so much about targeted individuals, who in turn are unaware that they are under watch. This chapter considers the very tangible future of policing on social media.

Summer 2011: Public Disorder, Public Surveillance

Game seven of the Stanley Cup Playoffs was a turning point for social media policing. As soon as rioting began in Vancouver, the hunt to locate and bring rioters to justice followed. People converged on Facebook to express their outrage. They submitted photographic and video evidence in the hopes of identifying suspected rioters. Users made use of ubiquitous mobile cameras, an element that was missing from previous hockey riots. These riots are not a novelty in Canada, but they have always had a degree of anonymity; they were never this visible. Yet in 2011, they yielded an unprecedented amount of social media content. Riot-themed groups grew on Facebook, and one entitled 'Vancouver Riot Pics: Post Your Photos' garnered over one hundred thousand users, over five million views and countless photographs in under five days. Its members believed that this kind of shaming through visibility is 'as strong as a deterrent you will find to prevent this [riot] from happening again' (VR Info 2011). While the admissibility and credibility of many of these photographs were questionable, the group marks a shift towards greater policing of social life through social media and mobile technology. Users directly contributed photographs, names and descriptions of incidents.

Police investigations do benefit from the thousands of photographs and hundreds of videos that they received (Rieti 2011). They may even visit the aforementioned Facebook groups to search for further evidence. But they are already using social media to locate evidence through other means, and these means suggest an entirely different engagement with social networks than what is anticipated by users, including Craig Lynch. Social media are typically defined as online locations where users build profiles and share personal information with each other. Sites like Facebook rely extensively on user-generated content, content that is contextually relevant and distributed through social networks. Social media are a de facto location for interpersonal sociality, and investigative agencies are investing their efforts to exploit these sites. In the aftermath, a report commissioned on the Vancouver riot pointed to the importance of social media in the above events. However, they acknowledged that Vancouver police did a suboptimal job of anticipating rioting based on social media activity, and recommend more aggressive intelligence gathering on social media (Furlong and Keefe 2011).

London experienced a more prolonged urban unrest that summer. Riots spread over four days in August, causing extensive property damage to storefronts as well as over 2000 arrests (Rees 2011). These events took place in the epicentre of CCTV surveillance, yet so much evidence came from the mobile devices that politicians and the press blamed for amplifying the riots. In fact, these very technologies were used to identify and prosecute suspects. The immediate pursuit and prosecution also marks a turning point in policing due to social media's growing presence. Public spaces are refit as more surveilled spaces not through government or private CCTV, but through individuals' own technologies and activities that are fed into software that is a fixture in their day to day lives. This assemblage of citizens, everyday devices and personal software makes otherwise anonymous gatherings very visible.

Social media features more and more prominently in policing and investigations. The 'social' quality of social media policing is based on a user engagement. Social media are designed for communication and interaction between users. In the case of the Vancouver riot, users draw on their social ties to identify and shame suspected rioters. Yet the police benefit from the ability to bypass these interactions to access evidence online. The Vancouver police partnered with the Insurance Corporation of British Columbia (ICBC), which offered their facial recognition technology to identify suspects online (CBC 2011). While they still rely on social media users to submit this content, it is only their content that matters. Facebook has also implemented its own facial recognition technology. This development further obviates the need to interface with social media users, bypassing them instead for their content. While Facebook is not publicizing its applications for police work, in-house facial recognition is a more effective way for police to gather evidence and identify people.

Sociological inquiry needs to uncover 'social' qualities of social media. These developments indicate as-yet unnamed features of social media that become observable only as these become default spaces for investigations. The increased scrutiny of sites like Facebook suggests that while users can be active agents through self-expression and social coordination, so too are they visible and accessible to institutions and governments, reduced to searchable and contextually relevant content. The use of social media by police and investigative agencies presents a different understanding of their affordances. The developments described below suggest that users are made visible as a result of the personal information on social media, all while they are decoupled from that evidence when it comes to investigative practices. In effect, social media content speaks on users' behalf.

The aftermath of the Vancouver riot is a distinctly Canadian example of policing through online surveillance. It is a response to a spectacular event, but it is representative of a more enduring security fuelled by everyday sociality. This heightened scrutiny of everyday life is noteworthy. What was formerly the remainder of modern institutional functioning (Poster 2004) is heavily scrutinized in late modernity (Haggerty and Ericson 2000) Everyday life used to be a product of institutional oversight. The homestead, the street and other non-commercial spaces used to be locations where people were free to behave as they wished. But the domestication of technology augments the visibility of these locations. Local interactions take place on global telecommunication networks. This development is heralded as the rise of the prosumer (Li and Bernoff 2008), as individuals can generate meaning and value in the content that they consume. Yet an unexplored possibility is how this mediated everyday activity is more visible to policing and investigations. Using social media technologies, investigators have a much better view of everyday life. Social media facilitate a more social policing. But what does this mean? Unpacking the 'social' in social media is an important task for sociologists, and we will return to this in Chapter 7. Already we may assert that the 'social' quality of social media is clearly linked to users, but in what capacity? Following scholarly accounts, social media enable participatory engagement and enhance social capital (Gueorguieva 2008, Ellison et al. 2010). This appears to be compatible with a community oriented view of policing, that privileges strong ties with the public. However, 'social' also suggests mere connectivity, and Surveillance Studies literature anticipates these services sidestepping individuals for their data, which then act on their behalf (Lyon 2007). Our understanding of the 'social' in social media is forming, as we grow accustomed to these ever-changing enclosures. But what is startling is that social conditions transform along with these technologies. Social media policing marks a heightened surveillance of online sociality.

Surveillance implies an overview. This refers to the vantage point of the guard tower, but also the overview provided by digital technologies. Domesticated technologies augment this vantage point. Whereas the guard tower and even the CCTV are a top-down attempt to envision social life, social media are an – often unwilling – collaboration between top-down and bottom-up efforts. Contemporary surveillance is heavily rooted in policing and control of 'risky' populations, but it is increasingly a feature of the regulation of everyday life. It is not surprising that police would turn to social media. Sites like Facebook are not only a new terrain where social life occurs, but they are a tool to search and locate social life. In other words, interactions, relations, events and other features of social life are mediated on social media, making them a more visible and useable kind of information. Police have always relied on evidence collection, and this is furthered with their adoption of social media.

A sociological understanding of social media policing comes from various sources of data. This chapter triangulates in-depth interviews with individual and professional social media users, recent developments in social media policing in Canada and abroad, as well as literature on the sociology of policing and Surveillance Studies. This data raises sociological concerns regarding social media policing that are considered below. Social media policing is a kind of community policing, but not what communities are expecting. It is a matter of watching citizens through their social media presence. This has consequences for police work, but also for social life on social media. Not only does this policing target new kinds of evidence, but social media and social ties are also reframed in terms of security and surveillance. The following section explores the origins of modern policing, and how it intersects with social media investigations. Next, this chapter focuses on three strategies currently used by law enforcement agencies on Facebook: investigations through interfaces, investigations through backchannels and managing their own visibility. It will then reconsider existing policing strategies in light of social media. This will include contemporary efforts to do community policing, but also undercover practices and the use of criminal informants. We then turn to new developments in this area, in recognition that emerging technologies and practices complicate the study of social media policing.

Origins and Context: When Policing Meets Social Media

The adoption of social media among police agencies is a novel development. But it is not surprising, as social life is increasingly taking place on these enclosures. Policing refers to the organized supervision of a population and upholding of laws. Modern policing is attributed to Robert Peel, who introduced the 1829 Metropolitan Police Act in London (Emsley 2007). This act modernized policing by centralizing and coordinating its efforts. Police became something distinct from society, as they possessed special designations to scrutinize communities. But relations with the broader public were tempered by Peel's approach. Modern policing, though professionalized and distinct from the broader public, was framed as symbiotic with the public. Maintaining public relations was paramount. This was a strategic approach, as the public was a source of invaluable information. Modern policing dictates that officers should be embedded in the public. They have to interface with the public in order to gather evidence. Although this evokes a noble sense of duty, being close to the public is also a pragmatic attempt to gather evidence, all while managing public opinion.

Despite popular visions of gunfights and car chases, policing is first and foremost about gathering information (Ericson and Haggerty 1997). Policing is surveillance in the most direct sense, and police agencies have long implemented technologies in order to augment their scope. Police technologies have distinct effects: while they seek greater access, often they further police from the public. Early biometric technologies like fingerprinting attempt to obtain better knowledge of an increasingly transient and heterogeneous population, but had a chilling effect on public relations (Nelson 2011). Closed circuit television is meant to augment visibility for police, but does not bring police closer to the broader population. In practice it is a barrier obstructing intervention, calling evidence into question and alienating relations with communities (Norris and Armstrong 1999). This tension is typical in post-industrial societies, where the loss of trust from communal ties is remedied with digital verification (Lyon 2001, Ball 2002). This culminates in a context where connections between police and the public are increasingly reliant on technologies, including social media.

Facebook is a unique police tool, as it was first designed for interpersonal relations. It began as a service for university students to socialize with each other. Separated from friends and family, these students enter a new environment at an impressionable age. Heavy drinking and wild parties often accompany their postsecondary experience. Social media augment the visibility of these events. Student indiscretions – a longstanding concern for universities – are thus brought out into the public. This visibility has a curious effect for campus security and investigations, as we saw in Chapter 4. Student incidents are by no means new, but their presence on social media now warrants a more public response. Campus investigators have long been aware of these indiscretions, but now that they have gone digital it is brought onto a new, more public terrain. Michelle, a human rights investigator at the university in Chapter 4, states that: '[T]he effect of [Facebook] has been to open up the realm of the public. So, it was much more likely for certain kinds of interaction, communication and that sort of thing, ten years ago, to be seen as private conversations. But now, less so, because it's out there.' Users are shocked and appalled by unintended visibility when it happens to them, but they also understand why campus security and other investigators will watch over the site. Social media users push social activity onto a public platform. Incidents are made visible and searchable on social media. This visibility will be further optimized and exploited by investigators as social media interfaces expand into social life.

Early adopters, especially student users, are familiar with police presence, or at least the spectre of police presence. Student parties are surveilled by police as well as university administration. This has been a historic concern, and this would be an obvious entry point for police presence and intervention. Among students, there is little outrage surrounding police presence on social media. Rather, respondents believe that their fellow students should be more responsible, given social media's quasi-public designation. Andrea comments on what she considers to be a lack of foresight: 'I think that it's pretty stupid, like, if you're going to have a kegger or something, to list your event as public and then, like, the police can see where all the parties are going to be for the weekend. Like, how stupid are you?' The above suggests that creating an event on Facebook means that everyone – including police – will see it, and failure to recognize this is nothing less than 'stupid'.

Some respondents believe that police shouldn't invest too much time on social media. Naomi states that police could probably do better things with their time, including preparing for events rather than simply searching them online. While this suggests a connection between social media and real life criminality, Naomi believes social media should not take too much importance in terms of police effort. Student respondents were generally not opposed to police investigating on Facebook, pointing to the agency of the user to avoid the site:

> I mean, again, no one's asking you to have a Facebook profile. … So yeah, I think that's fair for law enforcement to be able to peek through your information. Provided, on a case by case basis, and they wouldn't have ready access to it and there would be a warrant, et cetera. I think that would be totally fair. (Gregory)

Other respondents are comfortable with a police presence on social media, so long as the police have warrants. This suggests that these spaces should be accessible to police, but with the same oversight mechanisms we would find in conventional private spaces. Yet as we have seen, privacy on social media is a disputed category. Other students stressed the nature of visibility and exposure online, claiming that any content that is online is effectively public. Visibility is a 'hazard of using the Internet' (Charlene), and users should expect this risk by virtue of being on these sites. These accounts present Facebook as a new public means of self-expression, free of restrictions as well as protections. Users are left to behave as they wish, and cope with the consequences.

More types of social media investigations emerge with Facebook's expansion beyond universities. In September 2006, Facebook allowed non-students to become users. With this expansion came an older, more heterogeneous population. Like students, these users were willing to share personal details, making their everyday life visible in ways that brought on troubling consequences. Insurance companies turned to social media to find evidence of fraud (Millan 2011). Nebulous measures like 'quality of life' also come under scrutiny, as when an insurance company asserted that a Québec woman's presence on Facebook demonstrated that she was not depressed enough to receive compensation (CBC 2009). 'Quality of life' is difficult to quantify, and this ruling took place at a time when people were uncertain about how much weight to attribute to Facebook evidence. Although these investigations are controversial, Facebook content is increasingly scrutinized, and assumptions are solidifying about how to interpret this content. It is also a prime source of information for divorce lawyers (Popken 2011). Here, it is not just the individual's profile that it used against them, but a combination of that presence and the spouse's access to their network of friends. A broad section of the divorced couple's social life is made visible through their use of social media. This gives some indication of the unique kind of visibility that Facebook offers investigations.

These developments recast social life. Everyday actions and conversations become online content. Archived and searchable, this content can easily become evidence. Users are increasingly aware of this visibility and react accordingly. Facebook is made up of heterogeneous user values and practices. Some users refuse to upload content, while others refuse to become users. Yet they are still implicated when their friends post information about them online. The public outrage surrounding these events underscores tensions and contradictions in public perceptions of social media policing: it is ethically wrong, but practically sound. It is during these formative conditions that police turn to social media as the latest tool in gathering evidence.

Investigating Through Interfaces

The aftermath of the 2011 Vancouver riot suggests that social media users are more than willing to cooperate with the police. However, investigators have not been waiting for this cooperation with users in order to scrutinize social media content. Police turn to Facebook for gathering evidence, a process that can be as simple as searching a name.

One of the easiest ways for police to obtain evidence is by mimicking how other users access information on the site. Because a lot of information is not protected by privacy settings, any investigator can log on and search for evidence. Contact details, photographs, lists of friends and wall posts may potentially be accessible to all users. Investigators can directly access social media, but they can also rely on other users to gather evidence. When a Wayne Gretzky jersey was stolen from a sports apparel store in Ottawa, the owner was able to identify one of the suspects using the store's fan page on Facebook (Butler 2010). Even though the suspect did not belong to the fan page, one of their friends was a member. Thus, the suspect was identified not through their own content, but that of their peers. These peers were not deliberate in their attempt to expose the suspect. However, simply by virtue of making a visible connection between the store and suspect, simply by connecting with both, they led to the identification of the suspect. The visibility of social ties is a source of evidence for investigators, and a source of insecurity for criminal suspects. This is an important feature of social media surveillance, because social ties and networking are the principal means of exchange on sites like Facebook. Indeed, having a profile without social ties, without an audience, is as implausible as living in complete isolation. By necessity, social media users put themselves at risk of police monitoring when they connect with their peers.

Interface-based investigations on social media take advantage of these sites' search features. On Facebook, evidence can be located by searching for identities, groups, events or other keywords. The accessibility of so much content by searching, coupled with its ease of use makes it an attractive first step when launching an investigation, or simply looking up a particular individual. Howard, the campus security coordinator we met in Chapter 4, describes this process:

> A number of times we will know people only by the name that comes across the desk in the context of a complaint or what have you. It might jog something for someone in the department "I think that might be individual A from a situation that I had dealt with Saturday night" in which case, a shot in the dark, somebody might pull up a Facebook page and say "individual A has a profile on Facebook, and this is the image that they put out purporting to be them", and lo and behold, it is the same person that I dealt with on Saturday night.

By virtue of being a low-risk and low-cost approach, Facebook is increasingly the default starting point for investigations as well as routine kinds of scrutiny. This produces a baseline surveillance technique for investigations. Much like the ease with which students creep and are creeped, police expend few resources in order to access to social media. While sites like Facebook do not contain all desired evidence, they are valued for housing time-stamped and geo-located biographies.

While profiles are the principal target for investigative scrutiny on Facebook, police may also direct their focus on events, groups and fan pages. These spaces contain conversations and photographs based on a particular topic. This produces a surveillance that is aggregate, allowing police to hone in on evidence surrounding a common theme. A prominent example is the rise of memorial groups on Facebook for people who have been murdered. The conversations on these memorial pages bring up scores of evidence, but they also violate media bans for ongoing investigations (CBC 2008, McLean 2010). Yet by virtue of their visibility, these violations are easily policed.

Even though this kind of investigation is based on one individual interacting with another, this information collection typically involves some degree of secrecy and deception. Police may gather evidence from a user's profile without making their presence known to that individual. Likewise, they may choose to scrutinize someone by befriending them using a fake persona (Zetter 2010, Kerrigan 2011). This is done to circumvent the individual's privacy settings. Police may use an entirely fictional persona, or they may choose to imitate a trusted colleague, although both approaches violate Facebook's terms of service. But whether or not they befriend the user, police are taking advantage of sociality and interpersonal exchanges for investigative gain. In the United States, Department of Homeland Security officials connect with applicants for citizenship on Facebook in order to scrutinize them (Lynch 2010). These agencies take advantage of social networks by placing themselves within a context of information sharing and personal disclosure. They claim to take advantage of users' so-called 'narcissism' (Cheng 2010), as even people who have something to hide want to share their lives with others.

Investigators clearly recognize social media's use-value when stating that they are taking advantage of narcissism. But this can also be framed in terms of capitalizing on social media users' interpersonal vulnerabilities. In other words, investigators are able to securitize social media by virtue of its users' insecurities that draw them to the site. Jess, a student from Chapter 3, framed Facebook as fuelled by insecurities, stating that it was a way to publicly display all the friends and attention a person had, in order to affirm that one was socially desirable. In a context of long-distance relationships and temporary social arrangements, users turn to social media to cope with solitude, maintain bonds and seek validation. This student identifies an insecure social climate that compels users to seek validation on a potentially leaky platform. Following this realization, Jess opted for a more selective visibility, that is, not sharing everything with everyone. While this approach will mitigate the worst effects of self-induced visibility, she will also have to scrutinize her friends, as their content also shapes her presence. In a more general sense, Janine from Chapter 5 cites the presence of peers as a source of security for users, not because they provide reassurance in any emotional way, but simply to make social media seem more like a trusted space. While scholars, users and investigators are still making sense of social media visibility, it seems clear that user visibility is fuelled by a peer-based security. These initiatives shape policing, but they also shape social life on social media. Given Facebook's legacy as an interpersonal service, peer-to-peer relations are used by institutions to watch over populations in a trusted context. Social ties – both strangers and seemingly trusted colleagues – are recast as a point of entry to formal investigations.

The above are instances where friends – both the concept of the 'friend' on social media as well as actual peers – are used as a point of entry for police investigations. This development extends from concerns in earlier chapters that users expressed about 'friends' on social networks. The friend has always been cast in a vaguely suspicious light on social media. Either users have never personally met so-called friends, or known friends are liable to damage their reputation. But now formal surveillance is embodied in the individual profile, as a result of both real and imagined friends. This amplifies policing because it provides a novel kind of surveillance that blends everyday intimacy with investigative scrutiny.

Backchannels and Legal Pathways

Investigations on social media interfaces violate users' expectations of privacy and exposure. These users may implement privacy settings to prevent unwanted exposure, but end up friending an investigator digitally disguised as a trusted peer. A further circumvention of privacy settings happens when police skip the interface and go straight for the data.

Police can obtain information on social media through direct requests. Social media services have established official channels for police to obtain private information from their servers. These services know their value as a source of evidence for these agencies, to the extent that Facebook, Twitter, MySpace and others have produced compliance documents (Lynch 2011) that dictate what kind of information can be obtained from warrants, court orders and other legal procedures. In the case of Facebook, police can obtain contact information, private messages, photographs uploaded by the user as well as photographs uploaded by others in which the user is tagged. The range of content also includes group affiliations and lists of friends, which users would not necessarily think of as personal information. However, this content is especially fruitful for investigations, and exemplifies an understanding of social media based on social ties between users. What is interesting here is that users are effectively removed from the process, as their personal information is handed over by social media companies to law enforcement agencies. While social media are supposedly synonymous with user-generated content, investigative surveillance distinguishes user from content, and privileges the latter to speak on behalf of the former.

Social media companies have established legal pathways for investigators to request user data. All the while, investigators are pushing for other kinds of backchannels in order to speed up this process. In the United States, the FBI is petitioning for greater access to content (Singel 2011). Such ambitions effectively extend wiretapping to social media, notably in the way they circumvent encryption. In Canada, the Conservative government is pushing a 'Lawful Access' bill, which would speed up the process by which investigators could obtain this information by eliminating the need for warrants (Berkow 2011). This legislation deputizes social media as an extension of policing and investigations in Canada (Kerr and Gilbert 2004). The ease with which police can obtain online data means that police will have faster and more expansive access to social media content.

These efforts amount to a paradigm shift in the way users perceive the Internet, and social media in particular. New legislation could transform online spaces from sites of relative anonymity to sites of heightened transparency. Advocacy groups have expressed concern over these backchannels, citing privacy issues as well as the loss of control over one's personal information (EFF 2011). Sociologists should also be concerned with these developments because social life increasingly takes place on enclosures that are so unstable. Users grow comfortable under particular conditions of visibility, and these conditions change as backchannels and other protocols are implemented. Student users do not expect their dwelling to be such a prominent extension of law enforcement work. Police presence changes the nature of the social media enclosure. While investigators do not own these dwellings, so far they have unrestricted access to their content, and this access is becoming more and more enshrined.

The move towards backchannel investigations is indicative of struggles between those who wish to limit their exposure on social media, and those who seek greater visibility of social media content. This struggle is multi-modal: as some tactics to limit exposure are adopted, other strategies that bypass these tactics are launched. Users will tweak privacy settings and develop an agreement among peers about appropriate conduct online, for instance, by restricting conversations to more private backchannels. But police and other investigators can increasingly access even private data. Social media offer complex pathways in terms of scrutiny, as well as resistance against this scrutiny. But the likely outcome is that one technique to mitigate visibility is met by other means towards further exposure. And these kinds of backchannels effectively bypass dramaturgical forms of identity management. People may attempt to avoid visibility by sending information through private messages, or hiding their information behind privacy settings. Police would be able to go straight to this content without having to negotiate the layers of privacy that regular users manage. Even false information like pseudonyms does not shield the target if police can see all their friends, and piece together an identity based on that knowledge. This marks a transition from police using social media like any other user, to having special access over this decentralized network. These processes allow for police to take advantage of user visibility, precisely by not being visible. For all the talk of mutual transparency through new technologies, and the visibility of police work in particular (Mann et al. 2003, Goldsmith 2010), social media policing furthers asymmetrical relations of visibility between police and the public.

Police Visibility and Outreach

Social media are useful for investigators to obtain information through increasingly covert means. These efforts give indication of new kinds of visibility between users and investigators online. However social media can also augment the visibility of police work. The ubiquity of digital cameras allows citizens to monitor police activity. Police agencies manage their own visibility in order to manage public relations. Part of this is done reactively through the criminalization of civilian photography of police work (Adetunji 2009). In response to a growing visibility of police work beyond their control, officers are reacting by intercepting unflattering photographs and video.

Police are also proactive through the maintenance of an official police presence on social media. As an example, consider the Edmonton Police Service (EPS), the municipal police service of a mid-sized Canadian city. Their official webpage (EPS 2011) contains mission statements, crime prevention tips for citizens and information about suspects at large. This serves the dual purpose of maintaining a credible public image and augmenting the visibility of suspects wishing to avoid exposure. The official site contains links to YouTube, Facebook and Twitter presences, which in turn provide links back to the official site. The EPS YouTube channel is sparsely populated, with forty-five videos uploaded in the past three years (EPSYouTube 2011). These videos uphold the EPS's public image, as they feature community outreach efforts, ceremonies and high-profile arrests. Their official Facebook page (EPSFacebook 2011) and Twitter feed (EPSTwitter 2011) reproduce the news items from the EPS website. In both cases, other users are invited to provide feedback. Facebook allows this in the form of comments and wall posts, while Twitter users can re-tweet police messages as well as publicly respond to them. Social media are used in this instance to push official content onto more visible social media spaces, while directing attention back to an official website. Social media are thus used to amplify an official public image of the Edmonton Police that is already maintained on their own home page. Interestingly, there are also unofficial Twitter feeds authored by EPS officers (CstAnderson 2011, CstKube 2011). The content on these feeds is more candid, in the sense that they offer details of on-duty and off-duty life. Tweeting officers disclose a range of emotions, and their feeds offer a glimpse of everyday patrolling, traffic and conversations with the public. These officers make themselves visible, sharing a more candid side of police work than is most often understood by the public through televised dramas. Yet these personal feeds are undoubtedly coached and policed to ensure they only broadcast appropriate content. These feeds have standardized display pictures, suggesting a measure of top-down control by the EPS.

Police are building a public presence on social media. As noted above, relations with the public have historically been important for policing. When public opinion – as well as social life in general – migrates to social media, it stands to reason that police agencies would establish a front stage (Goffman 1959, Ericson 1989) on these services in order to maintain a positive perception. This is the nature of impression management, most notably on social media. Giving off the right impression through visual and textual cues is privileged over fostering proper relations. In Chapter 5, Ben suggested that giving the impression of trying to serve a community is sufficient on Facebook. Being present on social media is a thin commitment to community policing, in the same way that social exchanges are more or less reproduced through Facebook.

Police also use social media to solicit information from others. For instance, Facebook has been used to further disseminate AMBER alerts (Hopkins 2011). These are framed as 'a voluntary partnership between law-enforcement, media, transportation and others to send bulletins about child-abduction cases' (FB Amber 2011). These have been used previously to alert large sections of the population with time-sensitive bulletins through multiple forms of media. The migration towards social media is a further extension of this logic. Social media can make crime and criminals visible by quickly broadcasting information about subjects to a vast audience. This suggests enrolling entire social networks to report suspicious activity, a move that is reminiscent of Daryl's assertion that sharing information with the public is 'the exact opposite' of an Orwellian model of policing. Public alerts are perceived by law enforcement as providing a service to the public. Such efforts are foregrounded in order to frame social media policing in terms of sharing information with the public, rather than gathering evidence. Daryl positions sharing information with a population in direct contrast to watching over that population. Yet these two operate in tandem, as social media users can be both a target and an extension of a surveillance apparatus. Users not only make themselves visible in a way that augments investigative surveillance, but they also directly contribute to this watching on behalf of the investigative agencies. Social media offer multiple avenues for individuals to augment institutional scrutiny.

The above initiatives provide a more comprehensive view of a social media surveillance diagram by police. Social media users are a target of surveillance efforts, but they are also an audience to a public performance of police on social media. Through services like Facebook and Twitter, police are able to maintain relations with the public, all while using it as a source of evidence. This furthers the view that social media are a tool as well as a terrain for investigators. Police continue to be skilled at public relations and media relations on social media. In fact, more granular relations with the public increasingly resemble media relations. It is not a matter of police getting closer to community, but rather otherwise local interactions are now taking place through media. This happens all while police get better at using these services, as well as forcing changes in legislation. The impact of these efforts is felt when this is paired with the criminalization of public and police photography by citizens. A domestic network of technologies, once thought to empower citizens, now amplifies existing inequalities. Empowering possibilities are cut off one by one, and conventional surveillance is a de facto condition.

Rethinking Police Tactics

Many police strategies converge on social media. At this stage we may wonder how they are incorporated or otherwise altered by their presence on social media. Sites like Facebook are uniquely saturated in social life, which offers new possibilities for police work. The mutual augmentation framework allows us to consider how a police presence benefits from social media surveillance. The pathways for visibility afforded to police by social media can be anticipated by looking at existing ways to gather evidence. Yet the fact that all these practices are at least partly reproduced in social media is striking. Because they are such broad platforms for social life, social media have the potential to become broad tools for police work. In the case of Facebook we see that existing strategies are extended onto these enclosures.

Wiretapping

The increased reliance of social media forces a reconsideration of longstanding police practices. Most obviously, it furthers the use of wiretapping, especially when subpoenas and legal backchannels are involved. Surveillance Studies have outlined the relevance of wiretapping as an investigative technology (Bloss 2007, Nunn 2009). These have a specific surveillant quality in that they intercept communications discretely. This provides an asymmetrical relation of visibility between watchers and watched. The potential to 'tap in' to communication on social media, especially without a warrant, means that wiretapping goes from being an exceptional strategy to a default one. The expansion of policing into social media means that wiretapping is a kind of baseline for investigations. Instead of planned interventions, wiretapping can happen retroactively. It is a matter of an archived and searchable representation of social life. As a much broader set of interactions occur through Facebook, this amounts to a more expansive capture of evidence.

Community Policing

The principles that underlie community policing can be traced back to Robert Peel, and his emphasis on maintaining relations with the general public. For Peel this meant that police should be embedded in the public. In the 1990s there was a renaissance of community policing in major Canadian cities. These initiatives sought closer relations between police and public, ostensibly to the benefit of both parties. This translated to a more visible presence of officers on streets in order to maintain a public image, but also to foster stronger ties with the public (Friedmann 1992). The public are thus a means, in that police rely on them to gather evidence. But they are also an end, in that keeping them satisfied is identified as an objective. The attempt to get greater access to evidence suggests a view of the public as a terrain as well as a tool for policing.

The increased reliance on social media has the potential of extending community policing efforts, notably through the curation of official spaces where symbolic exchange can ameliorate public relations. Yet this is a minute part of investigators' broader agenda on social media. Whereas a community policing model would treat the public as a partner and stakeholder in public security and safety, a reliance on social media bypasses these efforts by placing the public's online traces above the public themselves. Instead, social media mark a bifurcation of public relations and evidence collection, with occasional appeals to the public for tips. Social media policing is shaped by covert scrutiny and pathways without public contact. This furthers a pattern in surveillance regimes to privilege digital traces (Boyne 2000) above individual, leaving these traces to speak on behalf of the individual.

Undercover Policing

Social media also force a reconsideration of the nature and effectiveness of undercover policing. This refers to a set of practices to infiltrate criminal spaces and obtain access to otherwise private and closely guarded information. Undercover approaches enhance police surveillance by using deceit and an asymmetry of visibility to locate and incriminate suspects. In particular, this is an asymmetry of disclosures: police conceal their identities while obtaining evidence from suspects. Policing becomes proactive and based on categorical suspicion, as undercover strategies enable a focus on suspects rather than incident-led scrutiny (Marx 1988).

Police efforts on social media greatly facilitate undercover investigations. Conversations and other exchanges between suspects and their peers are accessible from an investigator's computer. As stated above, investigators can also impersonate trusted peers, a further deception in order to access and watch over suspects in a candid state. Undercover policing becomes low risk, as police visibility and exposure on social media are negligible. This is distinct from conventional forms of undercover work, as embedded fieldwork becomes office work. Police and other investigators can expand these efforts because of the ease with which this can be performed. Undercover policing is normally an exceptional practice, because of risk and deception. Now social media enable a kind of lurking, during or after an incident. Although it also has the potential to foster mutually transparent relations, an increased reliance on covert investigations bypasses the need for community relations.

Most organized criminals will not post their exploits on their Facebook profile. But more and more social life passes through online interfaces, all while police and security develop a better grip on these interfaces. It is incumbent on sociological research to follow this development. Social media policing forces a reconsideration of covert police work. This kind of interception more closely resembles conventional undercover work because social media sociality is composed of a richer set of information than a telephone conversation. An investigation can quickly reveal a suspect's biography as well as social ties. Moreover, it enables the investigator to migrate along this social network, to see if a suspect's peers can yield evidence. This is considered below.

Criminal Informants

Social media also transform the use of criminal informants, or 'snitches' (Marx 1984, Natapoff 2009). Snitching is a kind of barter system between police and the public. Informants will offer information leading to evidence in exchange for lessened prison time or financial gain. Because of their cooperation with police, informants face a backlash from suspects. It is reasonable to assert that the prevalence of criminal informants is tied to a failure of community policing. Central to a community policing strategy is a reliance on an entire community, rather than singling out a few gatekeepers. If police have atrophied relations with the public, they will have to compensate with a greater reliance on criminal informants, who stand out because of this unpopular designation.

Social media policing resembles snitching in the sense that investigators direct their attention to a suspect's peers in order to obtain information. Yet this marks a shift in procedure, as these 'snitches' are seldom aware of their involvement in this process. In other words, snitching becomes involuntary. The costs associated with both undercover police work and snitching are lowered through social media (cf. Shirky 2008). As more users live more of their lives on sites like Facebook, their interpersonal visibility among peers becomes an increasingly valuable component of police investigations. Of particular concern is that users may not be aware of these kinds of exposure.

Just as informants can provide information to police, police may obtain evidence from a suspect's peers, as a result of what those peers display on social media.

In light of the costs and risks associated with snitching, suspects can potentially assess social networks as risky. Police efforts on social media can put users at risk of the backlash facing criminal informants. Suspects may recast social relations as a vulnerability. Suspects and fugitives already cope with strained relations with friends and family (Goffman 2009). But these strained relations become a lot more mainstream when suspects' peers are used against them in social media policing. In turn, social media users are obliged to watch over their own content, but also police their friends.

Furthering Social Media Policing with Emerging Technologies

The police practices described above are a concern for sociologists. But social media enclosures are dynamic, as are its uses. Services like Facebook routinely implement new features, which in turn can become new tools for policing social life. Moreover, these services interface better with other technologies as they become common fixtures in social life. Facebook's facial recognition service, Tag Suggestions, will feature prominently in future conversations about social media policing. This feature was quietly ushered in by Facebook in December 2010, and entered the public view primarily through outrage from users and advocacy groups (EPIC 2011). Tag Suggestions uses a facial recognition algorithm to identify users in photographs, and by default will then publicize their identity. Facebook frames this as a matter of convenience, as users uploading lots of photographs will not have to repeatedly tag their friends (Mitchell 2011). What is especially troubling about Tag Suggestions is that the public can only speculate about potential applications. Embedding facial recognition into Facebook enriches a database of users and content, and automates the identification process. Following the Vancouver riot, the ICBC volunteered its own facial recognition technology, coupled with a database of provincial drivers' licenses, in order to identify suspects. Facebook's move towards this technology suggests a vision of social media visibility that most users might not recognize. While many users were eager to bring rioting suspects to light through naming and shaming, a growing database and algorithms bypass the need to engage with these users. Contemporary policing on social media follows a logic of 'search first and consult the public later'.

Other technologies take advantage of the cumulative presence left by social media users across a range of services. Metropolitan police in the United Kingdom have begun to employ software that tracks individuals' activity on a range of online services, effectively mapping their social life (Gallagher and Syal 2011). This technology capitalizes on the volume and breadth of personal information online, assembling it to produce a robust portrait of user activity. Not only is this software useful for gathering information following a criminal event, but it also provides a persistent visibility of users in general. Technology like facial recognition or aggregate tracking is an easy sell when security is invoked, but its implications have already provoked civil insecurity (Snyder 2011). Social media users, and digital media users more generally, have established an extensive presence on these spaces with certain expectations of exposure and anonymity, and these developments directly violate those expectations. The technology currently available to police complicates the investigation techniques described above. If facial recognition and real time tracking are also at their disposal, policing will become even further linked to personal information and everyday life. Searching and social sorting on social media will grow from an investigatory technique to a persistent mode of visibility. This will impact categorical suspicion and enable new kinds of profiling. As social media policing grows, it is imperative that researchers focus on emerging as well as reinforced categories of suspicion.

Discussion

This chapter focused on the most recent addition to social media enclosures. Policing is increasingly central to a broader social convergence. Current developments in Canada, the United Kingdom and elsewhere suggest that it will continue to complicate life on sites like Facebook. An increased police presence means that targeted suspects are more visible. In addition, any single event or detail can be accessible by investigators, and it is all readily searchable through social media. In interviews with personal as well as professional users, uncertainty was a consistent theme to life on Facebook. Few respondents were willing to speculate about how social relations would change as a result of social media. Yet when they report their experiences, the convergence of social contexts and unexpected kinds of exposure were persistent themes. These features reinforce a mutual augmentation model of social media surveillance, and these are sociological consequences that scholars and users can anticipate with a growing police presence on social media. Indeed, this convergence is precisely why social media is policed. It represents a kind of assemblage (Haggerty and Ericson 2000), where the boundary of policing tools is extended, and police are able to employ a service also used by the general population.

Users think of social media policing in terms of officers watching over them. But citizens are involved in their own watching, and that of their peers, to the extent that social media policing is an assemblage of top-down and bottom-up efforts. The latter may be involuntary, as when users upload content in an entirely different social context. A user who uploads photographs from her most recent vacation is simultaneously providing evidence against her own insurance claim. Likewise, a user expressing controversial political views may also contribute to her own profiling as an unwelcome visitor to a neighbouring country. This is a product of the social convergence associated with the rise of social media. Both individual users and institutions have embraced Facebook. Yet this enthusiasm is mixed with uncertainty about what can be expected from these services. Social life is represented in great detail on these spaces, but the practices that surround this presence are being negotiated. These services are used extensively for communications. Police can take advantage of this and foster relations with the broader public. But, perhaps more importantly, social media are a great source of information. With the right techniques and access, police can effectively bypass privacy barriers and other attempts to maintain secrecy.

Social media policing is indicative of contemporary surveillance. This is an early stage of a new paradigm of visibility. Social media users produce staggering quantities of information on domestic technologies that are currently not fully visible to conventional watchers. A number of new police technologies and practices are ensuring a heightened surveillance of everyday life. A mix of domestic, decentralized technologies like social media and ubiquitous mobile devices, coupled with centralized databases and mandates, amounts to an exponential increase in visibility (ibid.). All are made more visible, but these developments also augment the possibility for profiling and anticipatory policing. Another risk is that the techniques above become standard and reproduced in other branches of social media sociality. Not only does social media visibility creep into policing, but social media policing may also creep into the rest of social media sociality. This risk is especially viable when users come to criminalize their content and connections, and begin policing their social networks.

These developments force a reconsideration of policing. But they also force a reconsideration of the social features of social media. They help pinpoint an evasive quality of social media: their access to social life. Scholars have pointed to the increased blurring of online and offline activity. Social life on the Internet was previously framed in terms of anonymity and flexibility but their continued growth, coupled with mobile and geo-locational technologies, means that these technologies are embedded in social life. The police are embedded in the public, but their use of social media does not resemble community policing. Evidence obtained through social networks is privileged over ties with community. Subsequent research requires multiple sites of focus. Investigative agencies ought to be under greater sociological scrutiny. Agencies that are able to know so much about social life should in turn remain visible to the public. In addition, research should focus on how these technologies and practices reshape relations between suspects and peers. As social media policing goes from exceptional and noteworthy to a given, criminal suspects will undoubtedly rethink their relations with peers. Under the rubric of security, social ties on social media will be reframed as insecure.

Chapter 7

What's Social About Social Media?
Conclusions and Recommendations

Introduction

Craig Lynch, the Facebook fugitive in Chapter 6, returned to prison, but the mundane visibility he maintained as a fugitive speaks to conditions to which social media users are exposed. He had an active presence for a vaguely defined audience, which began to contribute to his presence. Eventually – and perhaps intentionally – his day-to-day visibility online impacted his life chances when he was apprehended. Most social media users will not be imprisoned, and many fugitives will avoid social media, but Lynch's everyday presence on Facebook is part of a mainstreaming of everyday visibility through social media. Moreover, this everyday visibility is increasingly tied to the allocation of life chances, as institutions and businesses have an increased engagement with the social media.

Social media have grown beyond university dormitories, and more developments are imminent. One of the consistent themes to this research has been uncertainty. User-centric accounts present Facebook as a dwelling, because users invest time and build an identity in this space. The idea of the enclosure captures the other side of experience: that personal information is used in a variety of surveillance efforts. In Chapter 3 we saw students coping with the uncertainties of living on Facebook: their dwelling changed as a broader public joined, as well as when they left the university setting. Chapter 4 focused on institutions, and its members faced comparable challenges. Respondents who were professionals at managing incidents were overwhelmed by the amount of information and visibility brought on by Facebook. And while social media is touted as the 'next big thing', business respondents in Chapter 5 were ambivalent about their involvement. Policing and investigations are also riddled with uncertainty. Chapter 6 outlined how this will impact police work as well as social life on social media. And despite all this uncertainty, social media continues to be a central platform for social life.

This chapter offers a concluding overview of social media surveillance. It does this by first returning to the notion of mutual augmentation in order to fully consider its properties as manifest in the previous four chapters. Exploring these features provides insight regarding the spread of social media into various social contexts, with the consequence that managing visibility for those involved becomes a much more complex task. This chapter examines this complexity by focusing on five key features of social media surveillance. These draw on our understanding of mutual augmentation, but also provide direction for subsequent research. Chapter 1 proposed a diagram of social media surveillance based on mutual augmentation. While the first two chapters underscore scholarly work being conducted on social media, these works overlook the context in which users are immersed. This includes their motivations for making themselves visible on social media, their perception of surveillance on social media, and the measures they take to manage their own visibility as well as to take advantage of the visibility of others. Chapters 3 through 6 address these concerns by exploring four sets of Facebook users: university students, employees working on behalf of a university, employees and consultants using Facebook as a business service as well as police and other investigators.

The research in this book provides an in-depth exploration of how different kinds of surveillance on Facebook not only co-exist, but also amplify one another. This chapter returns to the concept of mutual augmentation in order to consider how it is manifest by these different groups on Facebook. This will involve Facebook's technical features, but also its ubiquity in social life. In unpacking the way that mutual augmentation is manifest between the various actors involved in Facebook, key features of social media surveillance emerge. Five features are considered in this chapter. First, users participate in a collaborative identity construction with other users. Second, friendships provide unique surveillance opportunities as users often engage with a particular audience in mind. Third, the construction of a personal social network means social ties become visible, measurable and searchable. Fourth, an ever-changing interface and privacy controls alter users' visibility though the site. Fifth, social media content is easily re-contextualized. Information leaks are now a common outcome. The first three features illustrate interpersonal aspects of social media with an emphasis on social ties. The final two highlight its growth into social life, institutions and culture. This chapter then returns to the notion of privacy. This is a concept that came up periodically in this book, and we have seen that it is complicated by social media. We can now return to this concept and consider not only why a private/public binary is insufficient, but also that users rely on other concepts and values to negotiate their visibility on social media. Finally, this chapter makes recommendations for users, for policymakers and for scholars. The latter will be informed by both the findings as well as the limitations of this research.

Mutual Augmentation of Social Media Surveillance

This research considers four kinds of surveillance: individuals watching over one another, institutions watching over a key population, businesses watching over their market and investigators watching over populations. Chapter 1 refers to mutual augmentation as a diagram where formerly discrete surveillance practices feed off each other through their prolonged engagement with Facebook. Based on the findings discussed in this research, mutual augmentation is a product of the social features of social media.

As a starting point, consider the features shared by these four surveillance practices. Individual, institutional, market and investigative scrutiny all rely on the same interface. Thus, familiarity with the site as an interpersonal user facilitates other uses. In addition to relying on the same interface, these practices also rely on the same body of information. This means that personal information that has been uploaded for any particular purpose will potentially be used for several kinds of surveillance. These practices are all tied to the authorship of specific information, yet each practice can use all information involved.

All four populations also share the potential of being watched. They may be visible as a result of information they uploaded, or because of content uploaded by others. Mutual augmentation results in shared risk and visibility as well as shared tools and features to watch over others. Individual, institutional and market users report that their own visibility on the site is a primary motivation to watch others on the site. The potential of being watched contextualizes their own surveillance. We may also speculate that investigators monitor social media for unfavourable publicity (Goldsmith 2010). Not only does this suggest that surveillance is rampant on the site, but it also dampens users' ethical concerns about covertly watching over others. The consultant's recommendation in Chapter 5 that users have to be on Facebook because they are already on Facebook encapsulates this point. Individuals, institutions and businesses cannot afford the luxury of contemplating the public and private aspects of Facebook. They believe that their reputation is on the line. Out of necessity they need to scrutinize what others are saying.

All four practices are augmented by Facebook's exponential growth. The social media service is rapidly approaching one billion users. Thus, more users are joining the site to watch over peers, customers, markets and brands. With every additional set of eyes affixed to Facebook, any content already on the site has a larger audience. Moreover, that increased audience is situated in a greater variety of social contexts, starting with Facebook's growth out of the postsecondary sector. In addition these users all augment each other's visibility by uploading content that implicates each other. How are different surveillance practices augmented by each other?

Individual users, especially students, were the first to join the site. However, they became aware that other populations were signing up. These users are more aware of tangible and visible forms of surveillance. They are more likely to be concerned with their parents watching over them than marketers, but they are increasingly aware of both, as well as universities and employers. They have a good idea of what kind of criteria these watchers are employing, and will self-scrutinize based on these criteria. Moreover, they will watch over others, including friends and family, with an eye for harmful content. Interpersonal scrutiny becomes professionalized in recognition that others are watching. Institutional surveillance on social media is a direct product of interpersonal scrutiny. Employees use their knowledge as personal Facebook users to watch over students on behalf of the university. Moreover, they were able to see content that was uploaded as a result of individual users wanting to remain visible to one another. This kind of interpersonal reciprocation augments institutional scrutiny. Businesses also draw on individual scrutiny by employing early adopters of social media to do this work. Not only do businesses take advantage of interpersonal scrutiny by watching over these conversations and exchanges, but a conversational approach is adopted as a best strategy for watching over markets. Investigators benefit from the visibility of social life brought on by the above developments. As social media become the default medium for social life, their ability to police social life is augmented. Moreover, their increased presence on social media triggers heightened self-scrutiny and lateral surveillance among users, who internalize the police gaze.

Mutual augmentation on Facebook illustrates some features about social media surveillance that warrant further inquiry. First, visibility on Facebook is an inherently collaborative act. Authoring information, commenting on other users' content, and adding friends to a social network are all actions that involve and implicate other people. This is evident, but it complicates the watcher-watched dyad in ways that are explored below. Second, social media enclosures themselves are dynamic. This is a product of the two-pronged invisibility of services like Facebook. While these sites serve to make their users visible to the social world, their own inner-workings remain opaque. As a result its users do not know what to expect from a site that hosts so much of their online presence. But Facebook is also invisible in the sense that it is ubiquitous. It is pervasive to an extent that it hardly evokes our attention. Its expansion into various social spheres elicits little concern or controversy. As a result, information contained on the site can easily migrate to new contexts. The following section considers these points in greater detail.

Key Features of Social Media

Five key features of social media highlight a shift in the collection of personal information on the Internet and illustrate the growing liquidity (Lyon 2010) of surveillance. New forms of visibility and transparency afforded by social media are coupled with user practices to manage these possibilities. The personal and professional users we met in earlier chapters return in this section to substantiate the proposed features.

Collaborative Identity Construction

Users increasingly participate in a collaborative identity construction with their peers. Facebook allows users to share information about their friends with those friends. Profiles are composed of fields where both users and their friends can add personal information about that user. By default this information is shared with the user's networks of friends. Thus, speaking to a colleague also means speaking about that colleague to an extended audience of users. This occurs in four principal locations: walls, photos, tags and comments.

Walls are a prominent feature on user profiles where friends can post messages and other content as a series of chronologically ordered entries. This serves a dual purpose: content is used to communicate with friends, but also offer a kind of public testimony about that person to their network of friends. Students acknowledge that the kind of postings a user will receive from friends is treated as a reflection on their personality and character: 'I guess the type of wall posts they get also kind of reflects who they are as well and, again someone who has a lot of really nasty wall posts from the people added on Facebook as friends might not exactly seem the most appealing person in the world' (Diane). With this reflection in mind, users are tactical about the content that they post on their friends' walls. They are careful how they portray their friends, relegating sensitive or compromising content to the private message feature:

> I love the walls and I post on people's walls all the time – but at the same time I'm very careful about what I post on other people's walls and I also send a lot of messages because it's like "This is wall appropriate, this is message appropriate." And … it's just a fact of life that people are going to read my conversations. … We all know what we're saying to each other. (Christina)

The above respondent suggests that scrutinizing other users' conversations is a taken-for-granted feature of social media. Likewise, users report having to scrutinize their own wall for problematic postings from their friends: 'Especially people have a tendency to throw things on your wall and you're like "Uh, you forget that I've got a dozen friends who are still friends with this person and they could see this and could see this on their News Feed" and that kind of thing' (Samantha). Users will not only monitor what other users will say about each other, but also actively monitor what is being said about themselves. In employing these tactics, users increasingly frame the wall as featuring content that is entirely public and visible to others:

> [W]hen you write, like, you know, a hilarious comment on one of your friends' walls, it's not necessarily to communicate with that person, but to show everyone who comes and visits their page that you are communicating with that person. So, it's intended to be viewed by others, in its very nature. (Katelyn)

Wall posts are partly a means to speak on behalf of a friend. Users can also upload photographs of their friends. With nearly eight billion photos uploaded to Facebook every month (FB Statistics 2011) it stands to reason that they are a central feature for interpersonal assessments. Indeed, most users report that when adding a new contact to their network they will immediately scrutinize the photos on their profile: 'You can get to know someone by looking at their information … you can see all the comments people have made on their photos and all the photos of them and all the photos that they've posted' (Christina). A user's collection of photos becomes another way to assess how someone is seen from the vantage point of their peers.

Friends can further augment a user's visibility by tagging them in a photo. By creating a link between the photo and the user's profile, tags facilitate browsing often hundreds or thousands of photos featuring any single user from dozens of sources. As an added feature, the act of tagging someone is itself content to be distributed. Following default privacy controls, if one friend tags a second friend in a photo – which may belong to a third friend – this will be featured on both walls as well as both users' friends' news feeds. The politics of tagging has become a sticking point for some users, especially those like Clancy who have struggled with incriminating material about them being publicized: 'There's a picture of me someone took randomly in an awkward position. It looks like I'm doing something bad to the teacher, but I was actually not. That was like a hundred comments on it. That took a week to get it off.' Through this experience, Clancy developed a series of tactics to cope with incriminating photos:

> First of all, especially people who are taking photos of you doing something destructive at parties, if I know they've taken it, I will go tell them like the next day after the party: "Do not upload these. Please delete them." And if they do upload, I would tell them again. And, first of all un-tag myself. And then, I would report to Facebook.

As this is a growing concern, campus security is increasingly involved in cases where students have been defamed through social media. Howard from campus security reports that: 'Within Facebook itself, if someone comes to us and says "subject A is slandering my name and has several entries on their Facebook sites about me that are grossly injurious to me", then we will check that out.' Through tagging users are publicly identified by their friends. This feature has been extended to text-based content like notes as well as status updates. When a user is tagged in someone else's note or status update, this content will then appear on both users' profiles as well as both friendship networks' news feeds. This feature has also raised concern for the tagged person's reputation. Many students are concerned with how their friends' opinions will reflect on them: 'You can make a note on Facebook … and you can mention people in the note. I find that a little bit difficult just because a lot of the time the views they'll sometimes post aren't something that you agree with' (Samantha). Being tagged in a note can be interpreted as an endorsement of the views expressed in that note. A friend's political or religious views may be perceived by others as the user's views.

Comments are another way users can be made visible by their friends. This involves adding a text-based response to content like photographs, status updates, notes as well as actions like adding a friend or joining a group. Comments add a conversational feature to activity on Facebook, such that users can comment indefinitely about any content or activity on the site. This feature ensures that users do not have exclusive claims over how they present themselves on social media.

Upon receiving an accusatory comment on a note she posted, one student used the comment feature herself to manage her online presence:

> But like an acquaintance of mine ... flamed my post and in the comments he accused me of being like tacitly supporting the murder of all these civilians and posted a pictures, a link to a picture of someone who I had participated in the murder of. I was just like "what the hell is this?" I didn't delete it. I instead wrote my response underneath it hoping that anyone who came across it was like "so he is a whacko". (Katelyn)

Users rely on what others say about their friends to make inferences about them. Given the difficulty involved in managing what potentially hundreds of friends are saying about a user, this is seen as a more authentic representation of a person. This is not to suggest that users are devoid of any tactics. They can choose to remove wall posts, photo tags or comments and can report inappropriate content. They can also disable their wall and hide all tagged photos as a means to minimize their friend's influence. But the absence of a wall or photos on a profile is often read as an admission of guilt in that the user is attempting to conceal something.

Lateral Ties Provide Unique Surveillance Opportunities

Marketers, employers, and other institutional watchers access a rich knowledge of users when those individuals are bound to a network of colleagues to whom they wish to remain transparent and trustworthy. Users have a particular audience in mind when uploading and sharing personal details. Yet that audience makes up only a small portion of the people who have access to their information.

Institutional surveillance typically occurs in fixed and readily identifiable settings, including the border crossing, the interrogation room, and the census form. These allow for a degree of deceit and subterfuge on the part of the person under scrutiny. In contrast, Facebook is a site of social convergence, with other users belonging to several social spheres. Personal information is not authored with all potential audiences in mind. Thus, other watchers can intervene in ties between a Facebook user and that user's intended audience. The majority of respondents claimed that they upload information for their closest friends and occasionally their relatives. There is some variance in terms of ideal audiences, as some use Facebook for geographically proximate ties while others use it mostly for long distance ones. With these kinds of friendship ties shaping the way users understand Facebook, they will provide information meant for a personal audience. As Christina notes:

> That's the best way to get a measure of someone ... when they think they're in their own space. The things people post on Facebook can be very telling. Right or wrong, if you want to know about someone, look on Facebook because that's sort of where they bare their souls to the world.

These social ties are experienced as a kind of soft coercion, with pressure from a network of friends pushing users to engage with the site. The majority of respondents report joining Facebook at the behest of their friends, and then being expected to submit biographical content. These friendship ties regulate the kind of information provided through a passive yet ongoing scrutiny. When uploading information, users only identify a portion of their audience. This suggests a self-presentation geared towards friends, ensuring a degree of comfort with sharing otherwise sensitive personal information. For example, users are routinely asked by friends to post their phone number on Facebook. Given the site's quasi-public status, this troubles some student users: 'I've seen a lot of people being like "I've lost my cell phone, please give me your phone number" and you'll just have walls full of people's phone numbers with their name attached and I think that's really stupid' (Claudia). A user's social ties with their friend network compel them to share personal information. What's more, the information they share is expected to be consistent with how they would otherwise present themselves to those peers. This is not to suggest that deception and identity play are absent from Facebook. Rather, this becomes the kind of deception that would normally exist between friends and colleagues. Instead of actively resisting online surveillance, these tactics are akin to self-presentation based on the use of explicit and implicit cues to maintain a favourable public image.

Social Ties are a Kind of Content

Sites like Facebook turn social connections into visible, measurable and searchable content. This adds a dimension of visibility to the study of social ties and social capital, which indicates that 'who you are' has always been a reflection of 'who you know'. With social media this has become a standard feature for profiling individuals. Not only are a user's social ties visible, but others can also make inferences about private information on the basis of friends' publicly accessible information.

The notion that social ties are a form of personal information often escapes users' scrutiny simply because they do not submit it in the same way they submit photographs and other content. As a result, friends and friends in common are visible on user profiles, even when most content is kept private. Following the default settings, everybody would be aware of the company that everyone else keeps. This information is used internally by Facebook to recommend new friends based on existing ones. Respondents look at other users' friends not only to confirm their identity, but also to make inferences about their reputation. Too few friends and too many friends are both seen as cause for concern. Several assumptions are made: too few friends suggests either the user is too socially withdrawn, or employing a false identity. Too many friends suggest social promiscuity, a lack of privacy concerns or lack of knowledge about privacy controls. As Claudia reports: 'You can't have that many friends. ... There were people on the site being like "Add me!" like, "I'll add anybody". And it's just like you're going to have way too many friends and way too many people who you actually don't know.' Christina suggests that the kind of scrutiny cast on friends also applies to the self: 'There are people who have over 1000 [friends]. And, okay, you can know a lot of people, but I have too many right now.' Christina's realization suggests that users learn the extent of their own exposure by way of their peers' exposure.

Beyond this immediate unease, there is a growing realization among users that friends, when taken in aggregate, can be used as a window into a user's innermost thoughts and intentions. Social ties are descriptive in and of themselves, but they also allow one user's personal details to reflect on their peers. Users may choose not to disclose their sexual orientation or political affiliations, either by omitting these details or hiding them with privacy controls. Yet a portion of their friends will openly share these details about themselves. By monitoring this information in aggregate, researchers claim that it can be used to make assessments about users. (Jernigan and Mistree 2009, Wills and Reeves 2009). If the average user has one hundred and thirty friends, and one fifth of those friends have partially transparent profiles, those users provide a substantial sample of information that may reflect on the individual. Current privacy settings are not able to prevent these exploits, as the user in question is essentially bypassed. The inferences made through users' friends may not be accurate, although that is hardly the point. Through social sorting this information shapes social outcomes.

The fact that a user's friends reflect them presents some unique challenges to self-presentation on social media. Many are clearly ambivalent about this kind of exposure, as evidenced by the number of users who hide this information. Yet, by default, users are sharing this information with the public. Users are beginning to realize the extent to which their friends reflect their identity, and many have expressed discomfort with this. Yet this discomfort is mixed with fascination about the insight these features provide. Angie states: 'I don't think everyone should be able to view who my friends are. Interestingly enough I do go look at other people's friends.' Visible social ties do trouble users, but they also take advantage of the visibility of others.

Interfaces and their Contents are Always Changing

Social media enclosures are dynamic. Not only do they perpetually solicit new input from users, but they also forge new avenues for that information. Likewise, user engagement is shifting in response to changes to the interface. This illuminates a broader vision of how Facebook operates, the culture in which it is situated and the way its users position themselves in it.

Users report that Facebook itself is continuously changing. Revisions to the interface push some information to the foreground while hiding other details. New features and third-party applications require further personal details from users. Facebook's front page prominently invites users to make new friendship connections and send new content to existing ties. Each revision to Facebook's interface is accompanied by new privacy settings, which by default are left open to a broad public. These changes indicate a tension where Facebook's developers purport to offer users greater control over their information while promoting open and unrestricted access to their personal information. The 2007 decision to make this content searchable through Google indicates that Facebook is increasingly linked to additional settings.

These changes to the interface and privacy settings are met with a degree of distrust among users, who link them to attempts to monetize personal information: 'I really don't trust Facebook at all because, they're there to make money, obviously, and it's like: "Oh, we don't sell your personal information" and then it's like: "Oh, headline story: Facebook selling your personal information"' (Christina). In addition to these features, research on the topic should consider the complexity of the users themselves, who may transpose this information to separate contexts. They may save a photograph to their hard drive and email it or upload it to a separate site, repost it in their own photo album or simply tag or comment on it. In all these cases that photo leaks from its original setting to another, and is thus made more public. Yet the latter methods require less user intervention, suggesting that these kinds of leaks are increasingly a built-in feature of the social media.

As users continually catch up with a changing interface, it stands to reason that information they post about themselves or others will be more widely distributed than anticipated. This suggests an ongoing learning curve for using Facebook that leads users to perceive each other as potential liabilities. Photos of a mature student's children were leaked when a day-care employee posted them online:

> Now I think she had intended to put them up privately and that was just the mistake. However still, she made those pictures available to everybody that goes to the day-care, all the other parents that were there and it was done without my consent and I was actually very upset by that. That's a violation of my privacy and my child's privacy. (Angie)

Recognizing these shifts, users themselves treat their engagement with Facebook as an ongoing project. Many users report revising their personal content, either modifying or removing content as well as pruning ties with their peers. These measures are framed as a way to cope with the emerging risks associated with Facebook's changes. Christina states that she goes 'through my privacy settings every couple months and just make sure that everyone is still how I want it to be', suggesting that routine self-scrutiny is necessary on social media.

While very few respondents are willing to predict how Facebook would change in the immediate future, they anticipate that its content will become more and more public with time. As for how they would use Facebook in the future, student respondents treat the job market as a catalyst for major revisions to their engagement: 'I will probably start locking down profiles and stuff, un-tagging myself from scandalous photos' (Ralph). Paula plans to 'turn off' her Facebook when she beings applying for jobs.

Despite uncertainties about new features and issues, respondents who approach Facebook from an institutional perspective regard it as a growing aspect of their responsibilities. Cindy, a university web coordinator, comments on the sudden emergence of a new set of responsibilities, citing 'an explosion in the last few months especially in the area of higher education'. This rapid growth in the university sector is only part of a progressive creeping by Facebook into numerous social spheres.

Social Media Content is Easily Re-Contextualized

The conditions described in the above section suggest that information on Facebook circulates to an ever-increasing amount of social spheres. Information is increasingly free from its initial context when uploaded to Facebook, augmenting the scope of any single act of surveillance. This speaks to some of the key features of most contemporary surveillance: where information is gathered in a particular setting and context, is scrutinized elsewhere and the consequences of this scrutiny may occur in yet another context. This in turn is why simplistic notions of privacy, including those relating to privacy settings found on social media sites, are inadequate to contemporary conditions. Context is crucial.

This is an acceleration of the leaks previously considered in information databases (Lyon 2001). The fact that information tied to a particular context may migrate elsewhere is not novel. Leaks are caused by technological error or the deliberate and often malicious intention of a particular operator. Yet social media enclosures privilege the open distribution of personal information through 'sharing' and 'publishing'. As a result, the leak becomes a standard feature for information exchange in social networks.

Facebook is especially susceptible to re-contextualization. Personal information is appraised in a distinct context, typically one that differs from the context in which it was authored. A profile may be treated as a personal – if collaborative – diary. Yet its contents are generally handled as a public broadcast. As Facebook gains prominence as a de facto location for self-representation, information found on user profiles will be assessed in several contexts. These features illustrate an interpretation of the social in social media: these services endeavour to bridge as many social contexts as possible.

Social networks first emerged as a service used exclusively by trusted colleagues. When it was limited to a number of American universities users were under the impression that they were sharing information with their fellow students. As a result Facebook was limited to a climate where university students were relatively comfortable sharing personal information with known peers. Starting in September 2006, their siblings, parents and non-university colleagues began to join the site. While this provoked some discomfort, they were more likely to use their privacy settings rather than remove personal information. As employers, politicians and other institutional representatives joined the site, users had grown accustomed to the degree of authenticity they offered. Facebook is now a hub of social convergence. A student's friend list still contains university colleagues, but they are situated alongside family, friends, co-workers and strangers.

Students author a wealth of information about themselves in a particular context. Many participants report either joining or augmenting their Facebook presence during the first few weeks of school. This activity is tied to a specific agenda: to create a publicized identity, make new friends and socialize in a context linked to recreational drinking and casual romantic encounters. The 'party photo' is a kind of interpersonal currency in this context, yet it is treated as a liability during job applications. In light of these possibilities, researchers should explore the principal trajectories by which information leaks. Conversations and photographs from this context are perceived as potentially leaking into a post-graduate context, whether that involves graduate school, law school or job applications. In a more general sense, respondents describe consistent leaks between personal and professional contexts:

> Obviously at work you have your professional self and at how you have your private self and your private life, but that's the part of you that gets reflected on Facebook. So, whereas before Facebook, there was this definite distinction between walking through the doors of the office and once you're out of there … with Facebook and with the Internet, your private life can follow you around 24/7. (Christina)

Mary offers a scenario where a childcare employee's photos are leaked into the public and the dilemma this presents for parents who are evaluating their professional image:

> And I'm thinking, you put that information on your page, that you happily work at a child care facility A and here you are in a drunken state – and that's not to suggest that I believe that people who work at child care facilities should live cloistered lives and not party and have a great time, but am I left with that one snapshot of this person and is that the person that I want to hand my child over to?

While the above respondent acknowledges that Facebook users have the right to their private lives, she also concedes that she will act on information about this lifestyle if made public. The kinds of leaks that are possible are difficult to anticipate, but it stands to reason that they will threaten interpersonal boundaries that users would prefer to maintain. Hannah, a human rights advisor, offers such a scenario:

> Let's say you're a person of a particular religious background that isn't particularly supportive of intimate relationships before marriage. Right? And somebody sends that out. Imagine how your family in Egypt is going to feel

seeing those kinds of things. I mean, there are huge ways to devastate people in very fast terms by using that technology.

Unlike more tangible kinds of surveillance regimes, it is the indeterminate nature of later scrutiny that evokes some anxiety. Users do anticipate this, but admit to not knowing the outcome, or being fully capable of preventing the exposure. Even if the user adopts some tactics to avoid the worst consequences, it is difficult to anticipate all the outcomes of publishing information. Different populations are engaging with the user's profile, different kinds of institutions are taking an interest in personal information, Facebook introduces new features, and users adopt new practices. Past activity is coupled with future conditions in a way that poses unique challenges for its users.

Returning to Privacy

Taken together, the above findings force a reconsideration of privacy. Privacy is a relevant social concern, a legal right, and a requisite for maintaining one's dignity. Yet there is more at stake when dwelling on social media than simply ensuring privacy. For one thing, the need for privacy can bring about greater surveillance and scrutiny around private spheres (Nock 1993). Maintaining a private space means securing boundaries, and scrutinizing those who enter and leave that sphere. Consider the gated community, or the private message board that requires visitors to identify themselves and make their activity visible while dwelling in that space. In the case of Facebook, we see that users will surveil their peers in order to restrict the worst kinds of exposure in their social life.

Consider the many ways that individuals understand privacy. Though some of these perspectives are more nuanced than others, they all hold conceptual and empirical purchase. Perhaps the most tangible approach to privacy presents it as a private/public binary. Binaries are a tangible and conceptually lightweight method to make sense of the social world. Indeed, we can return to Goffman's front and back stages in order to divide the social world into 'private' and 'public'. For instance, Facebook users readily make distinctions between private regions like their inbox and public regions like an event wall. Likewise, users experience privacy violations when information in a private space leaks to a public one. This distinction is helpful for comparative purposes. But not all private spaces are identical. An initial corrective moves away from absolutes like private and public, and instead situates privacy on a continuum. Users do make these distinctions in a comparative sense: an inbox message on Facebook is private compared to a wall post, but it is still public in the sense that is has been shared with an audience of one or more. Likewise, a photo on an event page may be considered public, but could be subject to further public exposure if it were published in a newspaper.

A further corrective states that a private/public continuum fails to fully address social complexity. Instead, legal scholars like Nissenbaum propose a contextual (2009) understanding of privacy. Users may be comfortable sharing some information with a marriage counsellor, and other information with close friends at a bar. Yet having either information enter the other context would be disastrous. A catchall social network site like Facebook facilitates this risk, as users struggle to find information they are comfortable sharing with friends, co-workers, family and former classmates. Multi-contextual services need to develop privacy settings that are robust enough to maintain contextual boundaries. Perhaps the most important contextual violation right now is the transition from online to offline. We expect a boundary that separates the two, but this is no longer the case. The famous 'on the Internet, nobody knows you're a dog' cartoon published by The New Yorker (Cartoonbank 2011) is indicative of an antiquated understanding of privacy once afforded by the Internet.

While respondents value privacy, they compromise their own because of competing or conflicting values. They may choose to expose private information for the sake of achieving publicity. When Rachel likens her exposure to being featured in a reality show, she suggests that exposure as a general concept can be desirable. Not only is the public exposure of otherwise private information seen as desirable, but it is also a reciprocal activity among peers. Users describe watching others in the same breath as being watched by others, and it can be assumed that one fuels and justifies the other. Users acknowledge that they may regret this visibility later on – if not immediately – but that other desires made this a beneficial or even rational decision. Many Facebook users report compromising their privacy in exchange for interpersonal security. They do not necessarily want their personal information to be public, but they want validation from social ties, and social media exposure is the most tangible way to obtain this. Some users may go public for the sake of feeling secure. As Jess, a first year student, reports:

> By having a Facebook profile – I mean, you're agreeing to have this information posted. Like, all this information available to people. Obviously if you're posting it, you want people to see it. Because why else would you put it up there? ... It's almost like an insecurity thing. And it's kind of like a way of saying, "Oh, look at me. Look at my life. Look at all the friends that I have and look at all of the people that want to talk to me" and I don't know. I guess in that way it made me really self-conscious about Facebook.

Interpersonal security is a positive value that pushes users to compromise their online privacy. In other instances, users feel social pressure from their peers to have a public presence on social media. Among the thirty students interviewed, there was a near-universal consensus that they joined Facebook at the behest of their friends, and now maintain an active presence because of this social pressure.

Privacy is an important and elusive concept, for scholars as well as social media users. Users invoke different kinds of imagery in order to make sense of their experiences and values on social media. These represent either compliance or discomfort with sites like Facebook. Users initially likened their Facebook photo albums to real life photo albums, and described privacy concerns as though strangers were breaking into their homes to browse through their photos. Other users object to this imagery, treating Facebook instead as a whiteboard on a residence door. Here, the profile is public, fundamentally social and meant to be shared. This imagery still links the profile to the individual's integrity, as it is still subject to abuse. Users also draw links between being on Facebook and being outdoors. This suggests that users should have limited expectations of secrecy, but still not be subject to invasive or humiliating encounters.

Academic research often rests on the assumption that users' motivations to harness social media are mediated and tempered by privacy concerns. It assumes that they are deliberately seeking a safe and sheltered space to be sociable. These concerns are valid for some, but the range of contexts and practices on social media suggest that other social values conflict with or compromise users' desires for privacy. Many users are not concerned with privacy when building a presence on social media. Some users will develop an awareness of these concerns if they experience privacy violations. Yet a lot of users will be oblivious to privacy – regardless of how private or public they regard their information. This is often contextualized by users: while university students feel privacy invasions are not an immediate concern, they acknowledge that these will likely be troubling when they move on to the next stage in their lives. Conversely, users who value privacy may lack concern on a per-use basis. This speaks to the risk of ubiquitous, everyday technology. Even vigilant people drop their guards around devices that are as pervasive as they are mundane.

The material above explores how users understand and negotiate with privacy on social media. But it is equally important to consider how these services are designed. The rapid expansion and transformation of sites like Facebook is indicative of how other kinds of digital media develop. First, social media are growing. Not only are they gathering a lot more users, but they also introduce new features that challenge previous understandings of 'what they do' or 'what they are'. These changes suggest that users may be comfortable sharing information at a specific point, but that its growth shatters their expectations. For instance, the 2006 launch of Facebook's news feed was met with heavy protest, but users came to see this kind of exposure as indispensable. On the one hand, this suggests users move from comfort, to shock, to retaliation and a returning comfort with their online presence. While they do occasionally scale back their presence and use more privacy measures, they also grow accustomed to new conditions of visibility. This points to the elasticity of the public's sense of privacy, and what they expect from technology (Rule 2011). Facebook deals in small doses that accumulate into a larger presence. Clancy offers the following:

> People like to have privacy. And, you know, there are secrets within a person that's like … for example … I myself even have secrets that nobody else knows. For example, I don't even tell my parents, I don't tell my friends, but you know, you leak out your secrets in droplets. And if people can collect enough droplets,

they could actually make a picture of what your secret might be. So, you know, you don't want people to know that.

The above quote points to how privacy can be eroded through small increments of disclosure and visibility. A user may have joined Facebook in 2005, and felt comfortable sharing a few dozen photos with a few dozen friends. But content and connections add up over time, spreading to new contexts. This may lead to an eventual shock and resistance against this exposure, but compliance is more likely.

For individual users, controlling their online presence is necessary but not sufficient. Privacy for users is often framed as an individual responsibility. Privacy settings for social media as well as public recommendations by the media and advocacy groups support the assumption that it is the user's responsibly to watch over themselves. Yet control over what is publicly known about them is largely out of their hands. Privacy is not enough to describe interactions on Facebook, but when it is employed, we have to consider interpersonal dynamics that are crucial to its functioning. In particular, the idea of collaborative identity construction explored above underscores how social media interfaces encourage users to speak on behalf of other users. Through wall posts, tags and comments, users routinely disclose information about their peers, exposing those peers to public scrutiny. Concern for the self should extend to a concern for how others are subject to exposure through our actions. Users routinely share data that they do not consider to be personal information, alongside information that they hold very dearly. These are pressing concerns for the study of privacy and social media. Moreover, these concerns are also relevant to other technologies. Facebook is just one kind of social media, and social media are just one venue for personal information. Many new initiatives enable personal data to be collected from new contexts. For this reason initial consent can still lead to protest and outrage by users. The more users are implicated, even when this information does not seem personal, the more we need accountability and mutual transparency.

Recommendations and Directions for Subsequent Research

Facebook's growth makes it a pressing concern for Surveillance Studies. A key tension underlies research on this topic: while managing personal information on social media is largely a user-initiated task, a lot of activity on these sites is beyond the control of users themselves, and may further the increased liquidity of surveillance. Recent scholarship has considered the surveillance consequences of social media. While some (Albrecthslund 2008) highlight the voluntary and empowering potential of managing online visibility, others (Andrejevic 2007, Fuchs 2010) warn that these services augment institutional surveillance while enabling new ways of exploiting everyday sociality. By exploring the key features of information exchange on Facebook, this research offers an understanding of the 'social' in social media based on the increased visibility of its user base. While the consequences that Andrejevic and Fuchs describe are a reality for users, many are aware of these consequences and are adopting tactics to prevent or at least manage the risks associated with living through social media.

Along with these tactics, users need to develop a responsibility that goes beyond the care of virtual self, in order to consider the care of virtual other. In practice, users are already watching over others, especially friends, family and associates. But this scrutiny needs to be infused with a consideration of how one's own activity reflects on those peers, as opposed to treating those peers as mere liabilities. The concern that users have about the content others post on their profile should be mirrored by a consideration of how their own contributions to another's presence reflects on that person. This recommendation is heavily based on this research, which focused primarily on Facebook. Yet a care for the virtual other extends beyond a single venue. Even if Facebook's prominence declines, it will be replaced by a similar platform. An individualistic care of the self needs to be augmented with a more holistic concern with one's social network.

Policies should be built on the premise that users have an extensive presence on social media. Although we perceive them to be single-purpose services, sites like Facebook are more like dwellings that encompass so many social contexts, and such a broad cross-section of our social lives. This social convergence brings some convenience and benefits to users, but it also raises a lot of immediate and long-term concerns. Even users who claim to be comfortable living in public value secrecy and autonomy. They take for granted the right to not be accountable for their personal lives, and to control how they are represented in public. Institutional policies and privacy laws should endeavour to uphold these expectations. Given the lasting social consequences of social media content, policies should support the right of users to manage, manipulate, and even delete (Mayer-Schönberger 2010) their digital presence.

Surveillance Studies research on sites like Facebook needs to consider the rapid mainstreaming of social networking services, particularly the exponential rise in membership and institutional involvement. The way it is perceived and utilized by businesses and other non-user actors is an underdeveloped field. As well, a nuanced understanding of ownership ought to balance perspectives that treat social networking services as either the users' or designers' exclusive domain. While users have invested time, energy and personal details into the collective act of 'Facebooking', they maintain a tenuous grasp over the future of the service. All of this will shed light on the new politics and dynamics of information exchange through social networks. Changes to the interface, coupled with emerging practices, complicate users' attempts to manage their online presence, although they are developing new tactics in response to these challenges. Despite this apparent growth, a director of campus security comments on how social media are still at an early formative stage of their development, claiming that 'it's like a toddler. It's not a newborn anymore, it's a toddler, it still needs some direction, some guidance' (Daryl). How such direction, such guidance, will emerge, and where from, remains to be seen. It is unlikely that those charged with responsibilities for campus security will be able to offer such tutelage for 'toddlers' without extensive collaboration with a number of other stakeholders. But this is an area beyond the scope of this research.

To conclude: this book considers social media surveillance as several distinct practices. By looking at how these practices share the same interface, this research locates the mutual augmentation of interpersonal, institutional and market scrutiny. Converging technologies, but also collaborative identity construction and vast social data, are driving forces for contemporary social sorting. This research contributes to sociological knowledge by looking at the continued domestication of surveillance technology. Of vital importance is its focus on the effects of everyday visibility and self-presentation. This will pose significant challenges to Surveillance Studies and related fields, as this technology is not only evolving, but is also being shaped through new approaches by individual, institutional and market users. This will also be an issue for policy and legal sectors, as issues of privacy and liability have to be reconsidered in light of these developments. Finally, through everyday practice users need to convey their priorities in terms managing their identity as well as the composition of their social network.

This research is limited to one particular social media and illustrates from a user perspective some of the novel dimensions and directions of today's liquid surveillance. Although Facebook's sharply growing population and emerging features justify this focus, subsequent research will expand this scope by contributing empirical findings from other platforms. Future research should also consider the increasingly taken-for-granted presence of social media, as this growth affects boundaries between social spheres. While the above focuses on peer-to-peer, institutional and commercial surveillance, it overlooks policing and national intelligence uses of social media. These are important studies in their own right, and are likely already being pursued by scholars. The growth of Surveillance Studies requires increased specialization, especially in the field of emerging 'social' technologies. While scholars scarcely understand the full consequences and potential of these technologies, they are rapidly accumulating a significant user population. As sites like Facebook become a mainstay in everyday life, indefinite retention becomes the de facto outcome for personal information, which has clear implications for surveillance research.

References

Abram, C. 2007. The changes are here … *The Facebook Blog* [Online, 11 April]. Available at: http://blog.facebook.com/blog.php?post=2327282130 [accessed: 17 February 2012].

Adetunji, J. 2009. Photographers fear they are target of new terror law. *The Guardian* [Online, 12 February]. Available at: http://www.guardian.co.uk/media/2009/feb/12/photographers-anti-terror-laws [accessed: 17 February 2012].

Agarwal, S. and Mital, M. 2009. Focus on business practices: An exploratory study of Indian university students' use of social networking web sites: Implications for the workplace. *Business Communication Quarterly*, 72(1), 105–110.

Albrechtslund, A. 2008. Online social networking as participatory surveillance. *First Monday* [Online], 13(3). Available at: http://firstmonday.org/htbin/cgiwrap/bin/ojs/index.php/fm/article/view/2142/1949/ [accessed: 17 February 2012].

Allen, N. 2010. Facebook privacy concerns overblown, suggests Mark Zuckerberg. *The Telegraph* [Online, 14 September]. Available at: http://www.telegraph.co.uk/technology/facebook/8001318/Facebook-privacy-concerns-overblown-suggests-Mark-Zuckerberg.html [accessed: 17 February 2012].

Andrejevic, M. 2003. Monitored mobility in the era of mass customization. *Space and Culture*, 6(2), 132–150.

Andrejevic, M. 2005. The work of watching one another: Lateral surveillance, risk, and governance. *Surveillance & Society*, 2(4), 479–497.

Andrejevic, M. 2007. *iSpy: Surveillance and Power in the Interactive Era*. Lawrence, KS: University Press of Kansas.

Andrejevic, M. 2009. Privacy, exploitation, and the digital enclosure. *Amsterdam Law Forum*, 1(4), 47–62.

Ball, K. 2002. Elements of surveillance: A new framework and future directions. *Information, Communication & Society*, 5(4), 573–590.

Barnes, S. 2006. A privacy paradox: Social networking in the United States. *First Monday* [Online], 11(9). Available at: http://firstmonday.org/htbin/cgiwrap/bin/ojs/index.php/fm/article/view/1394/1312 [accessed: 17 February 2012].

Barney, D. 2004. *The Network Society*. Cambridge: Polity.

Baudrillard, J. 1995. The virtual illusion: Or the automatic writing of the world. *Theory, Culture and Society*, 12(4), 97–107.

Beer, D. 2009a. Power through the algorithm? Participatory web cultures and the technological unconscious. *New Media & Society*, 11(6), 985–1002.

Beer, D. 2009b. Can you dig it? Some reflections on the sociological problems associated with being uncool. *Sociology*, 43(6), 1151–1162.

Beer, D. and Burrows, R. 2007. Sociology and, of and in Web 2.0: Some initial considerations. *Sociological Research Online* [Online], 12(5). Available at: http://www.socresonline.org.uk/12/5/17.html [accessed: 17 February 2012].

Bennett, C. 2008. *The Privacy Advocates: Resisting the Spread of Surveillance.* Cambridge, MA: MIT Press.

Black, D. 1995. The epistemology of pure sociology. *Law and Social Inquiry*, 20(4), 829–870.

Bloss, W. 2007. Escalating U.S. police surveillance after 9/11: An examination of causes and effects. *Surveillance & Society*, 4(3), 208–228.

Boase, J., Horrigan, J., Wellman, B. and Rainie, L. 2006. The strength of Internet ties: The Internet and email aid users in maintaining their social networks and provide pathways to help when people face big decisions. *Pew Internet & American Life Project* [Online]. Available at: http://www.pewInternet.org/Reports/2006/The-Strength-of-Internet-Ties.aspx [accessed: 17 February 2012].

Bogard, W. 1996. *The Simulation of Surveillance: Hypercontrol in Telematic Societies.* Cambridge: Cambridge University Press.

Boltanski, L. and Chiapello, È. 2005. *The New Spirit of Capitalism.* New York: Verso.

Boon, S. and Sinclair, C. 2009. A world I don't inhabit: Disquiet and identity on Second Life and Facebook. *Education Media International*, 46(2), 99–110.

Borsook, P. 2002. Cyberselfishness explained, in *Uncanny Networks: Dialogues with the Virtual Intelligentsia*, edited by G. Lovink. Cambridge, MA: MIT Press, 336–347.

Bowker, G., and Star, S.L. 1999. *Sorting Things Out: Classification and its Consequences.* Cambridge, MA: MIT Press.

boyd, d. 2006. Friends, Friendsters, and MySpace top 8: Writing community into being on social network sites. *First Monday* [Online], 11(12). Available at: http://firstmonday.org/htbin/cgiwrap/bin/ojs/index.php/fm/article/view/1418/1336 [accessed: 17 February 2012].

boyd, d. 2007. Why youth (heart) social network sites: The role of networked publics in teenage social life, in *MacArthur Foundation Series on Digital Learning – Youth, Identity, and Digital Media*, edited by D. Buckingham. Cambridge, MA: MIT Press, 119–142.

boyd, d. 2008. Facebook's privacy trainwreck: Exposure, invasion, and social convergence. *Convergence: The International Journal of Research into New Media Technologies*, 14(1), 13–20.

boyd, d. and Hargittai, E. 2010. Facebook privacy settings: Who cares? *First Monday* [Online], 15(8). Available at: http://firstmonday.org/htbin/cgiwrap/bin/ojs/index.php/fm/article/view/3086/2589 [accessed: 17 February 2012].

boyd, d. and Heer, J. 2006. *Profiles as conversation: Networked identity performance on Friendster.* Paper to the Proceedings of the Hawai'i International Conference on System Sciences (HICSS-39), Persistent Conversation Track, Kauai, HI, 4–7 January.

Boyne, R. 2000. Post-panopticism. *Economy and Society*, 29(2), 285–307.

Brighenti, A.M. 2010. *Visibility in Social Theory and Social Research*. Hampshire: Palgrave Macmillan.

Burrows, R. 2009. Afterword: Urban informatics and social ontology, in *Handbook of Research on Urban Informatics: The Practice and Promise of the Real-Time City*, edited by M. Foth. Hershey: Information Science Reference IGI, 450–454.

Burrows, R. and Gane, N. 2006. Geo-demographics, software and class. *Sociology*, 40(5), 793–812.

Butler, D. 2010. Facebook helps store owner track thief: Security video checked against business's 'friends.' *Calgary Herald* [Online, 31 October]. Available at: http://www2.canada.com/calgaryherald/news/story.html?id=a5cce40d-fff5-4915-90d6-a6cc24ea784c [accessed: 17 February 2012].

Cartoonbank. 2011. *On the Internet, Nobody Knows You're a Dog* [Online]. Available at: http://www.cartoonbank.com/invt/106197 [accessed: 17 February 2012].

Castells, M. 1996. *The Rise of the Network Society*. Oxford: Blackwell.

CBC. 2008. Facebook phenomenon latest legal obstacle, say critics. CBC [Online, 4 January]. Available at: http://www.cbc.ca/news/canada/toronto/story/2008/01/04/rengel-facebook.html [accessed: 17 February 2012].

CBC. 2009. Depressed woman loses benefits over Facebook photos. *CBC* [Online, 21 November]. Available at: http://www.cbc.ca/news/canada/montreal/story/2009/11/19/quebec-facebook-sick-leave-benefits.html [accessed: 17 February 2012].

CBC. 2011. B.C. authorities discuss Vancouver riot charges: Family moves out to avoid vigilante threats. *CBC* [Online, 20 June]. Available at: http://www.cbc.ca/news/canada/british-columbia/story/2011/06/20/bbc-riot-prosecutions-monday.html [accessed: 17 February 2012].

Cheng, J. 2010. Govt relies on Facebook 'narcissism' to spot fake marriages, fraud. *Ars Technica* [Online, October]. Available at: http://arstechnica.com/tech-policy/news/2010/10/govt-takes-advantage-of-facebook-narcissism-to-check-on-users.ars [accessed: 17 February 2012].

Cohen, N. 2008. The valorization of surveillance: Towards a political economy of Facebook. *Democratic Communiqué*, 22(1), 5–22.

Cote, M. and Pybus, J. 2007. Learning to immaterial labour 2.0: MySpace and social networks. *Ephemera*, 7(1), 88–106.

CstAnderson. 2011. *Cst. Anderson* [Online]. Available at: http://twitter.com/CstAnderson [accessed: 17 February 2012].

CstKube. 2011. *Cst. Adam Kube* [Online]. Available at: http://twitter.com/CstKube [accessed: 17 February 2012].

Dandeker, C. 1990. *Surveillance, Power and Modernity*. Cambridge: Polity.

Davenport, T. and Beck, J. 2001. *The Attention Economy: Understanding the New Currency of Business*. Boston: Harvard Business School Press.

de Certeau, M. 1988. *The Practice of Everyday Life*. Berkeley: University of California Press.

Deleuze, G. 1995. *Negotiations, 1972–1990*. New York: Columbia University Press.

Dodd, V. 2009. Facebook murderer jailed for 22 years. *The Guardian* [Online, 9 March]. Available at: http://www.guardian.co.uk/uk/2010/mar/09/facebook-murderer-jailed-paul-bristol [accessed: 17 February 2012].

Dyer-Witherford, N. 1999. *Cyber-Marx: Cycles and Circuits of Struggle in High-Technology Capitalism*. Urbana and Chicago: University of Illinois Press.

EFF. 2011. Social Networks. *Electronic Frontier Foundation* [Online]. Available at: https://www.eff.org/issues/social-networks [accessed: 17 February 2012].

Ellison, N., Lampe, C., Steinfield, C. and Vitak, J. 2010. With a little help from my friends: Social network sites and social capital, in *A Networked Self: Identity, Community and Culture on Social Network Sites*, edited by Z. Papacharissi. New York: Routledge, 124–145.

Ellison, N., Steinfield, C. and Lampe, C. 2006. The benefits of Facebook 'friends': Social capital and college students' use of online social network sites. *Journal of Computer-Mediated Communication* [Online], 12(3). Available at: http://jcmc.indiana.edu/vol12/issue4/ellison.html [accessed: 17 February 2012].

Elmer, G. 2004. *Profiling Machines: Mapping the Personal Information Economy*. Cambridge, MA: MIT Press.

Emsley, C. 2007. *Crime, Police, and Penal Policy: European Experiences 1750–1940*. Oxford: Oxford University Press.

EPIC. 2011. In re Facebook and the facial identification of users. *Electronic Privacy Information Center* [Online]. Available at: http://epic.org/privacy/facebook/facebook_and_facial_recognitio.html [accessed: 17 February 2012].

EPS. 2011. *Edmonton Police Service* [Online]. Available at: http://www.edmontonpolice.ca/ [accessed: 17 February 2012].

EPSFacebook. 2011. *Edmonton Police Service* [Online]. Available at: https://www.facebook.com/edmontonpoliceservice [accessed: 17 February 2012].

EPSTwitter. 2011. *Edmonton Police* [Online]. Available at: http://twitter.com/edmontonpolice [accessed: 17 February 2012].

EPSYouTube. 2011. *Edmonton Police Service Video Service Online* [Online]. Available at: http://www.youtube.com/epsvideoonline [accessed: 17 February 2012].

Ericson, R.V. 1989. Patrolling the facts: Secrecy and publicity in police work. *The British Journal of Sociology*, 40(2), 205–226.

Ericson, R.V. and Haggerty, K.D. 1997. *Policing the Risk Society*. Toronto: University of Toronto Press.

FB About. 2011. *About Facebook* [Online]. Available at: http://www.facebook.com/facebook?sk=info [accessed: 17 February 2012].

FB Amber. 2011. *AMBER Alert* [Online]. Available at: https://www.facebook.com/AMBERalert [accessed: 17 February 2012].

FB Statistics. 2011. *Statistics* [Online]. Available at: http://www.facebook.com/press/info.php?statistics [accessed: 17 February 2012].

Ferdig, R., Dawson, K., Black, E. et al. 2008. Medical students and residents use of online social networking tools: Implications for teaching professionalism in medical education. *First Monday* [Online], 13(9). Available at: http://www.uic.edu/htbin/cgiwrap/bin/ojs/index.php/fm/article/view/2161/2026 [accessed: 17 February 2012].

Fogel, J. and Nehmad, E. 2008. Internet social network communities: Risk taking, trust, and privacy concerns. *Computers in Human Behavior*, 25(1), 153–160.

Foucault, M. 1977. *Discipline and Punish: The Birth of the Prison*. New York: Vintage Books.

Foucault, M. 1980. *The History of Sexuality*. New York: Vintage Books.

Friedmann, R. 1992. *Community Policing: Comparative Perspectives and Prospects*. New York: Palgrave Macmillan.

Fuchs, C. 2010. Class, knowledge and new media. *Media, Culture & Society*, 32(1), 141–150.

Furlong, J. and Keefe, D.J. 2011. *The Night the City Became a Stadium: Independent Review of the 2011 Vancouver Stanley Cup Playoff*. Government of British Columbia.

Gallager, R. and Syal, R. 2011. Police buy software to map suspects' digital movements: Geotime software, bought by the Met, collates data from social networking sites, satnavs, mobiles and financial transactions. *The Guardian* [Online, 11 May]. Available at: http://www.guardian.co.uk/uk/2011/may/11/police-software-maps-digital-movements [accessed: 17 February 2012].

Galloway, A. and Thacker, E. 2007. *The Exploit: A Theory of Networks*. Minneapolis: University of Minnesota Press.

Gandy, O. 1993. *The Panoptic Sort: A Political Economy of Personal Information*. Boulder: Westview.

Gandy, O. 2009. *Coming to Terms with Chance: Engaging Rational Discrimination and Cumulative Disadvantage*. Farnham: Ashgate.

Gane, N., Venn, C. and Hand, M. 2007. Ubiquitous surveillance: Interview with Katherine Hayles. *Theory, Culture & Society*, 24(7–8), 349–358.

Gates, B. 2006. *The Unified Communications Revolution* [Online]. Available at: http://www.microsoft.com/mscorp/execmail/2006/06-26unifiedcomm.mspx [accessed: 17 February 2012].

Geist, M. 2011. Public debate on lawful access misses real concerns. *MichaelGeist.ca* [Online, 26 September]. Available at: http://www.michaelgeist.ca/content/view/6037/159/ [accessed: 17 February 2012].

Giddens, A. 1994. Replies and critiques: Risk, trust, reflexivity, in *Reflexive Modernization: Politics, Tradition and Aesthetics in the Modern Social Order*, edited by U. Beck et al. Cambridge: Polity, 184–197.

Glanz, J and Markoff, J. 2011. Egypt leaders found 'off' switch for Internet. *New York Times* [Online, 15 February]. Available at: http://www.nytimes.com/2011/02/16/technology/16Internet.html [accessed: 17 February 2012].

Goffman, A. 2009. On the run: Wanted men in a Philadelphia ghetto. *American Sociological Review*, 74(3), 339–357.

Goffman, E. 1959. *The Presentation of Self in Everyday Life*. New York: Anchor Books.

Goffman, E. 1963. *Stigma: Notes on the Management of Spoiled Identity.* New York: Simon & Schuster.

Goldsmith, A.J. 2010. Policing's new visibility. *British Journal of Criminology*, 50(5), 914–934.

Google. 2001. *Google Acquires Usenet Discussion Service and Significant Assets from Deja.com* [Online]. Available at: http://www.google.com/press/pressrel/pressrelease48.html [accessed: 17 February 2012].

Graham, S. 2004. Beyond the 'dazzling light': From dreams of transcendence to the 'remediation' of urban life: A research manifesto. *New Media & Society*, 6(1), 16–25.

Graham, S. and Marvin, S. 2001. *Splintering Urbanism: Networked Infrastructures, Technological Mobilities.* New York: Routledge.

Grannovetter, M. 1974. *Getting a Job: A Study of Contacts and Careers.* Cambridge, MA: Harvard University Press.

Greenfield, A. 2006. *Everyware: The Dawning Age of Ubiquitous Computing.* Berkeley: New Riders.

Grimmelmann, J. 2009. Saving Facebook. *Iowa Law Review*, 94(4), 1137–1206.

Grint, K. and Woolgar, S. 1997. *The Machine at Work: Technology, Work and Organization.* Cambridge: Polity.

Gueorguieva, V. 2008. Voters, MySpace, and YouTube: The impact of alternative communication channels on the 2006 election cycle and beyond. *Social Science Computer Review*, 26(3), 288–300.

Hacking, I. 2002. *Historical Ontology.* Cambridge, MA: Harvard University Press.

Haggerty, K.D. and Ericson, R.V. 2000. The surveillant assemblage. *British Journal of Sociology*, 51, 605–622.

Hardey, M. 2008. The formation of social rules for digital interactions. *Information, Communication & Society*, 11(8), 1111–1131.

Harvey, D. 1990. *The Condition of Postmodernity: An Enquiry into the Origins of Cultural Change.* Malden, MA: Blackwell.

Hearn, A. 2008. 'Meat, mask, burden': Probing the contours of the branded 'self'. *Journal of Consumer Culture*, 8(2), 197–217.

Henley, J. 2010. Facebook fugitive: the story so far. *The Guardian* [Online, 6 January]. Available at: http://www.guardian.co.uk/uk/2010/jan/06/craig-lynch-facebook [accessed: 17 February 2012].

Hewitt, A. and Forte, A. 2006. *Crossing Boundaries: Identity Management and Student/Faculty Relationships on the Facebook.* A paper presented at Computer Supported Cooperative Work 2006, Banff, 4–8 November.

Hier, S.P., Greenberg, J., Walby, K. and Lett, D. 2007. Media, communication, and the establishment of public camera surveillance programs in Canada. *Media, Culture and Society*, 29(5), 727–751.

Hill, A. 2005. *Reality TV: Audiences and Popular Factual Television.* New York: Routledge.

Hogan, B. 2008. Analyzing social networks via the Internet, in *The Handbook of Online Research Methods*, edited by N. Fielding et al. Thousand Oaks: Sage, 141–160.

Hopkins, C. 2011. Amber alerts come to Facebook. *ReadWriteWeb* [Online, 14 January]. Available at: http://www.readwriteweb.com/archives/amber_alerts_come_to_facebook.php [accessed: 17 February 2012].

Jagger, E. 2005. Is thirty the new sixty? Dating, age and gender in a postmodern, consumer society. *Sociology*, 39(1), 86–106.

Jenkins, H. 2006. *Convergence Culture: Where Old and New Media Collide.* New York: New York University Press.

Jernigan, C. and Mistree, B. 2009. Gaydar: Facebook friendships expose sexual orientation. *First Monday* [Online], 14(10). Available at: http://firstmonday.org/htbin/cgiwrap/bin/ojs/index.php/fm/article/view/2611/2302 [accessed: 17 February 2012].

Keen, A. 2007. *The Cult of the Amateur: How Today's Internet is Killing our Culture.* New York: Doubleday.

Kelemen, M. and Smith, W. 2001. Community and its 'virtual' promises: A critique of cyberlibertarian rhetoric. *Information, Communication & Society*, 4(3), 370–387.

Kerr, I. and Gilbert, D. 2004. The role of ISPs in the investigation of cybercrime, in *Information Ethics in the Electronic Age*, edited by T. Mendina and J.J. Britz. Jefferson: McFarland & Company, 163–172.

Kerrigan, S. 2011. US gov. software creates 'fake people' on social networks. *Examiner.com* [Online, February 18]. Available at: http://www.examiner.com/social-media-in-national/us-gov-software-creates-fake-people-on-social-networks-to-promote-propaganda [accessed: 17 February 2012].

Kim, K.-H. and Yun, H. 2007. Cying for me, Cying for us: Relational dialectics in a Korean social network site. *Journal of Compuer-Mediated Communication* [Online], 13(1). Available at: http://jcmc.indiana.edu/vol13/issue1/kim.yun.html [accessed: 17 February 2012].

Kirkpatrick, M. 2010. Facebook's Zuckerberg says the age of privacy is over. *ReadWriteWeb* [Online, 9 January]. Available at: http://www.readwriteweb.com/archives/facebooks_zuckerberg_says_the_age_of_privacy_is_ov.php [accessed: 17 February 2012].

Kittler, F. 1996. Technologies of writing/rewriting technology. *New Literary History*, 27(4), 731–742.

Knorr Cetina, K. 1997. Sociality with objects: Social relations in postsocial knowledge societies. *Theory, Culture & Society,* 14(4), 1–30.

Koskela, H. 2006. 'The other side of surveillance': Webcams, power and agency, in *Theorizing Surveillance: The Panopticon and Beyond*, edited by D. Lyon. Collumption: Willan Publishing, 163–181.

Lash, S. 2002. *Critique of Information.* London: Sage Publications.

Lash, S. 2007a. New new media ontology. Presentation at *Toward a Social Science of Web 2.0*, National Science Learning Centre, York, UK, 5 September.

Lash, S. 2007b. Power after hegemony: Cultural studies in mutation. *Theory, Culture & Society*, 24(3), 55–78.

Lash, S. and Lury, C. 2005. *Global Culture Industry: The Mediation of Things*. Cambridge: Polity.

Latour, B. 1999. *Pandora's Hope: Essays on the Reality of Science Studies*. Cambridge, MA: Harvard University Press.

Lazzarato, M. 2004. *Les Révolutions du Capitalisme*. Editions les Empêcheurs de Penser en Rond.

Lessig, L. 2006. *Code: Version 2.0*. Unpublished [Online]. Available at: http://codev2.cc/download+remix/ [accessed: 17 February 2012].

Lewis, K., Kaufman, J., Gonzalez, M. et al. 2008. Tastes, ties, and time: A new social network dataset using Facebook.com. *Social Networks*, 30(4), 330–342.

Li, C. and Bernoff, J. 2008. *Groundswell: Winning in a World Transformed by Social Technologies*. Boston: Harvard Business Press.

Ling, R. 2004. *The Mobile Connection: The Cell Phone's Impact on Society*. San Francisco: Morgan Kaufmann Publishers.

Liu, H. and Maes, P. 2005. *InterestMap: Harvesting Social Network Profiles for Recommendations*. Paper for the Proceedings of *IUI Beyond Personalization 2005: A Workshop on the Next Stage of Recommender Systems Research*, San Diego, 9 January, 54–59.

Lury, C. 2004. *Brands: The Logos of the Global Economy*. New York: Routledge.

Lynch, J. 2010. Applying for citizenship? U.S. citizenship and immigration wants to be your 'friend.' *Electronic Frontier Foundation* [Online, 12 October]. Available at: https://www.eff.org/deeplinks/2010/10/applying-citizenship-u-s-citizenship-and [accessed: 17 February 2012].

Lynch, J. 2011. Social Media and Law Enforcement: Who Gets What Data and When? *Electronic Frontier Foundation* [Online, 20 January]. Available at: https://www.eff.org/deeplinks/2011/01/social-media-and-law-enforcement-who-gets-what [accessed: 17 February 2012].

Lyon, D. 1994. *Postmodernity*. Minneapolis: University of Minnesota Press.

Lyon, D. 2001. *Surveillance Society: Monitoring Everyday Life*. Buckingham: Open University Press.

Lyon, D. 2002. Surveillance in cyberspace: The Internet, personal data and social control. *Queen's Quarterly*, 109(3), 135–149.

Lyon, D. 2007. *Surveillance Studies: An Overview*. Cambridge: Polity.

Lyon, D. 2009. *Identifying Citizens: ID Cards as Surveillance*. Cambridge: Polity.

Lyon, D. 2010. Liquid surveillance: The contribution of Zygmunt Bauman to surveillance studies. *International Political Sociology*, 4(4), 325–338.

Mann, S., Nolan, J. and Wellman, B. 2003. Sousveillance: Inventing and using wearable computing devices for data collection in surveillance environments. *Surveillance & Society*, 1(3), 331–355.

Manovich, L. 2001. *The Language of New Media*. Cambridge, MA: MIT Press.

Manovich, L. 2008. *Software Takes Command.* Unpublished [Online]. Available at: http://lab.softwarestudies.com/2008/11/softbook.html [accessed: 17 February 2012].

Marx, G. 1984. Routinizing the discovery of secrets: Computers as informants. *American Behavioral Scientist*, 27(4), 423–452.

Marx, G. 1988. *Undercover: Police Surveillance in America.* Berkeley: University of California Press.

Mayer-Schönberger, V. 2010. *Delete: The Virtue of Forgetting in the Digital Age.* Princeton: Princeton University Press.

Mazer, J., Murphy, R. and Simonds, C. 2007. I'll see you On 'Facebook': The effects of computer-mediated teacher self-disclosure on student motivation, affective learning, and classroom climate. *Communication Education*, 56(1), 1–17.

McGonigal, J. 2008. *Engagement Economy: The Future of Massively Scaled Collaboration and Participation.* Institute for the Future [Online]. Available at: http://www.iftf.org/node/2306 [accessed: 17 February 2012].

McLean, J. 2010. Does Facebook break the law? *Toronto Star* [Online, 11 January]. Available at: http://www.thestar.com/news/ontario/oshawa/article/748973--does-facebook-page-break-the-law [accessed: 17 February 2012].

Millan, L. 2011. Insurers and social media: Insurers' use of social networks impinges on privacy rights. *The Lawyers Weekly* [Online, 25 March]. Available at: http://www.lawyersweekly.ca/index.php?section=article&volume=30&number=43&article=2 [accessed: 17 February 2012].

Miller, D. 2011. *Tales from Facebook.* Cambridge: Polity.

Miller, D. and Slater, D. 2000. *The Internet: An Ethnographic Approach.* Oxford: Berg.

Miller, V. 2008. New media, networking and phatic culture. *Convergence: The International Journal of Research into New Media Technologies*, 14(4), 387–400.

Mitchell, J. 2011. Making Photo Tagging Easier. *The Facebook Blog* [Online, 30 June]. Available at: https://blog.facebook.com/blog.php?post=467145887130 [accessed: 17 February 2012].

Monahan, T. and Torres, R. 2010. *Schools Under Surveillance: Cultures of Control in Public Education.* Piscataway, NJ: Rutgers University Press.

Moreno, M., Fost, N. and Christakis, D. 2008. Research ethics in the MySpace era. *Pediatrics*, 121(1), 157–161.

Mosco, V. 2004. *The Digital Sublime: Myth, Power and Cyberspace.* Cambridge, MA: MIT Press.

Mosco, V. 2009. *The Political Economy of Communication.* London: Sage Publications.

Murakami Wood, D. and Webster, C.W.R. (2009). Living in surveillance societies: The normalisation of surveillance in Europe and the threat of Britain's bad example. *Journal of Contemporary European Research*, 5(2), 259–273.

Natapoff, A. 2009. *Snitching: Criminal Informants and the Erosion of American Justice.* New York: New York University Press.

Nelson, L. 2011. *America Identified: Biometric Technology and Society.* Cambridge, MA: MIT Press.

Nippert-Eng, C. 2010. *Islands of Privacy.* Chicago: University of Chicago Press.

Nissenbaum, H. 2009. *Privacy in Context: Technology, Policy, and the Integrity of Social Life.* Palo Alto: Stanford University Press.

Nock, S. 1993. *The Costs of Privacy: Reputation and Surveillance in America.* New York: Aldine de Gruyter.

Norris, C. and Armstrong, G. 1999. *The Maximum Surveillance Society: The Rise of CCTV.* New York: Berg Publishers.

Nunn, S. 2010. 'Wanna still nine-hard?': Exploring mechanisms of bias in the translation and interpretation of wiretap conversations. *Surveillance & Society*, 8(1), 28–42.

Nye, D. 2006. *Technology Matters: Questions to Live With.* Cambridge, MA: MIT Press.

O'Reilly, T. 2005. What is Web 2.0: Design patterns and business models for the next generation of software. *O'Reilly.com* [Online, 30 September]. Available at: http://www.oreilly.com/pub/a/oreilly/tim/news/2005/09/30/what-is-web-20.html?page=1 [accessed: 17 February 2012].

Oreskovic, A. 2010. Facebook IPO likely after late 2012 – board member. *Reuters* [Online, 27 September]. Available at: http://www.reuters.com/article/idUSN2717146120100927 [accessed: 17 February 2012].

Papacharissi, Z. 2009. The virtual geographies of social networks: A comparative analysis of Facebook, LinkedIn and ASmallWorld. *New Media & Society*, 11(1–2), 199–220.

Pearson, E. 2009. All the World Wide Web's a stage: The performance of identity in online social networks. *First Monday* [Online], 14(3). Available at: http://journals.uic.edu/fm/article/view/2162/2127 [accessed: 17 February 2012].

Popken, B. 2011. Facebook is number one tool for divorce lawyers. *The Consumerist* [Online, 18 May]. Available at: http://consumerist.com/2011/05/facebook-is-number-one-tool-for-divorce-lawyers.html [accessed: 17 February 2012].

Poster, M. 1990. *The Mode of Information: Post-structuralism and Social Contexts.* Chicago: University of Chicago Press.

Poster, M. 2004. Consumption and digital commodities in the everyday. *Cultural Studies*, 18(2), 409–423.

Putnam, Robert. 2001. *Bowling Alone: The Collapse and Revival of American Community.* New York: Simon & Schuster.

Rees, J. (ed.) 2011. *Reading the Riots: Investigating England's Summer of Disorder* [Online]. Available at: http://www.guardian.co.uk/uk/interactive/2011/dec/14/reading-the-riots-investigating-england-s-summer-of-disorder-full-report [accessed: 17 February 2012].

Rheingold, H. 2000. *The Virtual Community: Homesteading on the Electronic Frontier.* Cambridge, MA: MIT Press.

Rieti, J. 2011. Vancouver riot photos spark identity probe: Police launch process of gathering thousands of images to nab vandals, thieves, arsonists. *CBC* [Online, 17 June]. Available at: http://www.cbc.ca/news/canada/british-columbia/story/2011/06/17/f-photos-vancouver-identity-investigation.html [accessed: 17 February 2012].

Robinson, L. 2007. The cyber-self: The self-ing project goes online, symbolic interaction in the digital age. *New Media and Society*, 9(1), 93–110.

Roper, M.F. 2010. The bosses who snoop on Facebook. *The Guardian* [Online, 24 March]. http://www.guardian.co.uk/commentisfree/2010/mar/24/bosses-snoop-facebook-twitter-blogs [accessed: 17 February 2012].

Roychoudhuri, O. 2007. Your privacy is someone else's profit. *AlterNet* [Online, 29 October]. Available at: http://www.alternet.org/module/printversion/66090 [accessed: 17 February 2012].

Rule, J. 2012. 'Needs' for surveillance and the movement to protect privacy, in *Routledge Handbook of Surveillance Studies*, edited by K. Ball et al. New York: Routledge (forthcoming).

Sanchez, A. 2009. The Facebook feeding frenzy: Resistance-through-distance and resistance-through-persistence in the societied network. *Surveillance & Society*, 6(3), 275–293.

Sassen, S. 2002. Bandwidth and accountability, in *Uncanny Networks: Dialogues with the Virtual Intelligentsia*, edited by G. Lovink. Cambridge, MA: MIT Press, 102–111.

Savage, M. and Burrows, R. 2007. The coming crisis of empirical sociology. *Sociology*, 41(5), 885–899.

Scott, J. 1998. *Seeing Like a State: How Certain Schemes to Improve the Human Condition Have Failed.* New Haven: Yale University Press.

Sessions, L. 2009. 'You looked better on MySpace': Deception and authenticity on Web 2.0. *First Monday* [Online], 14(7). Available at: http://firstmonday.org/htbin/cgiwrap/bin/ojs/index.php/fm/article/view/2539/2242 [accessed: 17 February 2012].

Shirky, C. 2008. *Here Comes Everybody: The Power of Organizing Without Organizations.* New York: The Penguin Press.

Shirky, C. 2010. *Cognitive Surplus: How Technology Makes Consumers into Collaborators.* New York: The Penguin Press.

Silverman, M. 2011. Top 10 Twitter trends this week [CHART]. *Mashable* [Online, 2 July]. Available at: http://mashable.com/2011/07/02/top-10-twitter-trends-this-week-chart-10/ [accessed: 17 February 2012].

Silverstone, R. and Haddon, L. 1996. Design and the domestication of information and communication technologies: Technical change and everyday life, in *Communication by Design: The Politics of Information and Communication Technologies*, edited by R. Silverstone and R. Mansell. Oxford: Oxford University Press, 44–74.

Simmel, G. 1955. *Conflict and the Web of Group Affiliations.* Glencoe: Free Press.

Singel, R. 2011. FBI pushes for surveillance backdoors in web 2.0 tools. *Wired* [Online, 17 February]. Available at: http://www.wired.com/epicenter/2011/02/fbi-backdoors/ [accessed: 17 February 2012].

Slee, M. 2008. Profile changes are coming soon. *The Facebook Blog* [Online, 21 May]. Available at: http://blog.facebook.com/blog.php?post=17573547130 [accessed: 17 February 2012].

Smith, G. 2007. Exploring relations between watchers and watched in control(led) systems: Strategies and tactics. *Surveillance & Society*, 4(4), 280–313.

Smythe, D.W. 1977. Communications: Blindspot of Western Marxism. *Canadian Journal of Political and Society Theory*, 1(3), 1–28.

Snyder, B. 2011. Facebook facial recognition: Why it's a threat to privacy. *PCWorld* [Online, 21 June]. Available at: http://www.pcworld.com/article/230790/facebook_facial_recognition_why_its_a_threat_to_privacy.html [accessed: 17 February 2012].

Social Media Report Draft. 2009. University withheld.

Stalder, F. 2006. *Manuel Castells: The Theory of the Network Society*. Cambridge: Polity.

Steeves, V. 2008. If the Supreme Court were on Facebook: Evaluating the reasonable expectation of privacy test from a social perspective. *Canadian Journal of Criminology and Criminal Justice*, 50(3), 331–347.

Steinfield, C., Ellison E. and Lampe, C. 2008. Social capital, self-esteem, and use of online social network sites: A longitudinal analysis. *Journal of Applied Developmental Psychology*, 29(6), 434–445.

Sweney, M. 2010a. Tories make the most friends on Facebook. *The Guardian* [Online, 23 March]. Available at: http://www.guardian.co.uk/media/2010/mar/23/conservatives-friends-facebook [accessed: 17 February 2012].

Sweney, M. 2010b. Advertisers should fear Twitter and Facebook more than regulators. *The Guardian* [Online, 19 March]. http://www.guardian.co.uk/media/2010/mar/19/advertising-twitter-facebook [accessed: 17 February 2012].

Tapscott, D. 2009. *Grown Up Digital: How the Net Generation is Changing your World*. New York: McGraw Hill.

Tapscott, D. and Ticoll, D. 2003. *The Naked Corporation: How the Age of Transparency will Revolutionalize Business*. New York: Free Press.

Tate, R. 2009. Facebook CEO's private photos exposed by the new 'open' Facebook. *Business Insider* [Online, 11 December]. Available at: http://www.businessinsider.com/facebook-ceo-mark-zuckerbergs-private-photos-2009-12 [accessed: 17 February 2012].

Terranova, T. 2004. *Network Culture: Politics for the Information Age*. Ann Arbor: Pluto Press.

Thelwall, M. 2010. Emotional homophily in social network site messages. *First Monday* [Online], 15(4–5). Available at: http://firstmonday.org/htbin/cgiwrap/bin/ojs/index.php/fm/article/view/2897/2483 [accessed: 17 February 2012].

Thompson, C. 2007. The see-through CEO. *Wired* [Online], 15(4). Available at: http://www.wired.com/wired/archive/15.04/wired40_ceo.html [accessed: 17 February 2012].

Thompson, C. 2008. Brave new world of digital intimacy. *New York Times* [Online, 7 September]. Available at: http://www.nytimes.com/2008/09/07/magazine/07awareness-t.html [accessed: 17 February 2012].

Thrift, N. 2005. *Knowing Capitalism*. London: Sage Publications.

Tonnies, F. 2002. *Community and Society*. Devon: Dover Publications.

Travis, H. 2011. YouTube from Afghanistan to Zimbabwe: Tyrannize locally, censor globally. *Florida International University Legal Studies Research Paper*, 11(10), 1–34.

Tufekci, Z. 2008. Grooming, gossip, Facebook and Myspace: What can we learn about these sites from those who won't assimilate? *Information, Communication, and Society*, 11(4), 544–564.

Turkle, S. 1984. *The Second Self: Computers and the Human Spirit*. New York: Simon & Schuster.

Turkle, S. 1995. *Life on the Screen: Identity in the Age of the Internet*. New York: Simon & Schuster.

Turkle, S. 2011. *Alone Together: Why We Expect More from Technology and Less from Each Other*. New York: Basic Books.

Turner, F. 2005. Where the counterculture met the new economy: The WELL and the origins of virtual community. *Technology and Culture*, 46, 485–512.

Urry, J. 2003. *Global Complexity*. Cambridge: Polity.

Van Dijk, J. 1999. The one-dimensional network society of Manuel Castells. *New Media & Society*, 1(1), 127–138.

Van Dijck, J. and Nieborg, D. 2009. Wikinomics and its discontents: A critical analysis of Web 2.0 business manifestos. *New Media and Society*, 11(5), 855–874.

Vogelstein, F. 2009. Great Wall of Facebook: The social network's plan to dominate the Internet – and keep Google out. *Wired* [Online, 17 July]. Available at: http://www.wired.com/techbiz/it/magazine/17-07/ff_facebookwall [accessed: 17 February 2012].

VR Info. 2011. *Vancouver Riot Pics: Post Your Photos* [Online]. Available at: https://www.facebook.com/vancouverriot2011photos?sk=info [accessed: 17 February 2012].

Wable, A. 2009. Facebook search improved for everyone. *The Facebook Blog* [Online, 10 August]. Available at: http://blog.facebook.com/blog.php?post=115469877130 [accessed: 17 February 2012].

Ward, K. 2005. Internet consumption in Ireland – Towards a 'connected' life, in *Media, Technology and Everyday Life in Europe: From Information to Communication*, edited by Roger Silverstone. Aldershot: Ashgate, 107–123.

Warren, S. and Brandeis, L.D. 1890. The right to privacy. *Harvard Law Review*, 15(5).

Weiser, M. 1993. *The World is Not a Desktop* [Online]. Available at: http://www.ubiq.com/hypertext/weiser/ACMInteractions2.html [accessed: 17 February 2012].

Wellman, B. and Berkowitz, S. 1988. *Social Structures: A Network Approach.* Cambridge: Cambridge University Press.

West, A., Lewis, J. and Currie, P. 2009. Students' Facebook 'friends': Public and private spheres. *Journal of Youth Studies*, 12(6), 615–627.

Westin, A. 1967. *Privacy and Freedom*. New York: Atheneum.

Whitson, J. and Haggerty, K.D. 2008. Identity theft and the care of the virtual self. *Economy and Society*, 37(4), 572–594.

Wills, D. and Reeves, S. 2009. Facebook as a political weapon: Information in social networks. *British Politics*, 4(2), 265–281.

Winseck, D. 2003. Convergence, network design, walled gardens, and other strategies of control in the information age, in *Surveillance as Social Sorting: Privacy, Risk, and Digital Discrimination*, edited by D. Lyon. New York: Routledge, 176–198.

Wittel, A. 2001. Towards a networked sociality. *Theory, Culture & Society*, 18(6), 51–76.

Young, J. 2009. How not to lose face on Facebook, for professors. *The Chronicle of Higher Education* [Online, 6 February]. Available at: http://chronicle.com/article/How-Not-to-Lose-Face-on/24101 [accessed: 17 February 2012].

Zetter, K. 2010. Undercover Feds on Social Networking Sites Raise Questions. *Wired* [Online, 16 March]. Available at: http://www.wired.com/threatlevel/2010/03/undercover-feds-on-facebook/ [accessed: 17 February 2012].

Zhao, S. and Elesh, D. 2008. Copresence as 'being with'. *Information, Communication and Society*, 11(4), 565–583.

Zhuo, X., Wellman, B. and Yu, J. 2011. Egypt: The First Internet Revolt? *Peace Magazine*, 27(3), 6–10.

Zuckerberg, M. 2006. Calm down. Breathe. We hear you. *The Facebook Blog* [Online, 5 September]. Available at: http://blog.facebook.com/blog.php?post=2208197130 [accessed: 17 February 2012].

Zuckerberg, M. 2007. Thoughts on Beacon. *The Facebook Blog* [Online, 5 December]. Available at: http://blog.facebook.com/blog.php?post=7584397130 [accessed: 17 February 2012].

Zuckerberg, M. 2008. Facebook across the Web. *The Facebook Blog.* [Online, 4 December]. Available at: http://blog.facebook.com/blog.php?post=41735647130 [accessed: 17 February 2012].

Index

Google+ 36
Googling 118
Greenfield, Adam 14
Gregory (student respondent) 68, 71, 74,
        76, 77, 111, 112, 142
Grimmelmann, James 22
group activity 72
GUI (Graphical User Interface) 36
guidelines, social media, *see* policy, social
        media
'gurus' 108

Haddon, Leslie 65
Haggerty, Kevin D. 19, 61, 74, 139, 141,
        153
Hamel, Alexandre 20
Hannah (university respondent) 166–7
harassment 72, 73, 79, 94, 97
hardware
        decoupling of software from 35, 36
        as dehumanizing 17
        as devices for social media 47, 59
        Facebook's reliance on 15, 39
        technological convergence of 13
        and ubicomp 14
Harvey, David 34
hate speech 102, 103
hierarchy 21, 43
Hollesley Bay prison (Suffolk) 135
Holly (university respondent) 96, 97
Homeland Security, Department of 144
Howard (university respondent) 93, 94, 96,
        97, 144, 160

ICTs (information and communication
        technologies)
        audience exploitation using 53
        as augmenting public exposure 51
        as lived experience in household 65–6
        as maintaining existing power relations
        60
        online/offline distinctions recede via
        engagement with 14
        Silicon Valley ethos of 53–5
        as ubiquitous and networked 42
        university surveillance via 87
identity, personal; *see also* interpersonal
        surveillance; social networks

as active management of public image
        51–2, 65
as anonymous 26
as brand management without
        compromising authenticity 120
as collaborative construction 8, 63,
        156, 158–61, 170, 172
complexity of managing on Facebook
        81
edited, strategic markers of 64
Facebook as distortion of 70
as false 162
impact on of information-sharing 62
management of 81, 147
as networked individualism 62–4
piecing together of by police via
        knowledge of friends 147
as playful, empowering performance
        21, 64
publicizing of 33, 166
quasi-corporate branding of 47, 49, 121
undercover policing as concealment of
        150–51
as virtual self 61
as 'who you know' 162
image, public, *see* profiles, user
impression management 68, 71, 148
individual surveillance, *see* interpersonal
        surveillance
individualization 43
industry literature 54–5, 107, 120, 124–5,
        128, 132
informants, *see* criminal informants
information, *see* personal information
information and communication
        technologies (ICTs), *see* ICTs
information architecture 34
information brokerage 48, 57
information collection 10, 49, 144
information database 17
information economy, *see* personal
        information economy
information exchange; *see also*
        investigative surveillance
        business control over 131
        diagrams of 40
        as domestic technology facilitating
        institutional control 105